WHAT THEY ASK ABOUT

MORALS

WHAT THEY ASK ABOUT

MORALS

MONSIGNOR J. D. CONWAY

56987

FIDES • NOTRE DAME, INDIANA

Library of Congress Card Catalog
Number: 60-8445

NIHIL OBSTAT:
Louis J. Putz, C.S.C.,
University of Notre Dame

IMPRIMATUR:
✠ Leo A. Pursley, D.D
Bishop of Fort Wayne, Indiana

COPYRIGHT: 1960
Fides Publishers Association
Notre Dame, Indiana

Manufactured by American Book–
Stratford Press, New York, New York

 I

Acknowledgments

The Publisher wishes to thank the editors of *The Catholic Messenger* of Davenport, *Our Sunday Visitor*, *The Catholic Digest*, and *Marriage* magazine for permission to reprint previously published articles of Monsignor Conway in this volume.

Contents

of the Excommunicated. Marriage before a J.P. Secret Sins. Limbo. Requirements for Heaven. Desire for Hell.

1. *Moral Theology*

What is Moral Theology? Who is a
Moralist? What is the Natural Law?

Q. *What is Moral Theology?*

A. It might be defined as the science which studies and determines the rights and duties of man as a child of God.

It is a science: that means a careful, logical, systematic and
accurate study. It's immediate subject matter is human acts;
and it tries to find out the exact course of action we should
follow, in a practical way, in order to please God and get to
heaven.

Christian morality is based on the call of Christ that we
should come and follow him. So a Christian Moral Theology
studies the nature and meaning of that call of Christ, and
how we should respond to it in the daily routine of our lives,
and in the special crises which sometimes confront us. That
call of Christ is based on love; he calls because he loves us;
we follow because we love him. Moral theology points out
the practical way to put love into effect in daily living.

When we reject the call of Christ we separate ourselves
from him, despise his wishes, spurn his love, and lose his
grace. We are guilty of sin.

When we respond alertly to his call, we prove our love for
him, unite ourselves more closely to him, and share the

1

divine life which he died to give us. We thus practice virtue in imitation of him.

The law of Christ is Christ himself. He is our Way, our Truth and our Life. We find his law in his words, his example and his person. We practice Christian perfection when we are like him and live in union with him.

This sounds fairly simple, and Christ's personal teachings on the subject of morality were usually plain and clear; but the practical application of his example and teaching to our daily lives is not so easy. Our lives are often complicated; they are lived in circumstances vastly different from his; and we get all messed up in desires and emotions, friends and enemies, and the intricate solicitations of the devil himself. Moral Theology tries to outline the rules for practical application of the principles and ideals of the Master to the turbulent situation of modern life.

Christian Moral Theology is complicated in that it draws its knowledge from a variety of sources. For many of its basic principles it relies on the sound studies of ancient philosophers like Aristotle and Plato, and on the ethical thinking of mankind throughout its history. Christianity did not cut itself off from the current of civilization; it rather perfected and elevated the good it found in that pagan society which it gradually supplanted.

Moral Theology is called a supernatural science. It is based on revelation, on the law of God as found in the Scriptures and in the teaching tradition of the Church. But it wraps these elements of divine knowledge around a solid core of natural ethics; so that it understands them in the light of human reason and experience.

Large portions of the Old Testament are devoted to moral teachings; the first five books of the Bible are called "The Law." The ancient Jewish Law represented the call of God to his chosen people demanding that they follow him, and acknowledge him as their Lord, Creator and unique Protector.

We find Moral Theology cropping out in the writings of the ancient Fathers of the Church, not in a complete and systematic way, but in special treatises, directives and moni-

2

tions, and in an exposition of the practices of Christians and of the Church.

St. Thomas Aquinas gave Moral Theology its greatest boost. He made it an integral part of his total treatment of theology and philosophy, and he presented it in positive manner, considering the various virtues which form the glory of Christian living: the detailed requirements for our imitation of Christ in all His perfection. Sins then come into his study as defects in these virtues, or as actions contrary to them.

St. Alphonsus Liguori, seventeenth century founder of the Redemptorists, gave Moral Theology the form it has generally followed in the past three centuries: a presentation of precise and detailed manuals for the use of the confessor. These manuals follow the order of the commandments, pointing out just what is a sin under each commandment, and how much of a sin it is. Thus the study has become negative in its immediate concern, concentrating on sins and considering virtues incidentally, as the opposite of sin.

In our own day there is a notable reaction to this negative approach, a tendency to revive the method of St. Thomas, and to go much farther: to make Moral Theology accessible to the layman, that it may be an inspiring guide to his daily following of Christ, to his sanctifying union with Christ, and to his practical love for the Divine Master.

No matter what method of presentation we follow the complete study of Moral Theology can hardly be made simple. It must diligently search the sources of its knowledge: those we have mentioned above: natural ethics, the Scriptures, the Fathers of the Church and the great moralists like St. Thomas, St. Alphonsus and a hundred others; and then it must take into consideration the laws of the Church and the laws of the State, decrees of the various Councils of the Church, decisions of many Popes, and the practice and spirit of the Church through the centuries: the liturgy, piety, customs and interpretations of the Christian people. The moral theologian must be thoroughly familiar with the principles of sound philosophy, and he must have a practical

3

knowledge of human life, so that his application of principles will make sense.

As we said before, the basic subject matter of Moral Theology is human acts: those free and deliberate acts which are distinctly human, of which only man is capable. It is by acts of this kind that we express our love for God, our adherence to his law and our conformity to his will. It is by faithful acts of this kind that we advance in perfection, acquire virtue and attain the rewards of heaven.

It is also by these free human acts that we reject God's love, defy his law, commit sin, and end up in hell.

So at the beginning of our study we must find out what a human act is: what makes it free, what makes it our own, so that we are responsible for it, and so that it is imputed to us, for our merit if it is good, or for our guilt if it is evil.

Then we must make a study of conscience, which is our practical, personal guide to right and wrong. How is conscience formed and how does it work? When are we obliged to follow it? How can it get fouled up in doubts, anxieties and scruples, or so stretched by laxity that it becomes unreliable?

Then we must study laws: The eternal law which is in the mind of God, and can only be known as he reveals it: the natural law, which is man's reasonable discernment of God's purpose in the plan of his creation; the divine law of revelation, which we discussed before, and the positive laws which are made by the Church and the State under the authority of God. All these laws have a direct bearing on the rightness or wrongness of an action.

Then we get down to a discussion of virtues and vices, of meritorious actions and sins, and of the practical details of right and wrong in our daily lives: our obligations to God, to ourselves and to our neighbor; our duties as parents or priests, as employers or employed, as Catholics or citizens.

Q. In your column you often refer to the opinion of moralists. Sometimes they agree. Sometimes one group is more strict than another. Where do they get their authority? And which ones are we obliged to follow?

A. Jesus Christ established His Church to teach us faith and morality—to tell us about the things of heaven, and to point out to us in exact detail the way of getting there. This teaching is a vast job; it covers everything God has revealed to us, and all the logical and practical conclusions to be deduced from His revelation. And the teaching must be done to millions of people, of diverse education and intelligence, throughout the entire world.

The Church has various methods of teaching. Jesus gave His authority directly to the Apostles, and especially to the leader of the Apostles, St. Peter; and this authority was passed on to their successors, the bishops; and in a special manner to St. Peter's successor, the Pope.

For the teaching of extremely difficult points the bishops sometimes meet in an Ecumenical Council, with the Pope presiding either personally or through a delegate. This does not happen often—only about once a century—but if an Ecumencial Council should teach some doctrine solemnly and officially it is protected by the Holy Spirit, so that its pronouncement is infallible.

On other important points the Pope may sometimes make use of the personal protection of infallibility which Jesus promised to him. He does this when he teaches the whole Church formally and officially some doctrine or some precept of morality, requiring in solemn manner that his teaching be accepted by all the faithful.

On other occasions the Pope may express his teachings in less formal manner, as when he is giving a talk to a special group in audience, or writing a letter to the bishops of some particular country. Such teachings have great authority because they come from the Vicar of Jesus Christ; but they are not infallible.

Then of course the bishops throughout the world are busy teaching day by day. Sometimes they do it by pastoral letters or personal sermons, but more often through the professors in their colleges, universities and seminaries; through the pas-

5

tors they appoint to preach to the people; through the Sisters in their schools, the official papers of the diocese, and books which are published with episcopal approval.

No single one of these teaching instruments is infallible. Even the bishop is humanly capable of error; and the professor, the pastor, the editor, and even the answer-man of the Question Box are almost sure to get off the narrow track of truth sometimes—on minor points, of course.

However, if you could take all these instruments of instruction together, throughout the entire world, they would represent the ordinary teaching authority of the Church. You would have the Mystical Body of Christ performing the daily routine function for which the Master put it on earth— and for which he keeps it faithfully from error.

The bishop is not infallible, but if he were to make any significant mistake in his teaching it would be quickly pointed out to him by his fellow bishops, or by the Holy See. If the pastor were to err notably the bishop would probably speak to him. And if I get out of line in my column my lay readers will punch me back to orthodoxy with the sharp barbs of their letters.

In other words, the minor errors of one teacher will be cancelled out by the truthful doctrine of a thousand others; so that his little aberrations will go unnoticed amid the total teaching effort. And if his error should be major he will quickly come into open conflict with the teaching authority of the Church. The individual may make mistakes, but the teaching Church, made up of many thousand such individuals, is infallible.

All this is background for my explanation of the moral theologian. He is the expert on the Church's teaching about good and evil, virtue and vice, merit and guilt. Before he is widely known, accepted and quoted he has spent most of a lifetime studying and teaching and writing on his subject. If any Council or Pope has ever spoken out officially on a particular moral problem he knows about it and has weighed its meaning. If the Church has made a law pertaining to the question at hand, he knows that law and has evaluated its application. He knows what other moralists have written through the centuries and are writing today. He knows what the worldwide Church has been teaching and practicing since the time of Christ. And he doesn't forget the moral law of the Old Testament.

The moralist holds no position of authority, unless he is also a Pope or bishop. He cannot make a law or command you to do what he says is right. But he does tell you what the Church of Jesus Christ teaches on the subject. And he knows what he is talking about. His authority is that of scholarship and mature judgment. Like anyone else he may be wrong, but he is expertly careful to be right; and he will not remain long in error without someone bringing him sharply to task.

There are many minor points of morality on which the Church has never given definite official pronouncement, and about which the world-wide teaching of the Church is not entirely clear. And even where the law is clear there may be divergencies of its application, due to differing circumstances in particular cases. It is on such questions that the authority of the moralist is most often invoked. No one in the Church is better qualified to know the answers than these men.

But as you say, the moralists sometimes disagreee on particular problems. What are we to do then? To put it plainly, we can follow the opinion which pleases us most, as long as it is soundly held by notable authorities, and as long as we are personally convinced of its reasonableness. Some day the Church may give an official decision on the subject, which will make our favorite moralists out of date. But until that day comes we remain in good safe company when we follow them.

Q. The Church tells us that birth control is contrary to the natural law. What is this natural law and where do we find it? How can we be sure of its meaning?

A. We believe that Almighty God has a plan and purpose in all of creation. Plants and planets, beasts and boulders, atoms and astral bodies all have a purpose. God makes these unreasoning things accomplish their purpose by the laws of nature:

7

growth and gravity, instinct and inertia. They have no choice about it; they are and act the way God made them to be and do. It is their nature.

God has a plan for human beings too. He gave us a definite nature, put us on earth for a specific purpose, and has a precise program by which we should accomplish that purpose. But God's plan works differently when it applies to man as a free, intelligent being. There are things God wants us to do, but will never force us to do. There are things God wants us to avoid, but will never directly prevent our doing. So God's plan as it applies precisely to us is a moral law: there are things we ought to do—duties, obligations; and there are things we ought not to do. This divine plan for man, as God makes it known to us through creation, we call the natural law, or the natural moral law.

If we observe the heavens, and study the atoms, and dig probingly into the rocks, we can learn much about God's plan for his unthinking creation. Our process of learning is science.

If we will observe and study and weigh and meditate man's intelligent nature, his situation and purpose in the world, his relationship to God and to his fellow men, it is possible for us to know the natural moral law. We call this study ethics; and we have to be as diligent at it as we would be at physics or biology. And since man's nature, purpose and relationships are all complicated we must be careful to take all factors of the situation into account; otherwise our conclusions may be faulty.

The general principles of the natural law are pretty well known to all men: simple basic notions like: good must always be done and evil avoided. And the majority of men can form some fairly accurate notions of what is good and what is evil.

However, when it comes to finding out the application of the natural law to particular problems we have some real difficulties. Problems can be intricately involved and present various facets. If we see only one facet we may reach conclusions which would be false for another phase. To help us we need the experience of the race and the centuries, the

8

careful studies of profound philosophers, and the wise decisions of parents, moral teachers and experienced judges. And above all we need the guidance of the teaching Church.

Left alone there are many moral problems which we could never solve surely by appeal to the natural law. We need the Church, but we can be sure that the Church is not going to rush into every problem which presents itself and hand out authoritative decisions with arbitrary abandon.

Most moral questions are solved by the ordinary teaching methods of the Church: the guidance of custom, the studies of theologians, the writings of bishops and the sermons of priests. But every now and then the Pope or a General Council may speak out in a definite and official manner— even calling upon that divine protection from doctrinal error which was promised by the founder of the Church, our Lord Jesus Christ.

Sometimes we can be sure of details of the natural law only because our divine Master remains with his Church, as he promised, and teaches us through her.

The main point of this natural law notion is not the clarity or extent of moral knowledge which it gives us, but the firm and objective nature of our obligations, once they are known. Murder is wrong; nearly all men are agreed on that. But we might find many reasons why it is wrong: it is anti-social, cruel, inhuman, unjust; it does not show a mature sense of responsibility and self-control; it provokes the punishments of society; and it is a messy business.

Depending on which arguments you adopt against murder, you may arrive at different conclusions. You may decide that murder is wrong for some people and right for others, wrong in some circumstances and right in others. Or you may even decide that the wrongness of it depends on a particular person's motivation, or on his subjective concept of his obligation.

In the natural law concept, murder is wrong because it is contrary to the plan of God, who reserves to himself dominion over man's life, who gives each man inalienable rights to his life, and who demands that we be just and charitable

9

one to another. In other words, things are right or wrong because of God's plan, not because of some love or aversion we may have personally, or because of some custom or taboo developed by society.

2. Sin

What is sin? Original Sin. The
Roots of Sin. The Degrees of Sin.
Acts of Mischief. Doubts about Sin.
Sins of the Spirit. Imperfections.
Culpability. Imputability.

*Q. Just what is a sin, and what is the difference between a
mortal and a venial sin?*

A. Sin is moral evil. That means evil produced by man's
free action. Most of us know what it is from our own personal experience, and from seeing it about us. It is only the
definition which causes us trouble. In order to arrive at
that we should recall that there is a double aspect to our lives
and purposes:

1. We are creatures of God here on earth as human beings,
to live happily with our fellow man, being honest, fair and
decent, as we expect our neighbors to be.

2. We are adopted children of God here on earth as saints,
to love God and our fellow man and to show that love by our
every thought, word and deed.

So we might first consider sin under its natural aspect: it is
something selfish, mean, obstinate, unfair, unreasonable and
generally despicable. It may be anti-social—harmful to others
—or it may hurt only ourselves, but in any case it is unworthy of a mature and rational person.

11

However, it is only from a supernatural viewpoint that we can really understand the meaning of sin. And for simplicity, I am first going to talk only of mortal sin. I will give several partial definitions, each revealing a phase of the nature and results of sin:

It is the deliberate, personal, free act of a rational being. Man is the only creature on earth capable of sin, because he alone has a mind and a free will.

It is an act by which we deliberately turn away from God, scorn his offers of love, and choose some creature in his place. We reject perfection and choose dross; we prefer an attractive little chip of goodness to infinite goodness.

With eyes wide open we turn away from our eternal goal in life and skitter off in panting pursuit of shining little mirages which we try to grasp as goals.

We say that sin is an offense against God. Of course it doesn't actually hurt him; nothing can scratch the surface of his perfection or detract in any way from his goodness and happiness. But sin does hurt us; it affects our relationship to God as profoundly as if we actually did offend and wound him. And of course our sins did contribute to the sufferings of Jesus Christ while he was on earth.

The most practical and revealing definitions of sin are in terms of sanctifying grace, of which sin is the negation and the destruction:

Sin is the rejection of God's free gift of grace, throwing it back in his face ungratefully. And once we have cast out that grace we can never get it back until God has forgiven our sin. We have no power of our own to bring it back. Only with God's grace can we repent; and sorrow only lays our soul open to receive grace; it doesn't create it.

Sin is separation from God. He lives in our soul in loving union when we love him. His presence there is sanctifying grace; it permits us to share his life, and trains us for heaven. But he will not force himself on us; he will not stay where he is not wanted. And when we love contrary things more than him we really do not want him.

Sin is supernatural death. Sanctifying grace is life: a budding form of our life of heaven. Sin kills it. And we remain dead to heaven until God's love resuscitates us; and he will never force his love on us.

So sin is not only an act, but a state resulting from the act: a state of death, as regards the life of heaven which God's love makes to sprout within us when we love him.

Sin can be committed in various ways: by thought, when it is deliberate and malicious; by word, when it is lying or vicious; by desire, when it seeks evil things, mentally reaching out to wickedness; by an act, which we perform with intentional malice; or by the omission of some good thing which love would have us do.

Only a mortal sin rejects God's love completely. Venial sin neglects and hedges on love. It seeks a compromise between the hearty love of God and the heedless love of self.

Only mortal sin drives God out and away from our soul. Venial sin seeks to make him uncomfortable right there in our soul.

Only mortal sin brings death. Venial sin only weakens the effectiveness of grace in the soul, and sets it up for the killing coup.

The difference between mortal and venial sin may result from any one of three factors:

1. The thing we do is a tiny thing in comparison with blasphemy or murder. It simply isn't big or virulent enough to kill a life so hearty as sanctifying grace. It is not entirely incompatible with love.

2. We commit the sin without really thinking, without being fully aware of what we are doing, or of the wrongness of it. It is not deliberate. You don't need an hour's time—or even a full minute's time—to think it over. But you do have to be awake and thinking; and you must know that your act is sinful.

3. You were not really free in committing your sin. Never are human beings completely free of pushes and pulls, which may come from their own passions and habits, from the enticements of companions, or from the allurements of the devil. There are always motivation forces within us which have been built up from our heredity and our environmental influences. But in spite of all these compulsions and con-

straints, most of us remain free enough to commit mortal sin in a big way. But in some people the pressures of habit, fear and emotion may be so abnormal as to reduce their responsibility.

Mortal sin is the worst evil on earth; it alone can lose us heaven. Venial sin is only the second worst evil; it chisels on our love for God and our chances of heaven.

Q. You said that sin is a free personal act by which we offend God and lose his grace. Where then does original sin come in? We had no part in it; there is nothing personal or free about it, and the Prophet Isaias says that children are not responsible for their fathers' sins.

A. The book of Genesis tells us about the sin of our first parents in eating the forbidden fruit, and St. Paul (Rom. 5:12-21) points out that this first sin of theirs affected all of us who are descended from them.

We cannot understand original sin unless we first grasp two basic facts about the human race:

1. In the beginning God created man in a state of innocence and sanctity. The Scriptures tell us that God found all of his creation good, but he was particularly pleased with man, whom he had made in his own image. He was so pleased, in fact, that he decided to adopt men as his own children. But you do not adopt a creature of an entirely different nature as a son. So God decided to lift man up to a higher level of life, to share with him a bit of his own divine life. In that way man would have a tiny part in the divine nature, and be so equipped with divine characteristics that God could make him a real son, take him up into his own home, and there share with him his life and pleasures.

2. The human race has unity and solidarity. We are all descended from one set of parents, and we share the same nature so thoroughly that the characteristics of Adam and Eve have come down to all of us. We are linked to them and to each other by our common heritage. This oneness of mankind is a common theme of St. Paul in his Epistles: humanity

14

is like a great sprawling tree, with branches, shoots, sprigs and twigs growing world-wide from the same gnarled and twisted trunk, which grew from Adam as its seed. So things which changed Adam profoundly had a continuing effect on the whole tree:

"Therefore as through one man sin entered into the world and through sin death, and thus death has passed unto all men because all have sinned. . . ." At the time of their sin Adam and Eve were the whole human race; so it was the race which sinned. The results of their sin are in us racially. Through them sin entered into the living fiber of humanity, which was entirely contained in them at the time, and which has grown out from them. We who are directly descended from them inherit the only nature they had to give us: one blemished and crippled by sin.

There is no question of our personal fault in original sin; it is a racial fault. We will not be punished personally, but we cannot escape from the blemishes of the race; we cannot inherit what the race has lost.

What was lost? Three great and special gifts which God gave to Adam and Eve right in the beginning—gifts which they might have kept and transmitted to their children if they had remained faithful to their Creator. The first parents had no right to these gifts; the human race had no right to them. They were entirely gratuitous; not a part of man's nature, but adornments added to it.

God's first gift was supernatural life. It has two marvelous aspects: (1) It is God living in the soul of man by intimate union in love. (2) It is man's sharing in the life of God, which is transmitted in this intimate union.

We call this supernatural life sanctifying grace, and we will understand it better if we consider its purpose. When God adopted man he invited him to share his own home, which is heaven. But man was not equipped to live in heaven. He had been created for earth: to breathe air and walk on ground, to see, hear, taste and touch. He was designed to know and love things in a human way, and to find his happiness in the things of the earth, the senses, and the mind.

15

Heaven is completely different. If we are to live there we must be able to know God and love him. But God is so far above our nature that we cannot know him directly in any human way. So to fit Adam to live in heaven God elevated his nature and gave him a higher form of life. It was grafted right onto his human life; he was to live it here on earth, and grow in it that it might be strong for heaven later. He was destined to share God's life for eternity; he prepared for it by sharing God's life here on earth. In heaven he would know and love God so closely and thoroughly that he would be entirely happy; he practiced for it by knowing and loving God in a super-human manner here on earth.

The Garden of Eden is a symbol of man's life in union with God, and of his sharing the life of God. It is paradise on earth, a practice and preview of the paradise of heaven. To prepare Adam for heaven God came down and lived with him on earth, sharing life and love with him, as they would later share more completely in eternity.

This elevation of Adam to a life of intimate union with God is called the state of original justice. Sanctifying grace was its greatest gift, but there were two others closely connected to it: immortality and integrity.

God promised Adam that he would never die, but it was a conditional promise which depended on his remaining faithful to God. Man by his nature is designed to disintegrate like all physical beings. His soul is immortal by its very nature, because it is spiritual; but his body is sure to wear out in time, and his soul would have to separate from his body in order to live. Only by special intervention of God could man be made immortal in his human nature. And man never did actually get this favor; he failed to fulfill the necessary conditions.

God's third gift to Adam is called integrity. It kept the human nature of Adam and Eve in perfect balance. Their passions were strong and a source of pleasure to them, but they could be easily controlled by the intellect and were under supple force of the will. Adam and Eve were vibrantly human, but they had no complexes or compulsions, no sense of guilt or shame.

16

The symbols of all these gifts were found in Eden, a place of pleasure and privilege, where God lived in love and happiness with his creatures. It had four rivers to supply it with water, was ornate with gold and precious stones, and had many trees which were pleasant to the sight and good for food. It portrays the spiritual richness and happiness of Adam's life while he remained in union with God.

In Eden was the symbol of man's immortality: the tree of life. It grew only in the garden; so man had to remain in the garden (i.e. faithful to God) if he was to eat the fruit of this tree.

But Eden had another tree, even more mysterious: the tree of knowledge of good and evil. God had forbidden the fruit of this tree to Adam and Eve; if they should eat of it they would die. It stood right in the middle of the garden, and it was attractive, enticing.

Just what kind of fruit did it bear? Certainly not apples. It seems to symbolize man's freedom: God would not force his great gifts on man. Adam and Eve could make their own free choice, and the tree was the means of their choice. They would choose between Eden, which was union with God, and the wide barren world outside, which was separation from God. As long as they avoided the tree they would remain in Eden, sharing God's life; once they ate its fruit they would have asserted their own wilfulness contrary to the wishes of God. In Eden they would be like God in his way, subject to him in love; outside they would be trying to imitate God in their own way, striving futilely for power and glory.

To eat the fruit of this tree was to learn about good and evil by sampling them.

The serpent is the symbol of Satan, who is evil in person. His temptation of Eve was clever and cynical. He had been through this decision business himself. His choice had been rebellion, and he was too stubborn to admit his error. He sought imitators to console his pride. He deceived Eve into thinking she could make herself like God by acquiring knowledge and power. She fell for his ruse, and she fell further than she planned.

The Scriptures do not tell us the exact nature of this

17

sin of Adam and Eve. It was mainly a matter of disobedience, but what was back of it? It could hardly have been a sin of passion, because our first parents had the gift of integrity which kept their emotional life under easy control. It must have been a type of pride, similar to Satan's own sin: a vain effort of man to reach beyond himself, a presumptuous refusal to remain subject to God in love and obedience.

Whatever the precise nature of Adam's sin, it was a real, personal sin. Genesis tells us the story of a factual happening, even though it tells it in figures and symbols.

Adam was guilty of sin; so he deserved punishment, and he did not wait long to get it. He was expelled from the garden. Eden is union with God; sin is separation from God. The two are incompatible. Eden symbolized Adam's sharing of the life of God—sanctifying grace. Sin destroyed it.

It was only in Eden that the tree of life could be found; so Adam lost his immortality. It was only in Eden that his emotional life was calm and happy under rational control. So Adam lost his integrity. Sin had tossed him into the turmoil and conflict which we all know so well.

But why should we be punished too? Remember that God's special gifts to Adam were entirely gratuitous. The human race had no right to them. So God's decision not to give them to the rest of us cannot strictly be called a punishment. Yet, in our ordinary understanding of words the human race does seem to be punished. It is worse off than it might have been. It limps, wavers and suffers. That is because it has lost something it might have had, and it is shocked by the loss.

It had been the plan of God that his great gifts—sanctity, immortality, and integrity—should belong to the race: that they should be transmitted to all the descendants of Adam in the process of generation. But Adam could not transmit what he had lost. We his children cannot inherit the wealth our father squandered. If we were members of some other race we might be born into the world with sanctifying grace, but as members of Adam's sinful race we are born without it. We are still destined to heaven by God's invitation, but the sin of Adam deprived us of the means of getting there.

18

By sin the human race lost its immunity to death, and we who get our human life and nature from this infected source must accept it as it is: subject to death. By sin our race also lost the gift of integrity; so we who are members of this weakened race must cope with desires and impulses often hard to control.

That is what we mean by original sin: in Adam it was personal sin; in the race it is a loss and a weakness; and each one of us individually inherits the defects of the race to which we belong. In a spiritual sense we might say that Adam's sin jumbled his chromosomes; and the mutations became a trait of all mankind.

But there is a happy side to all this. As a result of sin we have a Redeemer. If Adam had not sinned God probably would not have become man. The human race rejected its Creator's love and gifts, but he did not abandon it. Even while putting Adam out of the garden God gave him an obscure promise of the Redeemer who would come to crush the head of the serpent. And that promise was renewed with increasing clarity in the course of centuries.

Should we be inclined to resent the solidarity of the human race, which makes us all participate in Adam's sin and punishment, we can rejoice in that same solidarity, which gives us each a part with Jesus Christ in the work and benefits of the redemption.

God's new plan for our sanctification is more personal and individual than his original plan. Each of us receives grace directly in Baptism. Each one may lose it by his own sin. And each has it restored by personal repentance and individual reception of the sacraments. But still it is because of the closeness of our union with Jesus Christ—beause of our oneness with him in race and life—that his graces flow into our souls.

We lost much by belonging to Adam's race, but we gained more when God became part of our race. He gives each of us a share of himself.

Q. How can I find out the roots of my sins?

A. By digging—deep down into your conscience. What should you look for while digging? Especially the seven capital sins:

Pride. Don't let it fool you; it often disguises itself as an inferiority complex. It is a DESIRE for self-aggrandizement; and that desire can be very strong and keen in the person who feels inadequate, self-conscious, and vain. It is the opposite of humility which is just plain honesty with ourselves and with others, and especially with God.

Covetousness. Are you always wanting things? A bit greedy, selfish, lacking in generosity? The opposite virtue is liberality.

Lust. Don't be surprised that you have strong normal instincts. But do you keep them under control? It is the inordinate, uncontrolled desire which leads to sin.

Anger. How's your irascibility? Is your temper choleric? Are you irritable? Does your wrath rankle and your ire irrupt?

Gluttony. Could you keep a diet? Observe the fast? Or do you live to eat? And drink?

Envy. Are you really happy when someone else is successful, gets an honor, or demonstrates superiority? Or do you begrudge them the things they have earned, the luck they have had, or the beauty and grace with which God has endowed them? Do you experience a feeling of discontent or ill-will in contemplating their advantages? Do you have an unpleasant feeling that their gain is your loss, that their success points out your failure, or that their evident superiority contrasts with your limitations. That, my friend, is the green-eyed monster.

Sloth. Before I studied theology I used to translate this as "laziness," and wonder what relation it had to the three-toed animal of the same name. Probably he is a bit sluggish as he hangs on a tropical tree. Theologians are technical and define sloth as a tedium for divine things, a distaste for doing good and for works of religion. Probably as a source of sin we can broaden the base: it is that indolence, that self-indulgence, that habitual disinclination to exertion, which leads to idleness, dawdling, shirking, inactivity, neglect of duty, tardiness, and general worthlessness. Diligence or zeal is the opposite virtue.

If you can't find some of the roots in this soil, you are really different.

Q. The degree of sinning confuses me. For instance, to steal $5 from a wealthy person is not nearly as sinful as stealing the same amount from a poor person, or so we were taught in school. If this theory is true, does it hold for all sin? For instance, would a couple with four or five children commit as great a sin by artificial birth control as a couple with only one or two children?

A. The seriousness of theft is measured, in part, by the harm done to the injured person. The wealthy man hardly misses the five-spot; but the poor man may go hungry all day if he loses it. But theft is also a sin against society; it is disturbing to security and order. It is contrary to the plan and justice of God. So regardless of the personal harm done to an individual, a major theft is a mortal sin.

Artificial birth control is something wrong by its nature; it is contrary to the plan and purposes of God. So when it is done deliberately it is a mortal sin. Various circumstances may add or subtract from the guilt of it, but it always remains a mortal sin. Some mortal sins are worse than other mortal sins; but they all destroy God's grace in the soul; they all mean the loss of heaven forever.

Q. If all the people in the world were good Catholics, how could kids have any fun stealing a couple of watermelons . . . or kisses? All kids do it, and it's part of the fun of growing up. But if these things are sinful, then no one should ever do them at any time.

A. Now, how can you answer a question like that? It catches you right between the horns of a dilemma. Either you shrug off little sins, as inconsequential, or you advocate raising children as inhibited little prudes.

On one side we know that the answer is categorical. Sin is wrong and can never be tolerated. Even venial sin is an offense against God's love and goodness. It is the second worst thing in the world—right next to mortal sin. So we cannot shrug it off, or smile with tolerance upon it.

On the other side, I think there are many partial answers.

First, not all acts of mischief and dare-deviltry are sinful. Maybe the owner of the melon patch is not seriously opposed to a bit of marauding; the kids can almost presume on his sense of humor and his tolerant philosophy that "boys will be boys." On the other hand they had better look out for his shot-gun.

It is a bit dangerous to carry this line of reasoning too far. It leads right into Blackboard Jungle.

Secondly, parents know well that they must be realistic. Not one brat in a million will grow up without some sin. It is simply a fact and parents face it. If wise, they choose carefully which manner of vices to tolerate—those which explode early with loud harmlessness, or those which grow insidiously in quiet goodyness.

Maybe we laugh off the pranks of youth with reminiscent tolerance because we are realists, who know that sanctity is not achieved in one unhampered leap, but is rather a struggle through trial and error, with always a new trial.

Thirdly, we are all sentimentalists, in a measure, apt to laugh at the devil if he is hearty, to smile at evil if it is cute, and to excuse the sin if it is done with love. And righteous as we try to be we just can't forget the fun we had—in the good old days.

Q. I read some time ago in a Catholic book or paper that when one is in doubt as to whether a sin is grievous or not, it isn't a sin, or it isn't grievous. I forget which. At least it isn't necessary to confess it. Am I right?

Here's my problem. I went to confession without confess-

ing this sin, if it was a sin. Now I am wondering if I did wrong.

A. First of all, you must give no more thought or worry to your past confessions. However, your moral theology confuses me a bit. Shall we try to get it all straight?

1. I am planning to do a certain thing. I am in doubt whether it is a sin or not. But I don't bother to find out, I just go ahead and do it anyway. In this case I am guilty of sin, even though the thing itself might be all right.

Example, I wonder whether there is meat in this soup which is served me on Friday. "Oh, well, so what? I'm going to eat it anyway." Actually the stuff was fish; but I am guilty of sin.

2. I am planning to do something wrong, but I doubt that it is really serious. Maybe it is though. I do it anyway. I commit mortal sin, even though the act itself were a small thing.

3. I have already done something. And now, as I examine my conscience I wonder if it was a sin? Did I do it freely and willingly? Did I realize at the time that it was wrong?

If this doubt is about a serious matter I might do well to talk it over with someone; but I have no obligation to confess it.

4. I have committed a sin, but I don't know whether it was a mortal sin or not. Strictly speaking, I am not obliged to confess it; but if I am smart and honest I will confess it for the good of my soul and my own peace of mind.

We may doubt whether our sin was mortal for two reasons:

a. Was the act itself serious? I stole a dollar. Is that a venial sin or a mortal sin? In such cases of doubt you are strongly advised to confess the sin and ask the priest for information.

b. Did I give full consent to it, or only partial consent?

If you are inclined to be a bit scrupulous, you certainly have no obligation at all to confess such sins of doubtful seriousness. Don't spend time trying to solve the doubt. Make an act of contrition and forget it.

If you are lax and careless you had better confess all doubt-

23

ful sins. It will do you good, and they are probably more serious than you think.

Q. *Why are sins of the spirit worse than sins of the flesh? Please name some sins of the spirit.*

A. Not all sins of the spirit are worse than all sins of the flesh. A burst of pride can hardly equal morbid murder.

However, in principle, other things being equal, considering only the spiritual and fleshly features, sins of the spirit are worse than sins of the flesh for the following reasons:

1. The appetites and desires of the body are concerned with created things—generally with things which are physical; so the sins which they induce are directly against God's creatures, and only indirectly against God himself. Sins of the spirit directly involve our reason and will—the very faculties which we use in knowing and loving God. So these sins are more directly against God himself.

2. Maybe it is mostly another way of saying it, but our sins of the flesh are generally against ourselves—our own bodies—whereas sins of the spirit are directly against God or against our neighbor.

3. We are apt to be less free and deliberate and malicious when we commit sins of the flesh. Passion pushes us. Our fallen nature pulls us down. Desire almost stifles freedom.

However, sins of the flesh are apt to be more shameful, more habit-forming, and more dangerously attractive.

Sins of the spirit are things like pride, disbelief, despair, presumption, and hatred that is cold and deliberate.

Q. *What is an imperfection? Are there any sins we just can't help?*

A. There are three kinds of imperfection, as the moralist uses the word:

(1) The failure to be as good as we might be: to love God less than we could, to lack humility without being sinfully

24

proud, to lack zeal without being lazy, to be a medium saint when we might be a great one.

(2) A failure to keep the law in minor matters and without deliberation: e.g., to be distracted in prayer without realizing it, to laugh too loudly and offensively without intending to, or to dally thoughtlessly when we should be working.

(3) The failure to comply with a counsel or recommendation. This might be deliberate without being sinful: as to omit your morning prayers.

If you are using words in their strict sense, we commit no sin when we simply cannot help doing a thing. By its very definition a sin must be our own free and wilful act. But we must be careful: it is so easy for the sinner to say: "Oh, I just can't help that; the devil makes me do it, or my passions push me, or I am so weak." Always excuses!

Q. My small child has been killed, and I feel that somehow I must have been very wrong, and yet I have always learned that to do wrong you must have the intention of wrong doing.

A. Cling to what you have always learned. If we start blaming ourselves for every catastrophe we will soon end up stark raving mad. Very often God imposes his heaviest burdens on those He loves most. And we can be sure He will never blame or punish us unless we do wrong knowingly and wilfully.

Q. I would like to ask your opinion in regard to people who are suffering from emotional and mental illness, which is not severe enough to require special treatment. Some people suffer from neurasthenia or mental depression to the extent that they find it almost impossible to practice virtue and to do their life's work with the perfection which is required if

25

one is to reach sanctity. Are these people displeasing God by their failures?

A. We offend God only by those failures for which we personally are responsible. But people with emotional and neurotic problems do have an obligation to try to find help or remedy for their difficulties. Sometimes it can be obtained through a confessor or advisor. Sometimes medical or psychiatric help is needed. Usually the basic work must be done by the suffering person. Others can only help, guide, listen and encourage.

Q. I have a bad habit of sin and have had it for about six years. I have tried to change on several occasions, but never could. I can keep away from this sin for about two weeks, but then when I fall I commit it so often that I make up for the two weeks. Because of this I doubt the firm purpose of amendment in my confession, and actually hate to go to confession, because I don't know from one week to another whether my confessions were good or bad. The more I go to the sacrament the more I have a craving to commit mortal sin, and actually feel a lot happier in the state of serious sin. Thus would it be better to stay away from the sacraments altogether, or go on receiving them, not knowing whether they are a means of salvation or damnation?

A. I believe that you need some help besides the sacraments. I would suggest that you talk the matter over carefully with a confessor who has time, patience, and wisdom.

The reason why you feel happier in the state of serious sin is that you are thus temporarily relieved of anxieties, indecision, and the effort of resistance. You know precisely what your status is—no pain of doubt! You have made up your mind and committed yourself to a definite course without reserve—no strain on your resolution! And temptations are no problem to you; you loll listlessly in them. But don't you rather hate yourself?

Then there are two things which you seem to be forgetting: one is the love of God, and the other is the eternal welfare of your soul. Better meditate calmly on those subjects.

And try to develop confidence in the sincerity of your own resolution at the same time you try to keep that resolution honest. Do you really want to quit? Really, now?

Subsequent failure does not mean that your confession was bad. Admit your weakness frankly; understand it, and realize how thoroughly you need God's grace to strengthen it. Then make use of the sacraments to obtain that grace. If you are honest grace will do the rest . . . in time.

3. Conscience

A Doubtful Conscience. Scruples.
Mental Health and Scruples. Scrupulous Child. Scrupulous Teenager.
Temptation. Sins of the Past. Confusing Sins. Fond Memories. Cure
for Scruples.

*Q. In our study club we have been discussing doubt. Will
you explain to us when there is true doubt, and whether or
not one may act while in doubt?*

A. I am in doubt, myself: about the answer I should give
to your question. It is a toughie; not because of inherent
difficulty, but because I can just see in advance the divergent
reactions my answer will cause. It will encourage laxists in
their looseness and create new doubts and tensions in the
scrupulous.

Doubt implies uncertainty, hesitation and indecision. It
leaves our mental question unanswered; it suspends judgment; it fluctuates between alternatives. We can doubt the
truth of a teaching, the reality of an idea, or the fact behind
an allegation, but your doubt concerns the goodness or bad-
ness of an act. It is a doubt in the moral order—a doubtful
conscience.

Our immediate moral guide is conscience. It is supposed
to tell us that this particular act is good, and to be done;
or that it is bad and to be avoided. Then after we have acted

28

conscience either nods in approval, or shakes a severe finger in admonishment.

Here we are concerned with conscience before the act. A good conscience usually knows for sure whether this particular act is wrong or right. It tells us definitely that we must not take this money—that we must go to Mass today—that we must not tell this lie.

When conscience is sure and certain the answer is easy: we must obey a sure conscience when it commands or forbids. If it tells us this thing is wrong we must avoid it. If it tells us we are obliged to do this thing, then we must do it. To do the opposite is sin.

Sometimes our conscience may be all wrong: for instance I think today is Thursday, and my conscience tells me I can eat this steak. Actually it is Friday. But no doubt ever enters my mind. I eat the steak and enjoy it. I have followed a certain conscience, and committed no sin—even though I ate a juicy beefsteak on Friday.

Sometimes our conscience remains in doubt. It can't be a guide; it doesn't know the way. As long as it remains that way it is no good. It must first find the answers. The question confronts us: I don't know whether this action is good or bad; may I go ahead and act—sort of hoping that it is all right?

The answer is: NO. You may not act in doubt. If you do something which you think may be a sin your attitude is something like this: I don't know; it may be a sin; but the heck with it; I'm tired of indecision; I'm going ahead and do it anyway. You are willing to do it even though it may be a sin. In other words, you are perfectly willing to commit sin—and you do. You commit sin even though you later find out that the act was perfectly innocent. You sinned by acting in doubt.

So what must you do?

1. Find out the facts. Get rid of the doubt. Inquire. Study. Call up the pastor—poor fellow!

2. If you can't get rid of the doubt, and you simply have to act one way or the other, then you must choose the safer course: don't eat the meat until you KNOW it is not a fast

day. Go to Mass unless you are SURE it is not a holy day of obligation. Leave the money there unless you KNOW you have a right to take it.

Sometimes moralists run into real tough problems, involving questions that are intricate and disputed. They follow reflex principles, the most practical being one of authority. I don't know the answer myself, but here is a first class moralist who holds this opinion; so I am perfectly safe in following his authority. Such reflex principles are of practical use to the layman too: I don't know myself, but the pastor says it is O.K.—or my confessor advises me to do this—or mamma says it's not a sin. Prudence and humility often encourage us to solve our doubts in this way.

This manner of solving doubts has particular value to the scrupulous person. The conscience of the scrupulous person is a mess. He is always in doubt. Fears get into his thinking process and foul it up so that he can't consider facts and reasons objectively. Anxieties get into the valves of his mind and won't let them close firmly on a decision. He can't make up his mind. So the best thing for him to do, temporarily, is to live on reflex principles until his fears subside. He should find a confessor or spiritual advisor whom he trusts, and humbly do what he is told—with confidence in another person's certainty. But this should be a temporary arrangement, until he can acquire responsibility. He must not remain dependent all his life.

This may give you a clue to the answer to the first part of your question: what is true doubt? Fears are not doubts. You are not in doubt when you are simply afraid you might be wrong. Doubt is intellectual—a judgment, or a suspended judgment. You simply don't know. There are the facts plain as day on the table; but they don't provide the answer. No prudent man could say for sure whether this act is good or or bad—not on the basis of the facts we have to work with. That is doubt.

This is entirely different from the fears and worries of the scrupulous person. He is not in doubt, really; he is simply afraid to be sure—worried that he might be wrong. This sort of person must gradually train himself to recognize his fears

30

for what they are, to understand them, and scorn them, and finally to act confidently in spite of them. It can be a long, tough process, requiring much help and encouragement.

So I will have to give a special answer for the scrupulous person: don't confuse your fears with doubts. You do not commit sin when you act in spite of fears that you might be doing wrong. You are doing just what you should do.

Another thing: What I have written does not apply to the conscience which is doubtful *after the act*. This is the conscience which asks: Did I commit a sin or not? Was it a mortal sin, or only a venial sin? Can I go to Communion? Or must I first go to confession? This conscience poses an entirely different question—and my answer is already long enough. In general, unless you KNOW it was a sin, forget it. Unless you KNOW it was a mortal sin, go on to Communion—after a good act of contrition for any sin you did commit. Unless you KNOW it was a mortal sin you are not OBLIGED to mention it in confession. But unless you are scrupulous, I would advise you to mention it and tell the priest of your doubt. If you are scrupulous you shouldn't even be reading this.

Q. I am scrupulous and find that the more I read on this subject the more confused I become due to controversy and disagreement in the advice given to those who are scrupulous. For instance, in one of your articles you stated: "Scrupulous people are NOT good people. They waste on useless fears the energy they should spend in loving God and their fellow-man. Many of them indulge in some big pet sins, without blinking and then lie awake nights worrying about past confessions."

Yet, in a pamphlet entitled: "Are you Scrupulous?" which is an interview with Francis J. O'Boyle, S.J., by Daniel A. Lord, S.J., it states: "I have never met a really scrupulous person who was not a good person. The fear you have of sin is your greatest assurance that there is no sin in your life."

May I please have your comments regarding this differ-ence of opinion?

A. I think we have been guilty—both the good Jesuit Fathers and myself—of making broad general statements which are true in many cases but false in others. I should have said that not all scrupulous people are really good people—and that those who are good would be much better if they could get rid of their scruples. Good scrupulous people are good because their fears scare them away from serious sins, but these same fears tie them up in such knots of worry and in-decision that they are prevented from accomplishing that positive good which results from love and confidence.

Many scrupulous people definitely try to be good. If they didn't care they wouldn't be afraid. But their motivation is apt to come from a vision of God the stern judge rather than God the loving and merciful Father. They see Christ on the throne of his glory, saying to those on his left hand, "Depart from me, accursed ones, into the everlasting fire," rather than Christ on the cross murmuring prayerfully, "Father forgive them for they know not what they do." In other words they are inspired by fear—a negative, restraining, inhibiting force—rather than by love—a positive, dynamic, impelling vigor. Fear may keep from sin; love sanctifies.

Again I must not generalize. Many scrupulous people have much love of God mixed in with their fears. And very often the scruples result from conditions of general health or are manifestations of a neurotic anxiety of early and for-gotten origins. They are, then, an affliction which causes much pain and suffering, and we all know that the patient bearing of our particular cross, for the love of God, is an effective means of sanctity. In this sense scrupulous people are favored by God in that they are afflicted with trials and a heavy burden, and can gain much merit for eternity if they bear that burden with patience, resignation and humility.

That does not mean that we should be content to accept our scruples and do nothing about them. Humility and patience are better exercised in trying to get rid of the scru-ples than in simply putting up with them. Fears do not produce sanctity, but they may well be steps on the way to sanctity.

This does not mean that I am retracting my statement that not all scrupulous people are good people. Very often we find people who are tensely scrupulous in some things and defiantly lax in others. It seems that they need an escape from the worry, tenseness and indecision caused by their scruples, and they find it in their pet folly or foible. Gossip is a frequent escape. They quench their own worries in the scandals of their neighbors. They worry themselves sick about distractions, but are blithely unconcerned about detractions.

Furthermore, scruples are not by nature designed to lead people to uniform goodness. They obscure our vision of God's goodness and love; they deprive us of peace and confidence, discourage us and torment us and tend to lead us to despair; they wear out our zeal and enthusiasm for holiness, and sometimes provoke defiance and revolt. They keep some people away from the sacraments or make the sacraments dreadful things to them.

And let me conclude by agreeing with you that scrupulous people are apt to be made more upset and uncertain by reading articles about scruples. They cannot tell temptation from sin, suggestion from consent, a venial sin from a mortal sin, or a good confession from a bad one; so how can we expect them to be clear and unperturbed on the very nature of their own ailment—and discussion of it agitates their perturbation.

Q. Some time ago you answered a question about scrupulousness. The question was whether scrupulous people are good or bad. As a person who became afflicted with this horrible condition in early adolescence, I am deeply interested in this problem. To be quibbling about whether scrupulous people are good or bad seems completely beside the point. This is a mental health problem, a very serious mental health problem. It is a condition on which priests

33

have too long turned their backs, and if they admitted it existed at all, attributed it to God's will, or to a neurosis in the person afflicted.

A. Surely a scrupulous person should know what it means to quibble. But I do protest that you accuse me falsely. I faced the question rather squarely and drew firm protests against my stand. When a person quibbles he evades the point at issue, or straddles it, or babbles all around it. I took a definite position that many scrupulous people are not nearly as good and holy as they think they are. They expend their energies worrying about being good instead of getting down to the task of doing good.

However, I did not take up your question for the purpose of more quibbling—to use your own word. I rather want my readers to profit by the wisdom you have acquired through suffering. Your letter is long and I cannot print it all, but I will relate some of its salient points.

First of all I agree with you entirely that this is a mental health problem. But it is not a problem on which priests have turned their backs. It is more like a festering thorn in their sides. Or, to complete the circle, a vexing difficulty they must face daily in the confessional, on the telephone, or in the parlor.

It would be a rare priest who would simply shrug off scruples as the will of God. But in steeling himself to hear another repetition of an anxious story, he may express a fervent prayer: "God's will be done!"

We do often give the name neurosis to a serious case of scruples, and doctors to whom we sometimes refer these problems accept the word, without argument. I am sure that scrupulous people do not like to be called neurotics, but let's face it: some of them are just that.

You appeal to our religion which preaches charity, love of neighbor and compassion to take a less heartless attitude. And you point out our obligation to do research to find the causes of scrupulousness, and to help these tortured people. I agree with you that such study must be made, and much

34

of it has been made. But precisely because serious cases of scruples are a mental health problem the research on them is out of the realm of the Church, and in the domain of the doctor.

For many years as a priest I thought I was giving much help to scrupulous people. Now I am not so sure whether I was doing much more than patting them on the head, figuratively, and saying, "there now don't worry." In more recent years I have sent some of them to psychiatrists, with varying results. One became worse; another was sent back to me with the recommendation that I could do as much as the doctor, because psychiatric help would be too long a process to be practical.

Your next recommendation interests me: "priests should listen with an open heart and an open mind to these people in confession. Rebuking them only adds to the confusion."

I couldn't agree with you more. And I am sure most priests try to do just that. If we sometimes fail it is because human patience can be stretched only so far before it snaps, and because the straining effort to help can stand no more frustration.

You tell me how your scruples have made you contemptuous and bitter towards religion. That is one of my reasons for holding that scrupulous people will not become really good until they get over their worries. Like you they come to blame religion that they are "so terrified that they become incapable of pursuing their rightful place in the world, or of having even a minimum of earthly peace."

Sometimes there may be reason for this blame; I will quote more of your letter, for the consolation it may give others who suffer in similar manner.

"I can trace the beginning of my scruples to a story which a nun told in class when I was eleven years old, about a child making a bad confession, and of its horrible result. This left such an imprint on me, that as I entered adolescence, this story, together with pressure about a religious vocation, and too much preaching about impurity (which in my innocence I could not comprehend), I became positively terrified of

35

forgetting some great sin in confession, and of burning in hell forever.

"Frequent confession only added to the confusion. There was no one to go to with the problem. My parents, burdened with the care of other children, had not the training, education, or any idea of the torture I was enduring. Life passed me by, and the youthful years which should have been opening to life and love, I remember as a horrible nightmare.

"You said in your column that 'often the scruples result from conditions of general health or are manifestations of a neurotic anxiety of early and forgotten origins.' I can assure you that in my case, I was always physically very rugged, and until adolescence I had no neurotic tendencies. I believe that most neurotics are so made by their elders. I had, until I became so obsessed with my confessions, always gotten along well, both at home and in school, where I had consistently had good marks. However, after having this difficulty, I could no longer concentrate in school, I became friendless, and eventually because of their pressure about my being 'odd' because I had no girl or boy friends, I became estranged from my family. This was followed by years of poverty, of the most bitter loneliness, of despair.

"To combat scrupulousness, I from my own experience, feel that Catholic educators, in their teaching of religion to children, should be careful how they deal with the problem. Children, girls and boys, should have emotional outlets, sports, music, active games. Too much examination of conscience and looking into oneself can do as much harm to the budding conscience as no religious training, and can produce equally dire results in the long run.

"When a child, who has always been a good student, begins having poor grades, and seems anti-social, parents and teachers should be made aware that worry about sins may be the seat of the difficulty. Remedial measures can be made before the child is so affected that his future life is imperilled."

Q. My little grand child is very scrupulous. She will spend some time brushing her teeth the night before receiving Holy Communion; and simply will not receive if she missed brushing her teeth the night before. She would not think of brushing her teeth in the morning before receiving; she thinks it would be breaking her fast to use tooth paste. I tell her that she could receive even if her teeth were not brushed. Also, if she uses face cream in the morning, she will not use it close to her mouth if she is going to receive.

A. Use every possible means of building up courage and confidence in this child. Make her aware of the love and goodness of Our Lord. Try to make her realize that there is nothing to be feared as long as we love Him.

There is absolutely no law of God or the Church which requires us to brush our teeth before Communion. There are, no doubt, many pious "betel-chewers" of the South Pacific who never saw a tooth-brush, but receive Holy Communion very worthily. And I am sure that many of the great saints of earlier centuries never heard of "irium"—or even of "that Dial feeling"; their devout reception of Holy Communion was more ecstatic than hygienic. But it gave them grace and love.

It is nice to be a clean little girl; but it is better to be a confident, sensible, and loving little girl.

Tooth-paste can be used freely in the morning without any fear of breaking the fast for Holy Communion—as long as you don't eat the stuff. If there should be little bits of it swallowed along with the saliva, that does NOT break your fast. And the same is true of face cream and lipstick, and gargles and mouth washes, and the bits of food which clung to your teeth the night before. The Church's law is sensible —strict, but not finicky. Let us not be fearful and worried when we receive our Lord; welcome him heartily, with love that is large and generous, like his own.

Q. I am a teenager and have been scrupulous for several years now. Due to my scruples I have dreaded confession. I have gone, but very infrequently. I have tried, but to no avail. I fear I will lose my faith, and I am certainly in need of the sacraments. Nothing I do seems to help.

A. I suggest that you go to some patient priest and talk the matter over with him. Maybe he can help you understand that scruples are fears that have become a habit. And maybe he can calm you down and teach you confidence in God's love and mercy sufficient to make you quit trembling.

In some cases, of course, scruples are anxieties which are too deep-seated to be calmed by simple confidence. Then the scrupulous person needs the help of a doctor.

What are you afraid of? Can you tell me? Is someone going to hit you? Is something going to fall on you?

Confession is the sacrament of God's love. Its only purpose is forgiveness—reunion—a spiritual embrace. God never scowls at a penitent; he smiles in sympathy and mercy. It is easy to fear God in his thunder and justice; but there is no reason to fear him when he invites you to love—and that is what he does in his sacrament.

No one can make a bad confession unless he really wants to. If you are honest you are forgiven. It is as simple as that.

Try to figure out just what frightens you; then pin it down and confront it. You can lick it if you can see it.

Q. In your article about scrupulosity you stated that temptation is not a sin. Do you mean that if one has premeditated murder, but doesn't actually murder, the premeditation is not a serious sin? Do you think it isn't a sin if one deliberately entertains impure thoughts? My prayer book and other Catholic literature says it's a mortal sin. You are the first priest I ever heard of saying temptation is not a sin.

A. You are confusing temptation with internal sin. Your premeditated murder is a mortal sin, certainly; even though you never actually pulled the trigger. But you might be strongly tempted to commit murder, so that you just can't

38

get the idea out of your mind; it torments you. But you never consent to it. You never once decide to kill. You would never do such a thing, for many reasons, but especially because it would be a sin. In all the torture of your temptation you have not committed sin.

Your deliberate entertaining of impure thoughts is a mortal sin, certainly. But suppose that these thoughts merely come through your mind, vivid but unsought. They are enticing; you would like to dwell on them; you have a hard time getting rid of them; and when you do they come back again. But you never once accept them intentionally. You have been tempted; but you have not sinned.

We can commit sin sometimes by dallying with temptation, coddling it and showing hopeful interest in it. We allow ourselves to get into needless danger of sin. And that is wrong. But I would not advise a scrupulous person, to spend much time worrying about this point. Their fears won't let them distinguish temptations from sin. They can't tell whether they are dallying or fighting. So the best practical rule for them is that they do not commit sin until they know definitely that they have committed sin—up until that point it is only a temptation.

Q. *I am troubled concerning sins of the past. I have made general confessions, but I can't forget the past. I keep thinking maybe I didn't make a good confession. Now that I am getting older it worries me more and more. I am wondering if I should make another general confession.*

A. Of course you know that you are scrupulous, and I have no hopes that I can cure your anxieties merely by answering your questions or telling you consolingly not to worry. But at least do not make any more general confessions; it merely aggravates your anxieties. Just try patiently, with the help of your confessor, to put your reliance on the goodness and love of our Divine Savior. When he says he forgives you he means it; and he has said it repeatedly to you through his priest.

39

Q. Lately I have been confusing venial sins, thinking they are mortal. I have been a daily communicant, but now I am afraid to receive. Does one have to go to confession before going to Communion if he is in doubt whether he has committed a mortal sin or not—if he is in doubt as to its seriousness—as to whether he did it with full consent of the will, etc.

A. No, you need go to confession only when you know definitely that you have committed a mortal sin. In your particular case you should make an honest little act of contrition, go to Communion with confidence and love, and after you receive ask our good Lord to help you get over the fears and scruples which confuse you and keep you away from Him.

Q. I am a very scrupulous person, and the more I read about the evils of beauty contests the more worried I get about one I entered many years ago. It was a picture contest, and a photographer, assisted by his wife, took my picture in a bathing suit and sent it to the paper. I won. And at the time I never had so much as an inkling that it was wrong. It was done in all innocence. Now each time I read that someone is forbidden to enter a contest I start worrying, and I am making myself a nervous wreck. Must I destroy all the pictures I have relating to this contest to prevent anyone else from learning about it. I am not in possession of all the prints.

A. Old memories never die—and sometimes they don't even fade away.

I would hate to see you crush this memory; rather inject into it some of the innocent pleasure you had in those early days. You might still win a handicap contest if you would get rid of those wrinkles of worry.

You have no slightest obligation, at this late date, to do anything about those early pictures. I am sure that age alone has sheathed their early glamor in its fading tints. And since that time various Marilyns and Bridgits have changed the fashion of display so that your early poses are now quite innocuous—and no offense intended!

Q. Through a long adolescent struggle with scruples I have learned some facts which might be added to your recent Question Box discussion.

The problem cannot be solved by anyone except the individual. Guidance may help.

It is a most serious problem. It is like a bull which must be taken by the horns and brought under control. Anyone plagued by it must take positive action. Let me outline a definite course briefly:

1. Any confession made in good faith must be regarded as good; because it is in fact good. You must not question it; you must resist that temptation to repeat it. Since you are in a continual state of examination of conscience, cut your examination short before confession; simply make it complete and definite. When the confession is over refuse to dwell upon the past. And also refuse to dwell on any sin which occurs before your next confession; simply make an act of contrition, honestly, and be done with it.

2. Stick firmly to this positive thought: "What I have done in the past that offended God I have confessed as I saw it. Of course I was sorry, or I would not have dwelt on it. I am forgiven. It is as though I am a different person."

Until you have faith in God's forgiveness and become a little indifferent to your past you will not be able to step forward in the life of grace. Rather than trying nervously to save your soul, try to achieve something for God and your neighbor; then the saving of your soul will take care of itself.

3. Stop meditating between scheduled confessions. It will

41

only lead to more self-examination. Briefly make offerings of your life to God; don't dwell on it; He will remember.

4. Keep the mind occupied and interested, and keep the body busy with the so-called emotional outlets: Sports, music and active games. An interest in these things cannot be injected by someone else; it must be acquired by the will of the individual.

With the grace of God, a person can overcome scruples, but he must learn that trying to think his way out is not the answer.

I will bet that most scrupulousness begins when communications between parents and children break down. If channels were kept open, so that children could take their problems to mother or father, in closeness and confidence, then scrupulousness would seldom get out of hand.

Cured alcoholics can often be the best helpers toward the cure of another; so also a cured scrupulous person may be able to assist another back to a healthy conscience.

A. I certainly like to have other people write my column for me, especially when they do it so well. Scruples are not entirely bad; they cause serious thought, and even though that thought often goes in circles, it does produce some clear insights—like those found in this letter. If a person can get over scruples, he may be better for having had them. But while he has them they certainly handicap and torture him.

I agree with you definitely that the scrupulous person must effect the cure himself; and I think your program is as practical as any I could propose—even after studying my books. The whole trouble is to get the scrupulous person to follow your rules. It is like keeping a fat man on a diet, or a drunk away from the bottle. Will power is the only answer; and that cannot be injected; though it can be greatly bolstered by God's grace.

Let me add one more bit of wisdom: It is much better for the scrupulous person to be wrong, but firm and definite about it, than it is for him to be right in a vacillating, agitated, fearful, doubting way. In other words he should make his decisions firmly and stick to them. It is more important that he be sure than that he be right.

If someone is about to jump on me for such subjectivism, then let me point out that I am giving advice to scrupulous people, not rules for calm moral judgment. After our friend gets rid of his scruples he can quickly see and correct his errors. While he keeps the scruples he gets little merit or satisfaction out of being right.

4. Cooperation In Sin

Approval of Wrong. Attitude Toward Invalid Marriage. Approval
of Marriage Outside the Church.
Approval of the Sin of Another. Ac-
cessories to Sin. Bartending. Stock
Owning. Divorcee. Loaning Money.
Joining Communist Party.

*Q. My son was married to a non-Catholic girl by a priest.
They have two boys both baptized Lutherans, as my son had
a set-to with a priest and left the Church. He does not go to
her church, but she and the boys attend her church. Now
this is what is bothering me: the oldest boy will be confirmed
in the Lutheran Church this coming spring, and I know
there will be lots of hard feelings if none of us go. Now can
we attend that ceremony in their church and take part in
the lunch afterwards and give a gift. We are all good church-
going people.*

A. It would be definitely wrong for you to attend this ceremony, or even to go to the lunch. And I believe you should
not offer a gift to your grandson on this occasion. Give him
a special Christmas present—or delay your gift until his birth-
day.

Your participation in this event could only be interpreted

44

as a measure of approval—even though reluctant—of various things which are wrong.

1. Your son and his wife have violated the solemn promise they made before the marriage that they would raise their children Catholic. Either they were dishonest at the time, and deceived the priest and the bishop; or else they have proven themselves unreliable.

2. Your son is subject to the penalty of excommunication which the Church inflicts on those Catholics who permit their children to be raised in another religion.

3. There would be at least a strong hint that you were putting the Lutheran ceremony of confirmation on the par with the Catholic sacrament.

Try to keep everything on a polite and friendly basis. Don't make yourself obnoxious or offensive; don't seem to meddle. But you can't do something wrong just to maintain harmony.

Q. There is a whole galaxy of questions and cases that I might bring up about mixed-up marriages and what kind of an attitude Catholics close to them should have toward them: supposing the invalid marriage involves a member of the immediate family; supposing it is a question of taking part in the ceremony and causing pain by not doing it; supposing one sincerely wants to help in straightening out such a marriage. Can you discuss the general principles involved and maybe some of the extenuating circumstances, along with some practical suggestions?

A. Cynics once maintained that even the most respectable family has some sort of repulsive skeleton hidden in the closet. Now, for Catholic families, many of these closets have been opened. Even the most proper and pious of us usually have some unfortunate member who is involved in a bad marriage. It is a source of worry and shame, of yearning and wrangling, and an incentive to persistent prayer.

Every week I answer questions; I have been doing it for

years, and I never run out of queries. Scruples, fasting, indulgences and rhythm are problems often proposed, but they all take a back seat to marriage: its nullity and indissolubility, the ways of getting into it—some glorious and some sordid—and the hopes of getting out of it—mostly forlorn.

The most persistent and plaintive among these questions involve the attitude and relationship of a family towards a stray member tangled in an invalid marriage. I find these questions hard to answer. The principles are fairly clear, but the prudent application of them is complicated. The moralist, if he is to be practical, must be a bit of psychologist. He must understand personal relationships, emotional reactions, and a maze of varied circumstances.

It is easy to fulminate principles. We may never cooperate in the sin of another person, either by encouraging it beforehand or by condoning it afterwards. We must all be wary of scandal, lest our words and actions lead others to think that sin is not so bad, or that good is not worth the sacrifice. And withal we must exercise justice and charity even towards the sinner who is not repentant.

When you try to apply these principles you get fouled up in the love of a mother for her children, in the bitterness which has resulted from family quarrels, in the natural need of a man for a woman, and in the hard facts of economic existence. Public attitude, accepted customs, and the civil law all play their part.

We will understand better by taking up some actual cases. The easiest to answer in theory, but sometimes the thorniest to handle in actual practice, involve the process of entering an invalid marriage: the publicity, the parties, the ceremony, the social amenities, and the bridal gifts.

The general rule is that whether you are relative or friend you should have no part at all in the formalities, functions or festivities which attend the contracting of the invalid bond. Even a doting mother is bound to show publicly and privately her disapproval when her darling daughter marries a divorced man before a justice of the peace.

In my experience the most flagrant violation of this principle involved a Catholic family whom I counted as friends

46

of mine. Their little blonde daughter fell in love with a Lutheran youth of firm conviction. He would have nothing to do with a Catholic marriage; so she agreed to have the affair in his church. The family argued, wept and pleaded—and then capitulated. It was a splendid ceremony, with pictures and stories on the society page; the father was arrayed in formal dress to give the bride away; her sister was beautiful as bridesmaid; the mother shed some tears, but she held fast to the front pew.

That is obvious, offensive and inexcusable. But lesser compromises take many forms: the most frequent are attending showers, offering gifts, and sending congratulations. There is always the worry lest offense be given or conventions be violated: "After all she sent a beautiful gift to me when I was married."

Standing on principle in these matters does cause trouble at times. A fellow chaplain of mine in the army was assigned to a hospital. One of his Catholic nurses fell in love with a divorced doctor. She begged the priest to find some loop-hole; but there was none; the doctor had been soundly and sacramentally married. The outcome: a marriage ceremony before the Protestant chaplain right in the hospital chapel.

My friend carried on no fruitless crusade about the matter, but when Catholic personnel asked him, he told them they should have nothing to do with the unfortunate affair. The Colonel in charge of the hospital was irate; to him this was bigotry, disruptive of the harmony of his command. He demanded the immediate removal of the Chaplain. The case had to go pretty high before his demand was overruled.

Problems attendant on the ceremony may be acute and bitter. The ones which drag uncomfortably through the years are the real cause of tensions, worry and heartache, particularly in the immediate family circle. No one is able to hurt us as deeply as the ones we love most. It is easy to give a frown of disapproval to a moment of sin, but it disfigures the visage to maintain that frown for years.

These problems are not made easier by their frequency. On the contrary the general tendency to social acceptance of invalid unions must make us wary lest we ourselves discount the seriousness of sin, and contribute to the general numbness of our society about the moral problems of marriage.

Here again we can easily outline the principles: never give approval to sin; never give scandal to others; never give needless or fruitless offense; try to figure out the attitude and line of procedure which will produce most salutary effects. But here also the application of these principles is all mixed up in family history, personal relationships, loves, hurts and resentments.

One basic rule I would propose: give your heart a loose reign, but don't let it rule your head. Don't let your feelings show too much—nor let them dig too deeply into your own innards. Sorrow and bitterness can be nursed into monsters. Clucking of the tongue is an annoying sound, which if long continued may incite to mayhem. A critical wagging of the head may make you dizzy if you keep it up.

You are not apt to effect the conversion of sinners by reminding them daily of their sin; you rather give them regular exercise in resistance and resentment.

Refusing to speak to them is childish and painful. They can hardly expect you to clasp them enthusiastically to your bosom. But you can't blame them for muttering occasionally that only people without sin should be slinging stones.

Here is a typical case:

"My sister has left the Church to marry a divorced man. What stand should the family take about writing to her and inviting her to their home?"

I replied by admitting that I didn't know the answer. If it is hard for the family to determine their own stand, it is harder yet for an outsider to indicate that stand for them. I outlined the principles of cooperation and scandal indicated above, and then cautioned them to be just and charitable toward their sinning sister. It is often hard to be fair to the sinner whom we know and love. We expect defections from the stranger; they do not touch us deeply. But with our sister there is so much hurt inside that we may be hard and cold in manner to cover up that hurt and ward off further wounds.

Here is one which strikes home:

48

"My sister is married to a divorced man. She has an aunt who is a nun. This good religious aunt keeps sending my sister gifts at Christmas, and prayers for her to say. She tells her to keep praying that things will work out in the end for her. Is this right? It looks to me like this nun is encouraging her to stay with this man and hoping against hope that it will work out for them."

Who is the pastor who should not join the good nun in saying: mea culpa? And yet how great is the fault? We are merely inured to frequent facts, reconciled to conditions we cannot change. We come to accept the sinful situation as inescapable. We know it is not really so, if people were heroic—if they fully realized that sin is the greatest evil on earth, if they really loved God above all else, if they rightly valued their immortal soul, and if they were to comprehend our Lord's warning query: "What does it profit a man if he gain the whole world, but suffer the loss of his own soul?" (Mark 8, 36)

We somehow feel that we must be practical about these matters. We can't expect heroic virtue or sacrifice. Why exhort with foregone futility? Keep them as close to the religion as they can be in the midst of their sin: keep them praying, even though much of their prayer must lack sincerity; keep them at Mass even though they cannot receive Communion; keep them hoping that the Lord will be as sentimental towards them as the rest of us are, and provide a happy solution.

The fact is, of course, that we are victims of the prevailing attitudes of our society which consider these situations respectable and decent, even if regrettable; and which holds heroism in matters of virtue to be a bit eccentric. It is strictly anti-social to try to disrupt a marriage which is working out well—no matter how sinful theologians may hold the union to be.

At least our attitude is often practical when children are concerned. Only from an ivory tower can you give a clear-cut reply to this poor woman who wrote me recently:

"For many years my religion meant little to me, but now I am desperate to get back into the Church and receive the

49

sacraments. However, my husband's first wife is still living, and the priest has told us that there is nothing we can do about fixing up our marriage. We have been happy together, but I wouldn't mind leaving him, except that we have six children. I am not well; my legs have bothered me ever since our third baby was born. I would not be able to work to support those children. . . ."

Another lady, whom I know quite well, has a different problem. She has lived with her second man for twenty-five years, and would leave him in a minute, except that she feels an obligation towards him. He is sick; he has been for ten years; and he needs someone to take care of him. She has worked like a drudge to support and sustain him; there is no one else to do it. She simply hasn't the heart to desert him after all these years; it would seem sinful to her.

And then there is the man who is convinced that it is better to live in conventional sin than to go on frequent drunks and run around with any woman he can find—as he was doing before he entered this invalid union—and as he would surely do again if he were to break it up.

Let me quote from another letter I received recently:

"Can I take those children away from their father? He loves them and is good to them, and he tells me he will take the matter to court and get custody himself. If he did that they would never be raised Catholics."

As a final example I am thinking of the non-Catholic divorcee who is now invalidly married to a Catholic man who is severely handicapped. Before their marriage he had been extremely lax about his religion, but now the two of them are at Mass every morning, and the woman studies books of Catholic doctrine and devotion every day. Her little daughter—by her former marriage—has been received into the Church and is a delightful saint.

I could go on all day. And I am sure you could add some interesting cases from your own circle of relatives and friends. Life is not a simple current to be easily controlled by rigid rules. Clamp it down in one area and it burgeons out in another. When you get down in the midst of it you will

50

find its morality all entangled in emotions, personalities, sentiments and inescapable weaknesses.

What then should be our attitude toward members of our own family—or towards close friends—who are involved in bad marrriages?

1—Do not ostracise them. Being distant and supercilious will never convert anyone—only antagonize him. You are probably on good terms with worse sinners outside the family circle.

2—Do not condone or excuse. Keep your own alertness to the reality of sin.

3—Be reasonably alert to the scandal you may cause others, who may interpret your acceptance of the situation as endorsement.

4—Pray incessantly that God's grace may work miracles in the souls of sinners—at the same time you beseech His Providence to find an easier solution.

5—Be sure that personal resentments do not influence your attitude: "I told you so," and, "You wouldn't listen to me," are futile and infuriating phrases.

You will have to interpret and apply these rules in the framework of your own family relationships. I should not be hastily critical of the way you express them. You should be charitable of my attitudes. We each have a problem, and there is as much of personality and psychology in it as there is of morality.

Q. May Catholics attend a wedding in which both parties are non-Catholic, but one has been divorced? Is there any law which says you are sinning if you send a wedding gift to these young people?

A. The only law which applies to this situation is the natural law of God. You may not give approval to the sin of another person. And you may not seem to give approval; so that the sinning persons or side-line observers will reasonably think that you are approving.

51

If you attend their wedding it looks like you approve of remarriage after divorce. At least in ordinary circumstances it looks that way. But there may be special circumstances in which it is perfectly evident that you have to be there even though you clearly disapprove of the sin involved. It is a difficult judgment to make, and I hesitate to give examples. Very often it is a good idea to seek advice from someone who can appreciate all the circumstances.

It would be much more easily excusable to send a gift. It could, in some circumstances, be quite evident that you are merely observing the social amenities, without any indication of approval.

It would be more excusable that you show graciousness to non-Catholics in these circumstances than toward a Catholic friend or relative. The non-Catholic is often convinced in his own mind that he is doing the right thing; and there is no question of a wilful, formal sin, as far as he is concerned. The Catholic knows full well what he is doing. He doesn't expect you to approve; but he would like for you to salve his conscience by seeming to approve. He might even boast that you were there, as proof that he is not as bad as he seems.

Q. A very dear nephew of ours married a year ago out of the Church. We felt very bad about this and did not attend the wedding. He married a very fine girl and she is an excellent housewife. We are very fond of her. Now they are expecting their first child. Is it permissible to send a card and gift when the baby arrives? We want to but hesitate.

A. So much of the personal element is involved in questions of this kind that it is hard to give a general answer which applies to all cases. Here are principles to keep in mind:

We must do nothing which would indicate to the parties that we approve of their sinful action or status. For this reason you did well to stay away from the marriage ceremony.

We must do nothing which would indicate to other people that we approve of this sinful situation. For this reason we must be careful of our public manifestations of friendship and acceptance. This was another reason for staying away from the ceremony.

We must be charitable and careful about giving offense. This applies particularly to your relationship with this young woman who is probably in good faith. To her your frown is merely unfriendliness; your disapproval comes from prejudice. We must always give due consideration to the honest convictions of other people. Besides any good you may do her will only result from kindness—not from a constant frown which she fails to understand.

Your nephew should receive much more properly the signs of your criticism. But sometimes, even here, we must accept with some grace a situation which we cannot change by being adamant.

We need not repudiate accepted social amenities in cases like this. Our society has found it necessary to adjust to many problem situations. Our adjustments may sometimes seem lax when judged by rigorous theory, but generally when we conform to common social customs we show no special approval of society's sore spots. I do not mean that we should go along with the crowd; but I do mean that in the midst of the crowd we will not attract attention.

You may still find that statement strange. I mean that in a conventional situation we can rule out danger of scandal and judge the particular issues on a personal basis. What is best for the spiritual good of this young couple—and ourselves?

I believe I would send the little note and gift without special comment or ostentation. The little baby to whom the gift goes is entirely innocent, and your kindness might lead to his baptism.

Q. I am a Protestant, married to a Catholic man by a priest. I have read the Question Box at different times. I know you give good advice; I now have a question to ask you. How can a Catholic couple in good grace stand up for an elderly divorced woman and man in a Protestant marriage cere-

mony? Do things like this help the Catholic Church or harm the Church?

A. Things like this harm the Church, and harm the Catholic couple who do them. Such actions not only create indignation, such as you express; they also contribute to the growing attitude of indifference about divorce and religion. There may, at some times and some places—where local laws permit—be reason for a Catholic couple to stand up for a Protestant marriage ceremony; but never if one of the parties is divorced.

Q. I must write this quick before I change my mind. Could you give me some help and advice on a problem which has long been a thorn between my husband and myself? We own a bar. How far should we go in letting a person drink? How much are we allowed to serve him and still be within God's law and the State law? I rebel at seeing a man stagger out of our place.

A. Charity requires that you refuse to cooperate in the sin of another person. So keep on rebelling; maybe you will get your husband to cooperate with you in trying to run a decent, lawful establishment.

I suppose you do have to be careful not to offend your customers; but isn't it more important that you be careful not to offend God—or cooperate in their offense against God?

Your obligation is stricter if yours is the only bar in the town or neighborhood. You will not do the individual much good if you refuse to sell to him when he can easily go next door and get plastered. But even then you will favor your other customers, your own self-respect, and the reputation of your emporium, if you sluff off the slobs to the joint next door.

Q. I have been contemplating buying some common stock in a drug store chain, or in a mutual investment fund which

holds such common stock among other values in its port-
folio. Suppose this drug concern makes or sells contracep-
tives or illicit drugs; would it be immoral for me to buy such
stock?

A. No, not if the company is otherwise honest and reputable.
Your ownership of a small piece of stock would not be an
endorsement of incidental immorality in which the firm
engages. You would search from mountain to ocean before
finding a company 100 per cent pure. If it does not make
illicit products, it is probably unethical in its advertising,
or it boosts its prices unjustly, or it chisels on quality here or
there, or it gouges its employees, or tries to throttle its competition.

If you took all these possibilities into consideration I
doubt that you could put your money in any mutual investment fund—or you would develop raving anxieties on the
subject.

But once you have acquired a controlling interest in that
drug company you will have an obligation of seeing that it
conforms to right morality.

Q. I am a practicing Catholic with a civil divorce; so I am
a target for many questions about the Church. I can under-
stand the non-Catholics who expect me to resent the position
of the Church on divorce and remarriage. The sincere ones
can understand that the Church is not to be blamed for my
situation. The Church didn't choose the man I married—I
did. Nor can the Church be criticized for not changing the
law of God, in a sympathetic effort to give one person "one
more chance," hoping that this time she will use better judg-
ment in making a decision which involves a vow "till death
do us part." Because my marriage was a sacramental mar-
riage it remains a sacramental marriage, and by its nature
can be dissolved only by the death of one of the contracting
persons. I can't expect the Church to set aside my marriage,

any more than I could expect the Church to execute my husband so I could remarry.

What I can't appreciate is the crocodile sympathy of the "sometimes Catholics" who set themselves up as theologians and try to persuade me that God did not mean for me to live alone. (It just looks to me that He did mean for me to live alone. If God expects that of me, He certainly will help me to do it—or rather He will continue to help me.)

The people who won't live up to the religion they profess to believe could at least "get off the backs" of the people who do want to live their religion in their daily lives. Maybe they act on the idea that misery loves company. If they are miserable with guilty consciences, perhaps they want other people to have guilty consciences too; it seems to justify their own actions.

The non-Catholics can readily understand that I intend to live according to my religion, although that means living as a single person. They mostly give me credit for the courage of my convictions.

The poor Catholics are the ones who "butt in" and even try to insist "for my own good" that I marry outside the Church. They accuse me of being stubborn. With the grace of God I intend to remain stubborn. But I would like to ask you to comment on this aspect of being accessory to another's sin by nagging another to commit sin. It would not surprise me to learn that many of the divorced Catholics who marry out of the Church have been nagged once too often in a weak and lonely moment, and mistook pity for their plight to be sympathy and understanding. The "re-married" divorced Catholics come in for a share of my prayers, and I hope some of them can return to the Church because of these prayers.

A. I like people who provide the answers to their own questions, especially when they do it in a manner so edifying. Your letter reveals to me a saint in the making; and I pray that you may keep on being stubborn—and happy. It is great to encounter a person who sees her own problem clearly, without rationalizing it, without seeking excuses, or looking for someone to blame.

As for those who give scandal, whether by nagging or pity or just plain malice, it is too bad some moral power cannot enforce the hint of our Savior: tie millstones around their scrofulous necks and drop them deep into the sea. It might fill up the sea, but it would do a lot to depopulate hell.

Q. I have a brother who drinks to excess. I don't approve and he knows it, but almost every week he will borrow a few dollars and I have a good idea that he uses it for liquor. He is working now, and has bought a car. Should we loan him the money?

A. I wouldn't loan him a single copper coin. Has he ever paid any back? The longer you pamper him the longer and stronger will be his demands on you. You have your own family. They need the money far more than he does.

Q. Would it be morally justifiable for a Catholic to join the Communist party as an undercover agent?

A. It would be a mortal sin to become a real member of the Communist party, and a Catholic would be excommunicated for doing so. But these facts do not have direct bearing on our problem. Here it is question not of real membership, but of faked membership, and I am sure that the good purposes of the undercover agent would justify his taking out a Communist card, simulating such oaths as might be required, attending meetings, and performing routine functions of membership. These are not things essentially evil, and sufficient reason may justify them.

But here we are concerned with deeper principles of morality—and I believe the best answer I can give to your question is simply to outline them and indicate the manner of their application. Such varied circumstances will surely confront the harried spy that no detailed answer can be given in advance to each problem which may arise.

1. The spy is thoroughly justified in prying into the secrets of the Communists. They are subversive, immoral and traitorous and have no valid rights to their secrets and plots, destructive of national welfare.

2. The aim of the undercover agent is essentially good, virtuous, even heroic. His services may even be necessary to the nation's welfare and security.

3. No matter how good our purpose we may never do an evil thing in order to achieve it. The end does not justify the means. This is the principle which will probably cause the most trouble for the undercover agent. He cannot lie, steal, be unchaste, commit murder, or deny his faith, however necessary these actions may seem to his heroic purpose. They are sinful, by their very nature, and no goal however glorious can make them right.

4. He may properly foresee and permit many evil results from his actions, provided that these actions are not essentially wrong and that they contribute directly to his good purpose. His aims are not childish, and his playmates are apt to be rough. The game is not nice and the action may be violent. Decisions must be instantaneous; the spy cannot dally with doubts, or hesitate with a scrupulous conscience. He must understand well and know how to apply with precise certainty this principle of the double effect. Here it is:

We may properly perform an act, good or indifferent in itself, even though we foresee that evil will result from it, provided that: (1) good also results directly from the act—not through the evil, (2) the good is fairly equal in importance to the evil and (3) we intend the good, and merely permit the evil.

That sounds very complicated, because it is complicated, and cannot be safely simplified. Its detailed application is even more difficult than the principle. And the conscientious undercover agent may well have to apply it daily to a new set of circumstances.

58

Spy stories tell us that intelligence agents frequently use immoral means to achieve their goals. Our conscientious agent may never do that, but if he knows how to use this principle of the double effect he may safely skirt the dangerous limits of morality without sin. He may not lie, but he may achieve deception. He may not be unchaste, but his strong purpose may make modesty flexible. He may not give direct scandal but he may permit startled wonderment.

We might imagine all sorts of circumstances for the application of this principle. Our imaginary solutions would probably have little practical value for our intrepid hero.

5. We may never directly and intentionally cooperate with others in their evil aims and acts.

This principle may well cause our agent nights of worry. Many party activities are sure to be morally wrong. Can our agent maintain his membership without taking personal part in these sinful activities? How far can he go in any particular endeavor?

Here again we might imagine a hundred circumstances. But we had best sum them up as follows: (1) His own personal acts must always be good; (2) His part in the cooperative activity must never be essential or integral, in such a way that the thing could not be achieved without him. Otherwise, his good purpose may justify some pretty close passive cooperation.

6. Scandal may never be directly given or intended. For sufficient reason scandal may sometimes be permitted. But this principle may well cause trouble. If a good Catholic starts missing Mass, neglecting his religion, and consorting with commies, how can he avoid giving scandal?

A man who volunteers to be an undercover agent with the Communists may be asking for heroic and virtuous work, but he is also asking for a multitude of moral headaches, and I hope he never selects me as his confessor.

5. Virtue and Vice

Reward of Virtue. Pride. Presumption. Temperance. Fortitude. Humility. Prudence. Vanity. Envy and Jealousy. Veracity.

Q. Would you please answer my question. I notice that some Catholic women who led a wicked and sinful life before marriage, and also got drunk, are now married and have everything anyone could wish for. And other women that led a clean Christian life are still single and don't have anything in this world. What do you think of this?

A. Thank God for his heaven! Virtue is not always its own reward; neither is it always rewarded in this world. Vice is not always its own punishment; neither is it always punished in this world.

St. Thomas Aquinas tells us (Sum. Theol., q.87,a.1) that sin fouls up the proper order of things; and it will receive its punishment like a recoil from that phase of proper order which it perverts. Sin is contrary to good common sense, and our violated intelligence tends to punish sin by remorse and feelings of guilt. Some sins are contrary to good social order, and society tends to punish them, by fines and frowns and prisons and hangings. All sins are contrary to God's law, and God will punish them in his own way, and his own good time, and his own merciful love. Sometimes he punishes in this life; more often in the next.

Virtue sometimes gives a good feeling, a sense of rightness and strength and adequacy. Human reason approves it and rewards it with a warming smile of conscience. Virtue sometimes pleases those with whom we live, and makes them love us and praise us; the social order heaps its own rewards. But you can't always count on these. Our good feelings get submerged; and society often fails to notice or appreciate, or it quickly forgets. Only God notes all with justice, remembers with mercy, and rewards faithfully with love. Sometimes his rewards are much delayed, but they are eternal.

Repentance is a forceful factor in this plan of rewards and punishments. Possibly those women who have "led a wicked and sinful life before marriage, and also got drunk" have realized deeply their guilt, and have humbly confessed, and deeply repented, and thoroughly reformed. But I fear much that those who sin by uncharitable judgments, bitter resentments, and frustrated envy may not realize fully the fact of their sin. Reform is rare for them.

Q. What is pride? How do we commit the sin of pride?

A. In ordinary usage the word pride indicates an inordinate conceit of one's own superiority, dignity, importance, or merit—an unreasonable self-esteem.

Moralists, considering pride as a vice, put their emphasis upon its volitional features—the desires which it generates. Following St. Thomas Aquinas they define it as an inordinate longing for one's own superiority.

You will notice that both definitions mention the word inordinate: whether you consider it as a notion or a desire, pride is disordered, out of due proportion, unreasonable, and often unwarranted by fact.

The proud person usually thinks he has superior talents, beauty, wealth, rank, or virtues. Occasionally he is factually correct; in that case his notion is inordinate because he makes too much of what he has, takes all the credit for it, values it out of sensible proportion, or openly displays it in manner offensive to others. Sometimes his superiorities are only

61

imagined; in this case his notion is inordinate because it is erroneous; and when he manifests it he is offensive and looks foolish.

The proud person is usually not quite secure in his exalted opinion of himself; so he seeks desperately to justify that opinion; and this is often the cause of volitional pride. He desires to convince himself beyond doubt that he is really as superior as he thinks he is. He vaunts himself for what he hopes he is, and yearns to prove the vaunting.

Pride is a general exaltation of self. Presumption overestimates abilities. Ambition tends to honor, position, or wealth. Vanity seeks fame, praise, and admiration. Self-respect is a decent virtue. A sense of personal power and the joy of achievement are essential to success. But pride embraces them all, adds a bit of arrogance and a hint of disdain, and cloaks the whole in haughtiness.

Gregory the Great pointed out that there are four varieties of pride, and his division is still accepted by moralists:

The first is the worst; the proud man gets the impression, or even the firm conviction, that all his merits and abilities come from himself and not from God. So he owes nothing to God—no subjection, love or allegiance.

The second proud man admits that he has received from God all the fine qualities with which he is endowed, but feels that he got them because of some personal merit—he deserved them. He is something special.

The third proud man deceives himself on the natural level. He thinks he is wise when he is actually dumb; he holds himself handsome while his face stops the clock; and he joys in his strength though his muscles are flabby. His pride attributes to himself qualities which he does not have.

The fourth kind of pride is maybe most common. We exult in the good things we have, wishing to overwhelm others with them. We play up our superiority with insolence and self-approbation, and take delight in our arrogant awareness that others suffer by comparison. We look down upon them with elation.

The first two kinds of pride may turn us directly against God, causing us to repudiate his laws and his authority, making us refuse to be subject to him. The third kind of pride can make a fool of us, and lead us to break various laws of charity and justice in frantic effort to establish the superiority we think we have. And the fourth makes us inconsiderate of the rights and feelings of others, since we look upon them with disdain. Since they are not our equals they do not have rights equal to ours.

That is why pride is called a capital sin, or a deadly sin. It leads us into many sins. Often it is not a serious sin in itself, because we are not fully aware of it; it is not deliberate. But it lies deep down, half hidden, as the seed and foment of many sins of which we rarely suspect the origin.

Pride is directly opposed to the virtue of humility, that sane, judicious awareness of our actual worth and position— that sure knowledge of self which places us in proper perspective in relation to God, to our neighbors, and to our own personality and purpose.

Pride makes us self-centered, and in its turn it feeds and grows on the seeking of self. Humility turns the mind outward so that it sees God and his vast world, and our little selves in the amazing midst of it, remaining conscious all the while of God's personal love for us, of the sublime importance of the human personality, and of our exalted destiny to share eternal greatness.

Q. Here is a question that I think very few of us know enough about. Just what does the sin of presumption consist of?

A. Presumption is a sin against the virtue of hope. So we should first recall what hope is:

Hope is a virtue given us by God. By it we desire the happiness of heaven and are confident of obtaining it. We are confident, too, that we will be given the means necessary to obtain it, like grace, and the sacraments, and forgiveness. The reason for our confidence is that God is ready to help us by his divine power. He is able to help us because there is no limit to his power. He has promised to help us, and we know that he is faithful to his promises. He is good and merciful, and he loves us; he has promised to forgive us. He has sent Jesus Christ to merit heaven for us, to obtain for us and give to us the means of getting there, and to lead us there personally. He had Jesus establish a Church to provide us the means and helps we need along the way. He gives us the love and help of his own Mother, Mary. He gives us the example, prayers and merits of the saints. And by his grace, he lets us gain merit for heaven by our own good actions, which have value because they are done for love of him and in union with the unlimited merits of Jesus Christ.

In itself hope is a very certain thing. We can never have too much of it. Our faith tells us absolutely that God is able and willing to help us. We need have no doubt, fear, diffidence or hesitation. He wants to help us, and just waits the chance. There is the difficulty. He can't help us until we let him. He has made us free and he will not force us. Our only danger of losing heaven comes from ourselves; and that danger may be great, indeed.

Presumption is not too much hope; it is a distortion of hope. It is a foolish, unreasonable, temerious expectation of heaven, or of the means of getting to heaven. It may be foolish, unreasonable, and temerious either because it puts too much reliance on your own human powers, or because it expects things from God which are impossible, contrary to his goodness, his justice, and his promises.

The first type of presumption is exemplified in the pharisee or in the self-righteous puritan. This type of presumption may result from heresy, as it did back about the year 400, when Pelagius preached that we didn't need grace to get to heaven; we could get there under our own power. But pharisees and puritans generally never believed anything like that; they knew that we get to heaven through God's power, not our own. But then knowing that, they seemed to forget it for all practical purposes. The pharisee worked his way to heaven by a meticulous variety of rigid external observances, and came to place all his reliance in those formalities. He would make himself a saint by strict and pre-

64

tentious legalism. The puritan had a similar attitude except that he relied on the practice of more sensible and essential virtues. By being rigorously and intolerantly right, he was determined to make a saint out of himself by his own grit and grimness. He was never willing to relax and let God's grace and love have a chance in him.

The second type of presumption may develop in proud and foolish sinners who build for themselves a happy delusion that God will save them in spite of themselves. He is so good and merciful and loving that he will forgive them even though they don't repent. He is simply too good to send anybody to hell. This kind of presumption, too, may be connected with heresy, as in the teachings of Luther that we would be saved by the redeeming merits of Jesus Christ and our faith in him regardless of our own sins.

This type of presumption is not to be confused with the foolhardiness of the habitual sinner, who knows full well that he is going to hell if he doesn't repent and straighten himself out. Like a gambler, he takes a chance, hoping for later opportunity of repentance, knowing that he has no assurance of that opportunity.

These two are the types of presumption which are directly opposed to hope. They are fairly rare as deliberate sins; they rather grow into unconscious attitudes.

There might be other types of presumption, which would simply be foolish, unfounded hope, like the following:

1. Hoping that God is going to give you such extraordinary graces as to make you like the Blessed Virgin.

2. Sincere, confident hoping that God will give you opportunity of final repentance, in spite of a life of sin.

3. Making hope of forgiveness a motive for sinning; e.g. a person might say, "Well, I have committed one sin; I might as well commit a dozen. God can forgive twelve as readily as one." This is different from the poor fellow who says, "Well, I have to confess this one sin; and it's as easy to confess a dozen as one, so here goes." It is also different from the poor fellow who commits sin with a sort of fearful natural hope that he may have the opportunity of repentance and reform. The first man makes his sin worse; he sins because God is

65

good. The last man makes his sin less, because his will is not all bad; he is simply going to do this bad thing and then go straight.

Summary: True hope is aware of two factors in salvation —God's grace and our free cooperation. Presumption forgets one of them and relies on the other alone. Presumption thinks God will save us without our efforts, or that we can save ourselves without God's grace.

Q. I would appreciate a column on gluttony. I weigh 250 lbs. but have a thin man's psychology. Our Catholic calendar has a scriptural text for each day, and one of these, seemingly quoting our Lord, said in effect, "More souls are lost through satiety than is believed." When we were boys if we did not come back for a second helping at meal times we were considered suffering from some form of illness. Most working men and women enjoy good nourishing and well-prepared food; and vast numbers, including myself, get up from the table feeling mighty full and content. I doubt if I ever rose from the table feeling hungry in my entire life; however for Lent I do give up my noon meal.

I discussed this with a priest who said that the amount of food does not constitute gluttony, but the WANTING of special items (pheasant under glass) constitutes the problem.

A. I believe this priest was being considerate of your generous girth and healthy appetite. The Wall Street Journal recently defined pheasant under glass as "a small bird with a large bill." Anyway, your manner of asking a question gives delight comparable to that of a choice cuisine.

Gluttony may be defined as an unregulated desire for food or drink. It is appetite out of order. The virtue of temperance would keep appetite reasonable—in accord with right reason. Gluttony disregards good sense; it simply longs for the pleasures and satisfactions of eating and drinking, for their own sake.

God gave us all our natural instincts and desires, and he

66

gave them all for good purpose. As long as they serve that purpose they are virtuous and the pleasure they give us is good and right. In the plan of God purpose and pleasure are joined; when we separate them the pleasure becomes purposeless, and doesn't make sound sense. Food has a purpose: our health, strength, growth, and general well-being. The fun of eating is designed to achieve that purpose painlessly. Gluttony separates the pleasure of eating from its purpose. It makes pleasure its own purpose; and that is unreasonable. Epicurus was an ancient Greek philosopher who taught that the highest good in life is pleasure. This idea made sense to him because he thought that the world had come together by mere chance and had no particular purpose. It does not make sense to us because we believe that the world was created by God for a definite purpose; and that purpose is not pleasure. Pleasure serves the purpose; it is a means to an end.

The excessive drinking of alcohol is a form of gluttony, but we are not considering it here, because it adds other vicious elements to our simple vice.

In its root meaning satiety would not necessarily denote a vice. In satiety desires are satisfied, and if the appetites are reasonable there is no excess. However, as actually used, satiety implies overloading, even to the point of disgust and weariness. It indicates a surfeit, which is quite the opposite of abstinence or restraint. So your quotation may have some validity, even though I fail to recognize it.

Since gluttony is a sin of excess, rather than something essentially wrong, it will seldom become a mortal sin: only when it seriously endangers health or impairs efficiency, or when it leads us into dangers of other sins, like stealing to get the money to buy pheasant under glass, or neglect of the family through squandering money in fine restaurants.

In his advice to you your priest friend does not agree with St. Thomas who says that there are five ways in which we can be guilty of gluttony:

1. Eating at the wrong time. So hungry you can't wait. This might lead us to break the law of fasting, or cause offense to our family and friends.

2. Eating too much. If you are in any way guilty, I would judge that this might be your manner of coddling the vice. You simply want food, and lots of it.

3. Eating too fast and greedily. Wolfing the stuff; acting like a pig.

4. Doting on fine foods. Avidly seeking the pheasant under glass, with a tendency to scorn ordinary meat and potatoes. The gourmet proudly distinguishes himself from the gourmand, but St. Thomas indicates that he shares the same vice; he is only more refined about it.

5. Being a finical fanatic about the way food is prepared, seasoned, cooked, or served. Making taste a cult, driving the chef to desperation or the wife to tears, and boring all guests with superior manifestations of culinary discernment.

St. Thomas also says that many other vices may also arise from gluttony. He indicates foolish talk and buffoonery, foulness and impurities, silliness, and loquacity often combined with dim wit and stupidity. But even while indicating these results he points out that the vice is not in the food itself, however abundant or seasoned, but in the inordinate desire for it.

Q. You often write about various virtues, especially modesty and justice, but I have never seen anything in your column about the virtue of fortitude, which is one of the four cardinal virtues, and is essential equipment for the strong and perfect Christian.

A. Fortitude is certainly one of the virtues we admire most in anyone, and especially in a man. It gives strength of character, firmness, courage, consistency and perseverence. It braces the backbone, strengthens the nerves, fortifies the heart, and steels the spirit. It puts a man on his mettle, sets him firmly on his feet, and girds up his loins. It makes his soul sturdy.

Fortitude can probably best be understood by comparing it with temperance. These are the two cardinal virtues which

68

permit us to run our own internal, personal lives in a sane and steady manner. They do it by keeping the emotional elements of our lives under control, so that sound reason can prevail and guide us directly to our goal of happiness.

There are two types of emotions which tend to make us deviate from the straight line of right reason. First are our desires: our driving urges for food, drink, sex and satiety. Temperance restrains these, keeping them in line with our goal. Then there are our fears and weaknesses: our timidity, diffidence, cares, anxieties, and misgivings; our lack of confidence in ourselves, our mistrust and suspicion of our friends, our loss of reliance on God; our fluttering and trembling, quivering and quaking; our dread of death, our horror of pain, and the cold feet we get when we walk into danger. Fortitude bolsters these frailties; it shores up the shaking hull of our character, and makes us firm in the face of life.

In a way temperance is a negative virtue: it restrains and inhibits those emotions which might lead us into sin. Fortitude is strongly positive: it give us the guts to do those things which right and duty command, to do them in spite of danger and difficulty, in the face of criticism and ridicule, notwithstanding aches and fatigue.

Like all virtues fortitude has two species: natural and infused. Natural fortitude is that courage, force and strength of character which some men seem to have by nature and others must struggle to acquire. It is that good habit which is built up by constant practice: by facing dangers firmly in spite of fears, by going ahead doggedly when you feel like folding, by standing up to men with forced confidence when they try to stare or shout you down.

Infused fortitude is one of those supernatural virtues which come from God as his graces. It is the Shepherd's support of his sheep; God's firm hand backing us up with gentle strength. In the ordinary course of events it is not very effective unless it finds in us a natural virtue of fortitude on which it can hook itself. But if the natural virtue is there God's gift fortifies it mightily, develops it, and raises it up to usefulness for heaven. God can make a coward a hero by direct action of his grace, but most of the time he doesn't do so. It is too much like forcing a man to be good; usually God only helps us when we want and try to be good. When we are struggling to develop habits of goodness, he bolsters those habits with his grace.

Like most virtues fortitude is the happy means between two extremes: fear and audacity. Most of the time it has to work with fear and its attendant vices: laziness, languor and lassitude; anxiety, apprehension and apathy; cowardice, cravenness and convenience. But a measure of fear is a good thing; it keeps us from crazy risks and dizzy dangers. We should at least be afraid of sin. We should fear God in the enormity of his love and the justice of his punishments. We should fear evil men . . . and evil women. And we should be downright afraid of the devil, unless we have God's grace to fling at him.

The man who sins by audacity does not have real fortitude. He has bravado and bluster; he vaunts his valor and swaggers his vanity; or else he has contempt for his own life and its mature responsibilities. Pride pushes his courage off the route of good sense. He sins by excess, while most of us falter by defect.

Fortitude has a long train of attendant virtues, typical of the man of strong character. If we possess them all we will be noble, generous, high-minded, tolerant, trustful, confident, forceful, constant, persevering, patient and kind. Fortitude is a cardinal virtue because it represents the basic strength and bigness in which all these glorious traits of the great and valiant man sink their roots.

Q. What is humility?

A. Humility is a moral virtue. It gives us the right attitude in our thoughts and feelings towards ourselves. It is based on an exact and objective knowledge of ourselves: our nature, our dependence on God, our sinfulness and weaknesses, our strength and abilities. It encourages a sensible ambition, without pride or vanity, without the seeking of personal glory. It protects our vulnerable sensibilities, and keeps us from wounding the feelings of others.

Humility is a distinctive Christian virtue. The Greeks and Romans did not even have a word for it. The Old Testament gives it little mention, except that the Psalms sing of the lowly ones whom the Lord will exalt at the same time he topples the mighty from their thrones.

The notion of humility comes from Jesus Christ. He first exemplified it in his human life and death, and then he taught it to us in his sermons and parables. Next to charity he made it the most characteristic and universal virtue of the Christian life. It is characteristic because we can never really imitate Christ without it; and it is universal because it permeates all other virtues and guides our motives and efforts in the right direction. St. Bernard indicates that it might be called the fifth cardinal virtue; indeed he would name it the Christian cardinal virtue, since the other four are prized by pagans also.

St. Teresa tells us why humility is so important in the eyes of God: He is Truth and humility makes us truthful; it makes us conform to truth in our thinking, in our feelings, in our memory of past failings and our hopes of future accomplishments. It makes us live honestly with ourselves, with our neighbors, and with God.

Our humility derives from two basic truths which we often tend to forget. First, we are creatures made from nothing by the power of God, completely dependent on God for everything we are or have or hope to be. And secondly, we are sinners, utterly unworthy of God's love, which we have often repudiated.

Humility is the frank recognition of these two facts of life, and the adjustment of our thoughts and actions to them.

Since these two facts are the basis of humility, it may seem strange that Jesus Christ could exemplify this virtue so well. Neither fact rightly applied to him. As a person he was divine, and as a man he was incapable of sin. But his human nature was created and dependent on God; so he used that created nature to acknowledge the divine omnipotence: "The Father is greater than I." And then he, the sinless man,

71

took upon himself all the shame, sorrow and suffering of your sins and mine.

Humility was first exemplified in the Incarnation itself, when God who was everything became a man who was made of nothing. And then the manner of his human living gave daily emphasis to humility. He, the master, came to serve. As king of the world he was born in a stable, made a refugee from his homeland, was subject to his humble parents, lived unknown as a common laborer, and then later was persecuted, reviled, humiliated and scorned, and finally was subjected to cruel torture and shameful death. And it was all done that the aims of humility might be accomplished: that God might be worshipped and sin expiated.

Since humility is truth it inclines us to an honest recognition of the faculties, talents and graces which God has given us. But we acknowledge that they come entirely from him, and that they are not given us for our exaltation, but rather that they impose on us an obligation to use them for God's glory and our neighbor's good.

Since humility is truth it inclines us to a frank admission of our faults, weaknesses and failings; it prompts us to admit our guilt and put the blame where it belongs—not to be seeking excuses, defenses, and justifications. It inhibits rationalization.

Humility avoids comparisons. It prevents that exaggerated concept of personal importance and ability which would lead us to set ourselves above others and treat them with disdain or condescension. And it likewise avoids that feeling of inferiority which might lead us to resentment, pretension or envy.

Humility gives us a true vision of our purpose in life, which is sanctity; and it shows us how far short of that goal we have fallen in the past, and how high we must aim for the future.

All the other virtues require humility for their proper functioning. Without it faith will falter, because we try to fit God and his eternal truths into the frame of our own limited knowledge and experience. With it we seek him amid the astounding mysteries of his transcendent greatness.

72

Pride rejects what it cannot grasp; humility knows its limitations and marvels at every intimation of the glories beyond. We need humility for a knowledge of self, an admission of guilt, and for repentance and reform. And above all we need it for charity—for that generous love of God and neighbor which is the inspiration of all sanctity. The proud man loves only himself, or where his love does embrace others it is only that he may pull them to himself. Humility is inspired by genuine charity which pushes us to give ourselves to others and to God, as in truth we were created to do.

Q. You dropped that question about rashness versus heroism, etc., as if it were a hot potato. I dare say that's just what it is. No one can possibly judge another person without knowing all the facts and all the motives. But it is a terribly interesting question, and I wondered if it couldn't be handled "theoretically speaking"? Abandonment and Prudence have to kiss somewhere along the line.

A. Prudence is a maligned virtue. It is invoked as excuse for fear, delay, indecision, and downright laziness. It is cited as reason for excessive worry, absorption in worldy affairs, preoccupation with security, cleverness in making deals, slyness with the truth, and sharpness in judging others.

It's a shame. Prudence is a beautiful virtue, a sort of judge, moderator, and guide of all the other virtues. It resides in the intellect, man's highest faculty; and is exercised by right reason and sound judgment. It is closely connected with courage, is inspired by love of God and neighbor, and is rudderless without faith and a complete trust in God's love, mercy, providence, and fatherly care of his children.

Not only should abandonment and prudence kiss somewhere along the line, they should, in the perfect man, proceed happily toward heaven in constant embrace.

Should we say that Jesus Christ despised the virtue of prudence? Yet he preached that abandonment which has been the inspiration and literal guide of great saints like

73

Paul the Apostle, Francis of Assisi, and Anthony the Abbot, to say nothing of the thousands of martyrs who sought death for Christ with prudent zeal.

Against the world's judgment he called blessed the poor in spirit, the meek, those who mourn and suffer persecution. He urged that "if one strike thee on thy right cheek, turn to him the other also . . . if he take away thy coat, let him take thy cloak also . . . if he force thee to go one mile, go with him two." Was he scorning prudence in advising such worldly foolishness?

"Give to him that asketh of you . . . and lend, hoping for nothing thereby . . . love your enemies . . . do good to them that hate you." Did he forget prudence in advising us to such worldly imprudence?

"Let not thy left hand know what thy right hand does. . . . Lay not up to yourselves treasures on earth. . . . Be not solicitous for your life what you shall eat or for your body what you shall put on. Behold the birds of the air . . . and the lilies of the fields. . . . Your Father knows that you have need of all these things. . . . Seek first the kingdom of God . . . and all these things will be added unto you. Be not solicitous for tomorrow . . . sufficient for the day is the evil thereof."

When he sent out the Twelve to evangelize Palestine he told them not to "possess gold or silver, nor money in your purses . . . nor two coats . . . nor shoes . . . nor a staff." And he gave them that advice which impromptu speakers regularly invoke: "Take no thought how or what to speak; for it shall be given you in that hour what to speak."

And then there are those words which have often inspired heroic prudence: "Fear ye not them that kill the body, and are not able to kill the soul. . . . He that findeth his life shall lose it; and he that shall lose his life for me, shall find it."

He did not advise recklessness. He advised faith and trust and confidence in the loving care of an omnipotent Father: Two sparrows sell for a farthing, and not one of them shall fall to the ground without your Father . . . the very hairs of your head are numbered . . . you are better than many sparrows. "If you being evil, know how to give good things to

74

your children, how much more will your Father in heaven give good things to them that ask Him."

In the face of such advice, most of us like to turn in defense of our conservatism to the Parable of the Prudent Virgins, or the story of the man to whom the Lord gave the five talents, or the comparison between the wise man who built his house on a rock and the foolish man who built his house on the sand. We like to remember that we are admonished to sit down and count up our money and resources before we start building the house, lest we find ourselves embarrassed with a gaping foundation.

If we really study these examples which we cite in defense of our worldly care and wisdom, we will find that Our Lord was urging true heavenly prudence in each case—the same type of trusting prudence which he recommended in his abandonment. The person who really believes that God is his loving Father, trusts him completely, and loves him without reserve, will understand that the greatest prudence is exercised in placing himself completely in the care and protection of that capable, solicitous, and provident Father.

Prudence is the habit of judging all actions in relation to the final goal of life: God and his heaven. Prudence judges carefully and surely of the particular means to reach this goal. It applies ideals and motives to the practical details of daily life. It helps us make the right choice of thoughts and actions each moment of the day, so that each thing we do will lead us nearer God. The imprudent man is he who chooses things which put him in danger of sin, or things which slow up his advance toward his final goal.

When prudence is thus understood in its true sense we see that it does not contradict that complete abandonment to Divine Providence which has characterized many of the greatest Saints. They have been supremely prudent. They have chosen the radical means which took them racing directly to their final goal—straight up the steepest part of the mountain, bouncing off the boulders, without thought to the pain of the climbing or the hurt of the bruises.

Most of us lazily admit that we are not capable of such supreme heroic prudence. So we distort the name and call

75

our slow plodding prudence. We say we are prudent when we avoid the dangers and hardships of the direct way, skirting deviously the sheer, jagged cliffs. We say we are prudent when we try to enjoy fully the way itself, and provide for its ease and security, lowering our gaze the while from the final goal.

We confuse worldly wisdom with the moral virtue of prudence. We may be sharp and sure and safe in secular judgments, but deviate far from the direct path along which prudence guides.

These are the reasons back of my earlier answer which seemed evasive. It would seem that the good lady who had her children under threat of death had that heroic, wholehearted, trusting, heavenly prudence of which most of us believe ourselves incapable. She gave her life in her heroism, but she is an affronting reproof to our tepidity, timidity, and worldly wisdom. We can't take such reproof without defense; so we characterize her direct, heroic, sacrificing love and confidence as imprudence. We who would not dare such dangers are simply prudent. That is why I say we ordinary sluggish servants will gaze upward in admiration at her and her daring, direct companions as they cluster closely around the Master in his celestial home.

Q. We live in a country parish. Is it a sin when I go to church on Sunday and see a lady wearing the same coat like mine, if I can't wear mine any longer and usually end up by buying a different one?

A. There are probably sins involved, but not serious ones, unless your foible leads you into furious fights with your husband, or makes you spend foolishly the money you need for your home and children. It might salve your conscience if you give the "old" coat to some deserving charity.

The most obvious sin involved is vanity—which theologians call "inane glory." The adjective is well chosen: inane means "empty, devoid of sense, silly."

Probably your good husband told you that you were

76

simply being empty-headed about this thing. He was expressing good theology. It is not necessarily a sin to BE empty-headed, but it may be a sin to ACT empty-headed. It implies reversal of values: putting foolish things ahead of important things—appearances above realities.

Little children are expected to be silly. They have not learned a sensible order of values. But age and experience are supposed to give us more prudent judgment and a mature sense of the relative importance of things. When we get the years without the maturity we are rightly called silly —or even inane.

My dictionary tell me that "silly" means—among other things—"good, innocent, guileless, or harmless." It once meant "happy" or "blessed"—or even "helpless." So it is evident that being silly can't be a very big sin. Silly vanity can be a sin though, because:

(1) It pushes us to make ourselves noticed and admired and praised by others for foolish, false, fragile, and flimsy reasons—like a coat that is just out of this world. And when that mundane Mrs. Cosmos gets the same model, it evidently remains no longer out of this world.

(2) It impels us to try to impress people whose taste and judgment have little value. Mrs. Cosmos probably has more appreciation of style and color than most other members of your parish, and she has paid you the sound compliment of endorsing your own choice. But your "inane glory" ignores that real praise and seeks rather the polite "ohs" and "ahs" of those other hicks, who don't know Dior from dandify.

(3) It urges us to seek glory, praise, honor, and applause, for our own personal pleasure—just to thrill us with a sense of superiority—so that we can momentarily look down on others, and breathe the rarefied air of admiration.

Glory, praise, honor and applause are "indifferent" things, neither good nor bad in themselves. They are made good or bad by the motives for which we seek them, or the purpose for which we use them. We can make them contribute to God's honor, our own spiritual well-being, or our neighbor's benefit. Then they become good things. But we can also use them to build up our own false sense of importance,

77

and demonstrate our "superiority" and make others feel inferior. Then they become evil.

St. Thomas Aquinas (q 132, a1, ad 3) said that it is essential to our well-being that we know ourselves, but not essential that others know us, and consequently this impression on others is not something to be desired in itself. However, it is to be sought in so far as it can serve a good purpose. Our good example may inspire others to praise God, or to imitate our virtues; or the good opinion of our neighbor may encourage us to be good, so that we can merit and keep that opinion; and a word of praise and flattery often inspires us to great effort in the practice of virtues. In such cases it is important and good that we be known by others.

The virtues of humility and honesty restrain us from trying to make a false impression on others. Their false opinion might possibly inspire us to try to make ourselves worthy of that opinion. But more probably it will encourage us in our pretense, and make hypocrites out of us.

The virtue of charity is involved in this coat deal too. If you really loved that neighbor, wouldn't you be glad she has such good taste and is able to wear such a nice coat? And if you didn't despise her a little bit, would you feel so keenly the disgrace of being her double?

Rather than causing sin of any consequence, your vanity problem results from mixed emotions (which are not a sin, but can cause sin) and a distorted sense of social values which you share with many members of your sex. Men consider themselves quite free of these foibles, of course.

One of the advantages of being a priest: I have no temptation to discard my topcoat because Father John has one of exactly the same color.

Q. That answer on the subject of envy was not bad; you apparently took it from St. Thomas. At least you gave him some credit. But one part was evidently your own, because you said that jealousy was the special failing of women, and it is different from envy. Now I am not trying to defend the fair sex; they are quite capable of wielding their own cudgels. But I want to know the basis of your distinction between envy and jealousy. In none of my moral books do I find a separate consideration of it. And I don't believe St. Thomas treats it expressly, as distinct from envy. Are you trying to write a new moral theology?

A. Even without the signature it is evident that this question does not come from a layman.

Possibly from a moral point of view jealousy does not much differ from envy. And if it does, its divergent moral problems are probably treated adequately under the various headings of its component emotions and reactions: anger, hatred, slander, murder, etc. For jealousy is a complex emotion. More accurately, it is a complex of emotions—many of them—in painful disorder and violent conflict.

Even if my new moral book doesn't need a separate heading for jealousy, I do aim to treat it specially in my psychology. And in so doing I will remedy a defect in the traditional manuals. I have gone through several of them trying to find justification for my statement that jealousy is different from envy, and in only one of them could I even find the word jealousy listed in the index. That one makes my complex emotion ridiculously simple. It defines it as a "combination of anger and dejection," and says no more about it.

How simple can you get? A combination of anger and dejection. That would hardly be good for one lively tantrum. What about fear, the basic ingredient of jealousy? Fear begets it, nourishes it, and spins it into its tempestuous gyrations. And then fear is itself generated anew from its own offspring.

And what about the nine other emotions named on the classical list? At least seven of them can crop up at any moment in a good lively fit of jealousy. Love and desire are there always. Their direct conflict with fear produces the violence of the explosion. Hate and aversion are normal results. Sorrow is intense. There is sure to be a mixture of hope and despair, with fear goading on the latter. And through it

79

all is anger, of course, as our psychologist said. But his simple mention of it gives little suggestion of the frantic intensity of frustration it may encounter. It might, in its confusion, even lead to a bit of courage, to be used in attack or retaliation. The only one of the eleven emotions which seems to escape jealousy's vortex is joy. And sometimes we may wonder if the expert cannot get that too from her clawing, and belittling, and destroying.

Bossuet has a beautiful treatment of these eleven emotions in which he suggests all eleven can be related to love, which embraces them all and excites them all. We hate evil and sickness because we love goodness and health. Desire is love for something one does not have; and joy is love in possession of the beloved. Sorrow is love deprived, and courage is love striking out to win. Anger and fear surge up when love is cheated or threatened.

Following this suggestion of Bossuet, we might say that jealousy is love in turmoil, splitting itself out into ten directions at once. But from another point of view, jealousy is not love at all—except love of self. The jealous person is essentially selfish. He does not give of self generously, but draws to self avidly. And withal we will not quite condemn if we understand that it is fear—almost helpless fear, at times—which makes his grip so tight that it threatens to strangle the love it grasps. Fear of losing is the cause of selfish seeking.

I said that envy differs from jealousy. And it does. It is more normal, natural, mature and respectable. Sometimes you even find people admitting they have it. But hardly anyone will admit jealousy. It is too shameful and childish. Perfectly normal for a two-year-old, it is ridiculous regression at twenty—or sixty.

Envy retains self-confidence and self-respect, hope and ambition. Jealousy despairs, loses self-possession, and whirls up a tempest of temper.

The basic difference is probably fear. Envy has little or none of it. Jealousy grows from it, feeds on it, and is inflamed and confused by it. Consequently envy is a simple, fairly honest sort of resentment, or hurt, or sadness, or hate.

Jealousy is a confusion of conflicts, anxious and often frantic.

Envy is a rather sensible sort of thing, humanly speaking. There is reason for it—if we are short-sighted enough not to see through and beyond that reason. Jealousy seldom has much sound reason about it, just the imagined things which breed fear. And even when it does have real cause it refuses to face the issue, but is apt to aggravate the very things which cause it.

If envy begets vengeance it is usually fairly open and frank about it. Jealousy is as devious in its methods as it is brindled in its origins and confused in its emotional composition.

Envy is apt to grow from strong, positive vices, like ambition and pride and vanity. Jealousy is a negative trait, based on insecurity, and feelings of inferiority, and suspicion.

Envy came off second best this time, and feels bad about it. But it still hopes for future victory. Jealousy fears that all is lost, and in its despair seeks comfort in resentment and retaliation.

Jealousy has just one redeeming feature. It does show strong attachment. It clearly does not want to lose the loved one. It is desperate to keep him. This fact is worth consideration by the poor victim gasping in its strangling clutch. But he can hardly help being aware that even in its intense desire to keep, jealousy is hardly proof of love. It lacks generosity and trust, both essential to love. And it adulterates its love with selfishness, letting fear defile it.

This intense longing to possess, and hold fast, and never lose, may be flattering at first to the inexperienced fly in the web. But he will soon tire of its enslavement, and fret under its restrictions and spyings. And this very tiring and fretting may soon give proof that jealousy is no guarantee of possession. It rather creates the very pressure which will burst its own chafing bonds.

As we agreed in the answer you cite, feelings alone do not count in the moral scale, but they can quickly lead to sin. So we judge the morality of jealousy by the voluntary consent it induces: to hate and aversions and despair and anger—to sarcasm and criticism and the knife in the back—to attack and resentment and retaliation and destruction. Most of its sins will be against charity. Some will be against justice. And some may be grievous. And all will cause grief. And the whole process will be self-defeating.

Do we sound completely unsympathetic? Our sarcasm is superficial. We sincerely pity the poor person tortured by jealousy. It is evident agony. Sometimes it may result from deep neurotic anxieties and need expert attention for its cure. But in other cases it can be cured by the sufferer, with a little friendly help. It must first be admitted and acknowledged frankly. Then there must be watchfulness to detect it, cool humor in analyzing it, and a firm desire to grow out of it. If the beloved victim understands too and is patient and sympathetic it helps greatly in the growth—and can save a tantrum. But he has to be a hero.

Q. I was recently in an argument with a Catholic lawyer who maintained that once a guilty defendant voluntarily takes the witness stand in court, he is bound to admit his guilt when questioned by either attorney. I said that my ethics professor in college (a Jesuit) had declared that a defendant, even though guilty, may deny his guilt and answer "No" to direct questions as to whether he did or did not commit the crime. This professor had said that this "No" answer is understood, by custom and tradition, to be a legitimate answer by a defendant in legitimate self-defense, and since it is so understood by both lawyers and jurists it cannot be defined as a lie. My attorney friend (also a Jesuit-trained man says that such an answer is perjury and that both the defendant and the attorney who advises him to say "No" are guilty of lying. Who is right? We are watching for your answer. No bets have been laid, though.

A. If my answer decides the argument then you are lucky that you placed no bets. I hold the lying defendant guilty of perjury.

This defendant is thoroughly protected by the law. He is not forced to take the stand and testify. If he chooses to give

82

testimony he is still protected by the rules of cross-examination. The prosecuting attorney is not permitted to grill him on any subjects not opened up already by the questioning of his own attorney. If he takes the stand it is for his own advantage; and if he decides to lie on the stand his only purpose is to deceive the court.

Actually, I realize that lying by the defendant in a criminal trial is rather common, and in trials for capital crimes it is half-expected, and probably does not deceive anyone very much. However, a lie remains a lie even if nobody believes it; and the fact that people expect you to lie does not excuse your lying; it may simply prove that you are a notorious liar.

Our Iowa laws make no exception from the penalties of perjury for the lying defendant. Prosecution would be very rare, but there are cases on record which show that a man can be found guilty of perjury for lying in his own defense in a criminal trial.

What about your Jesuit professor? It is my guess that he had in mind third-degree procedures to extort confession, or those unjust processes which exist in some countries in which the defendant is forced to take the witness stand and be grilled without restriction. In such cases it is generally accepted that a guilty person may deny his guilt when he is questioned in an unjust manner, or by one to whom he is not obliged to confess.

What is a lie? Moral theologians agree that every lie is a sin, but sometimes they have difficulty deciding just which equivocations, evasions, and circumlocutions are lies. It is obviously not a lie to tell the obnoxious salesman that mamma is not at home, or to tell a plain girl that she looks beautiful. However, we all know that if your line gets too heavy it may submerge you socially. Insincerity does not bear true witness.

The traditional definition of a lie is "an assertion contrary to your mind." You say what you do not believe. It is not strictly necessary that you intend to deceive; and less necessary that you actually deceive. The habitual barefaced liar is not less a liar because nobody believes him.

Veracity (truthfulness, honesty) is the virtue which inclines us to speak the truth—to speak what we really believe in our own minds. We can sin against it by excess or defect. We would sin by excess if we went around indiscreetly telling everything we know, just because it happens to be true. We would violate secrets, ruin reputations, and develop black eyes. We sin by defect of veracity when we lie.

We cannot really understand veracity and lying unless we consider them in the full light of their social implications. God created us as social beings. He expects us to live together in harmony and trust. We cannot live happily and securely with people unless we can believe what they say. So the very fact of our speaking carries with it an implied promise to our listeners: that we will honestly tell them what we really believe. In exchange for this promise we expect them to believe us. We become traitors to our neighbor's trust when we speak falsely or insincerely.

On the other hand, our neighbors do not expect us to tell everything we know. Social harmony demands discretion. And many of us have strict obligations of keeping secrets committed to us. If someone tries to pry a secret from us he is not asking that we be a witness to truth but a traitor to trust. We are allowed to evade as best we can. He has no right to expect truthfulness in our answer. Our speaking carries no promise with it. We are trustworthy and truthful because we have kept our secret.

So the criminal on the witness stand, if he were questioned unjustly—if his rights were not protected by law—might be justified in denying his guilt, as he has already done in his formal plea of "not-guilty." His denial would not be a lie. But in our courts, as they normally function, since he can only be questioned on subjects he wants to be asked about, his denial can only be for the purpose of deceiving the court. It is a lie. And since his lying is done under oath he commits perjury. Lying and perjury can never be a legitimate defense against conviction.

6. *The First Commandment*

The Practice of Religion. Participation in Non-Catholic Services. Bringing Children to Mass. Talking in Church. Perfume in Church. Bobby Pins in Church. Sunday School. Position at Prayer. Non-Catholic Socials. Bake Sales. Alms to Salvation Army. Congratulating Non-Catholics. Teaching in Non-Catholic Schools. Obeying Your Pastor. Grace before Meals. Making Retreats. Chain Letters. St. Malachy's Prophecy. Myth of St. Joseph.

Q. *Is is wrong to believe just in God and not belong to any Church?*

A. It is, because you do not believe in God entirely—as he really is. Neither do you live in accordance with his plan, and his commandments.

Ordinarily the person who merely believes in God is a semi-agnostic. He knows that there is a Supreme Being of some kind. There has to be some kind of Creator; some sort of transcendent Providence. But he figures that we can never know much more than that about God. Consequently he is not much interested in the three Persons in God, or the fact that one of these Persons became man.

This sort of agnostic indifference must offend God, who has taken loving care to tell us much about himself, so that our knowledge would inspire and console us and lead us to loving him in his goodness. We must not scorn his truth and his love. If we do that we don't really believe in God at all—not in the real God.

The Lord has created us, adopted us as his children, and plans eternal happiness for us in his own home in heaven. He became one of us to lead us to his home. He mapped out the way to get there, and He gives us constant personal help along that way; lifting us when we fall, retrieving us when we stray, strengthening us at each step.

Do you think we really believe in God if we throw away his map, reject his loving help, and tell him, in effect, to leave us alone and let us find our own way, under our own power, to his home? We will be his children when we get there; we aren't interested in adoption now. We will love him when He meets us at heaven's door; we see no reason to learn to love him now.

You see my point: God's plan for our right living on earth and our eternal happiness in heaven includes his Church. He established that Church, himself, when He was on earth, as Man. He put it into the world to teach his truths and dispense his graces. It has his map of the way to heaven; and it acts in his name—or rather he acts through it—to lift the fallen, retrieve the strays, and fortify each wavering step.

Our Lord Jesus Christ told his apostles they must make disciples of all men—bring everyone into his Church—that there might be one sheep-fold and one shepherd. And he sent word to us by them that if we hear the Church we hear him, and if we despise the Church we despise him. If we believe and are baptized we will be saved. (See Matt. 28, 19; John 10, 16; Luke 10, 16; Mark 16, 17.)

So we may not simply make up our own minds whether we will join a Church or not. God has established a Church for us and told us that we must belong to it. If we really believe in God we will follow the commandments of God.

Q. Will you please give me a good reason why Catholics cannot attend Protestant services? How about taking part in their funerals and weddings?

A. Our attitude toward the Church and its official method of worshipping God must necessarily differ from that of most Protestants. We believe that Jesus Christ established only one true Church, and that the Catholic Church is it. And we believe that Jesus Christ designed the method of worship which he wants his Church to use; it centers around the Mass, as the continuation of his Sacrifice of the Cross, and around the Sacraments as his own instruments for our personal sanctification. And we believe it is not at all a matter of indifference to him whether we use his methods or others which we might think up to replace them.

Most Protestants do not believe these things. They generally give a measure of recognition to dozens of different Churches, all of relatively recent origin, and all claiming in one way or another to be a part of the Church of Christ. Most of them would explain that Jesus did not establish a precise, tangible Church, but only a spiritual union of faith and grace, and the Catholic Church just happened to be the first form of putting this union to work. Few of them would admit that Jesus gave us any method of worship; they repudiate the Mass, and discard most of the Sacraments. In the place of the Mass and Sacraments they have built up worship-services of hymns, prayers, sermons, and Bible readings, sometimes beautiful, edifying things, but a long way from the methods which the Apostles used because they got them from the Master.

Since these modern methods of worship supplant the Mass and the Sacraments they are direct rivals of the methods of Christ. We cannot be indifferent to this rivalry, and if we encourage man's methods we take sides against Christ. These new methods claim to be the true worship of God; but the method of Jesus Christ is the only true one. So their claim is false. God may be pleased when these false methods are used by sincere Protestants, who devoutly express in them

87

their faith and love. But He would not be pleased if we used these same methods, because we would not be honest or sincere, unless we were terribly ignorant; we would know that we were offering false worship instead of the true he asks of us.

This explains why we cannot take active part with non-Catholics in their official worship service. But why, cannot we go to their churches and remain passive, and see what goes on? The answer is that we can sometimes, for special occasions or special reasons. But the reason we cannot do it often is that we would encourage religious indifferentism. Outside of the Catholic Church there is a general notion in this country that one religion is essentially as good as another. You prefer yours; I like mine; but it is mostly a difference of tastes and needs. Since the Holy Spirit directs each one of us in our different interpretations of Christ's message, our personal internal faith is the important thing, and it doesn't greatly matter what we believe as long as we are sincere and live by our beliefs.

This is entirely contrary to the Catholic doctrine of the one true Church established by Jesus Christ. We believe that it is eternally important that we belong to this Church, which is the Mystical Body of Christ, and that we accept her teachings as coming from Christ, who remains constantly with her to keep her teaching truly. Yet our frequent attendance at non-Catholic religious functions would seem to give our support to indifferentism. Our non-Catholic friends would certainly understand it that way; and we might gradually come to adopt the notion ourselves and spread it to our Catholic friends.

The First Commandment forbids us to worship false gods, and it also forbids us to offer to the one true God any type of false worship. Canon 1258 of the Code of Canon Law outlines this prohibition in more detail:

"It is not licit for the faithful, in any manner to actively assist or take part in the religious functions of non-Catholics.

"It may be tolerated that they be present in a passive or material manner for reason of civil office or honor, and for a serious reason, which must be weighed by the Bishop in case of doubt, in the funerals, weddings, and similar solemnities of non-Catholics, provided that there is no danger of loss of faith or of scandal."

It is rather difficult to translate the precise Latin of the Code into accurate and readable English. But that is the general tenor of the law. Now what does it mean in practical application?

First of all, we are dealing here with formal, official, public worship of non-Catholic churches. You can say prayers privately with non-Catholics, or join with them in common prayer at civic functions. However, funerals and weddings, when they take place in Protestant churches are public religious functions. There is no doubt about that. So our law applies to them. We cannot take ACTIVE part in them. For instance, it would not be permitted for a priest to join with the minister in the service, or for Catholics to sing the hymns of the service with the choir.

PASSIVE presence may be permitted, however, in various circumstances. This does not mean that you have to sit with a blank stare on your face. You can be interested, look about you, listen attentively, and even move about. In other words you can be physically and mentally active as long as your activities do not contribute directly to the religious services —as religious services. Sometimes it is hard to distinguish. A pallbearer carries the body of the deceased into the church that a religious ceremony may be performed over it. An usher shows people to their places that they may assist at a religious service. But neither of them need have a direct part in the service as such.

Best men and bridesmaids at weddings have a much more prominent part in the function. They add to the splendor of the occasion; they are necessary in most States that the civil marriage may be contracted validly; and they are intimately near to the center of religious activities. However, considering the attitude of most non-Catholic churches on the subject of marriage, their functions are not strictly religious. In most Churches marriage is not considered a sacrament; and even where it is so considered, the witnesses do not participate in the administration of that sacrament. From

89

a religious point of view the marriage could take place without them. By their prominent presence they are evidently approving of the proceedings, and if there were any scandal to be given thereby they would certainly be broadcasting it. But essentially their function is civil, social, festive, honorary, decorative and ostentatious, rather than religious.

Canon 1258 indicates that you must have a serious reason just to be present at a wedding or a funeral. So it is evident that you must have a doubly serious reason to be an usher or a pallbearer. And your reason must be at least three times as serious if you are to be a bridesmaid or attendant.

We must often take circumstances into consideration in evaluating reasons and dangers of scandal. If you lived in a strong Catholic community eyebrows might well be raised and talk caused by your being attendant at a wedding in a Protestant church. But you actually live in a strong Protestant community, where Catholics have it rough enough without their aggravating the situation by seeming to insult their Protestant neighbors.

I mentioned that wedding attendants give seeming approval to heretical proceedings. In that might lie the principal source of scandal. It tends to foster religious indifference. Actually of course, they are not approving the heretical features of the program, but sanctioning the legitimate marriage of two people before God, in good faith. They would never be permitted to give such apparent approval to the attempted marriage of Catholics outside the Church, or to the marriage of divorced persons.

Q. For the first time in ten years I am able to attend daily Mass and receive Communion. But I must do it under a handicap, since I must bring my two youngest children with me. If you were to think of all the noisy, active, squirmy children you have known and roll them into one, that would be the image of our 15-month-old. She will sit and play only until the time of the Gospel; then she must move. If we can get the last pew in a side alcove to ourselves, I let her walk

*back and forth and ignore her until she becomes rowdy.
That usually happens between the Offertory and Consecration.*

*From then on, I hold her, playing finger games and trying
to keep my mind on the Mass. Communion is a diversion.
We go for a walk. After that she is usually tired and content
to be held. But I can follow only about half the Mass from
my Missal, with the rest only from memory.*

*Under these circumstances—half attention on my part,
and disturbing the other worshippers—should I content myself with a visit, or should I continue attending Mass, wor-
shiping as best I can, teaching the other child, and doing
my best to keep the baby from distracting others.*

A. The Lord love you; keep going to Mass. We have several
good women like you in our parish—and several duplicates
of your 15-month-old. But we have few complaints from our
other parishioners, and when we do we mostly ignore them.
Some churches may be neat little sanctuaries of quiet and
devotion; but those are not family parishes. The Church
urged you to have those children; she shares your patience
in raising them. Those little brats of the Gospel seemed to
annoy our Lord; the Apostles were for getting rid of them.
But Jesus said: Let them come to me.

Q. Is it a sin for people to talk and converse in church?

A. Much depends on intentions and circumstances. Does
your talking show any sign of disrespect for our Lord present there in the Blessed Sacrament? Does it distract other
people from their prayers? Are you talking about pious subjects or profane ones? Are you being charitable in everything
you say?

Conversation that is reasonable, respectful, proper and
charitable may well take place in church, as long as it does
not distract others who are at prayer. Our Lord would want
us to be at ease in his house, but never to forget that it is

91

HIS house, and that it is a house of prayer. We come there primarily to visit him. It is not polite to come into a person's home and then ignore your host, turn your back on him, and gossip with others in such ways as to exclude him.

Q. In regard to your recent article as to why the women put on such loud perfume when they go to church, will say that it is to drown out the awful cigarette smell that many men carry with them when they come to church. It seems that they must have one last "drag" before stepping in church, as shown by the large number of cigarette butts lying just outside the door.

A. Ladies, I want you to know that this letter was written by a man. And he is so courteous that he makes no mention of all those cigarette butts which have lipstick on them.

Q. Why don't you make a little comment in the Question Box about these young girls who go to Mass with their hair full of bobby pins or aluminum clippies? I admit that it is a wonderful thing to see so many young people at daily Mass during Lent, but some of them look terrible. I don't believe they would go on a date or even greet their boy-friends at the door looking the way some of them do when they approach the Communion rail. To my husband and me it seems downright disrespectful—and we have teen-age daughters of our own.

Of course they might have to get up a few minutes earlier to remove the clippies, but if they could see how they look to us I am sure they would fix their hair before coming to church. Why do their parents allow it? These girls come from nice families. Perhaps, if the priest who gives their retreat, or the nuns who teach them, would bring this up they might do better.

A. What comment is there left for me to make? I only hope we do not discourage those budding beauties from coming to Mass. It is surely much better for them to come with their clippies showing than not to come at all. And most of them are still quite attractive, bobby pins, babushka shawl and all. We chew these teen-agers out about so many things that I prefer to concentrate my campaign on more important issues; but I am happy to publish your question as a sharp hint. No need to scorn perfection!

Q. *My little girl likes to go down to the farm to spend several weeks in the summer. The people there are Methodists and last year, without my knowledge or consent, they took her to Sunday school. This year I haven't allowed her to go to the farm because they would take her again. Would it be a sin to allow her to visit them knowing that they probably would take her to Sunday school?*

A. Couldn't you just ask them not to take her and save me the trouble of answering your final question?

Q. *Is it necessary to kneel down to say morning and night prayers?*

A. It is not absolutely necessary, but is, by far, the best position for prayer; and a healthy person who habitually neglects to kneel for prayer is slipping badly in his religious fervor and duties. Next thing he will be neglecting the prayers entirely; and then he will be wide open for temptations; and soon his faith will start wobbling. Better be faithful about kneeling down humbly and devoutly.

Q. *Why are Catholics not permitted to attend socials and dinners given by non-Catholic Churches? We have been told that we are committing sin when we do so. It is difficult to explain the reason for this since Catholics expect these non-Catholics to attend their affairs.*

A. I fail to see why Catholics should not attend such dinners or social events, particularly in small communities where neighborly friendship and cooperation seem to demand it.

Some segregated rigorists may object that by attending and paying for our supper or entertainment we are giving encouragement and aid to a false religion. I think they have a distorted evaluation of the situation. Such aid and encouragement is merely an incidental "evil," permitted for good purposes: namely, charity, friendliness and community solidarity. It does not create religious indifference; it merely breaks the walls of our papist ghetto, fosters a sense of friendly fairness, and shows respect for our neighbor's sincerity.

Things may be different in a big city, or in strong Catholic centers, but in most small towns and rural areas, our Protestant neighbors must need great charity to tolerate our repudiation of them—our "holier-than-thou" exclusiveness. And then we wonder why bigotry blossoms!

Q. Am I right in believing that it is all right to buy things from bake sales that are put on by non-Catholic Churches?

A. I doubt very much that their cup cakes will be contaminated by heresy. The good-neighbor policy should start in our own little community. And only a fanatic would interpret your friendly little purchase as the promotion of a false religion.

Q. Recently our Superintendent of Schools (a Catholic man) acted as chairman of the Salvation Army's fund-raising campaign and sent our Catholic students to canvass the town door to door for funds. This seems wrong to me. Wouldn't this be taking an active part in another religion? Funds might be used to build churches, etc., as no special

94

project was mentioned. I feel I have a duty to find out the right and wrong of this, as I have two children in high school here.

A. I am confident that this campaign was for funds to be used by the Salvation Army in their welfare and relief work and not for their religious activities; so I don't think that individuals who contribute need to be troubled in conscience about cooperating in religious activities. However, I do think it is entirely out of order for our public school officials to assume leadership in campaigns of this kind supported by denominational or semi-religious groups. Imagine what a cry of protest would be raised if the superintendent became chairman of a Catholic Charities campaign and sent his little minions out to canvass the town. There would be frantic charges of "union of Church and State" and of violations of the first and fourteenth amendments to our Constitution.

Even as a Catholic layman, apart from his official position, I think your superintendent was letting his zeal outweigh his prudence. Unless the circumstances were exceptional, a Catholic layman should not assume a chairmanship of this kind. We are apt to get a bit maudlin about the Salvation Army because they are good to bums. Indeed, they are generous and often selfless in their charities. We approve, applaud, encourage, and lend our occasional conventional support. But their activities are directly sponsored by an heretical Church. They will feed a Catholic derelict and help him to sober up; but they have no special use for the Church of Rome. If they form a part of Community Chest we do not hesitate to include them in our support; but there is no reason why we should single them out and make them representative of the community—any more than Jewish Relief or Catholic Charities. Let them conduct their own campaigns, as we do ours.

Q. A difference of opinion has come up on the following question, not only between members of my family, but also

95

among the different members of the clergy whom we asked about it:

A member of our family was going to send a small present and a card congratulating a non-Catholic friend of ours on being confirmed. I said it was wrong to congratulate a non-Catholic on anything he does in the line of faith, because the non-Catholic teachings are contrary to the teachings in the one true faith. And if we congratulate them we say that a faith founded by man is equal to the faith founded by Jesus Christ. A priest I consulted agreed with me; but several priests said that they could see nothing wrong in sending the congratulations.

What is your opinion? And in a case of split opinions among the clergy whose advice should one follow?

A. I would send the little present and the card and make my friend happy. What is wrong with it? What harm can it do?

It would be wrong if we were to take active part in a non-Catholic religious service, or to positively encourage others to take such active part. It would do harm if we were to lead others to believe that we were indifferent about matters of religion, or that we really do equate man's religion with that of Christ. Your harmless congratulations do nothing of the kind. Here is the way I would interpret that card and gift—and the way I am sure my non-Catholic friends would interpret them:

They would show that I am thoughtful. I appreciate the joy of my friends and join them in it.

They would show that I am tolerant. I appreciate the sincerity of my friends, their good faith, their holy intentions, and their honest efforts to serve God. They know well that I do not agree with them in the way they go about it; but they don't expect me to taunt them constantly with their errors, to show a stern and reprimanding face toward their every devout effort.

My courtesy would show that I want to live in peace and

harmony with my friends; that I do not set myself up as judge over them, simply because I have been blessed by God with the true faith.

My little gift would show that I appreciate the social amenities by which people of different faiths live together happily and charitably in a mixed society, with mutual respect for firm convictions.

I don't believe any average American would interpret my gift and card as showing my approval of Protestant confirmation services. The danger is rather that my friends may sense a patronizing note in my congratulations; because they know how vacuous I hold their ceremony to be.

If your convictions are less firm than mine, or your position less clearly defined, then you might hesitate about sending the gift and card.

Even moral theologians sometimes disagree; and it is a generally accepted principle that, in case of such disagreement we are at liberty to follow the opinion which pleases us best. Possibly the same principle might apply to your question. Go right ahead and follow the opinion of the priest whom you consulted, since he agrees with you. But do not try to impose this opinion on others who have good authority for their position also.

Q. What is the Church's position regarding Catholics teaching in non-Catholic (public or religious) schools? Is any distinction made between lower grades and college level teaching?

A. I know of no legislation or pronouncement which reflects an official position of the Church in this matter. On general moral principles I would give the following answers to your question:

In normal circumstances there should be no reason for a Catholic to restrict his teaching in a public school at any level: from kindergarten through advanced graduate studies.

The question of teaching in denominational or church-

97

affiliated schools may be much more complicated. I would hesitate to give any general answer, except that I believe a Catholic would ordinarily feel more at home and at ease in another environment. Much depends on the nature of the school and the subject taught. Each case had best come up for individual consideration.

Q. A friend of mine who is a professional singer was singing in a Jewish temple (for pay) with the permission of his pastor. His conscience troubled him on the matter, and he consulted a missionary. The missionary became quite disturbed and told him he could do no such thing. My question has nothing to do with singing at Jewish services. What concerns me is whether, when your pastor makes a decision, it does not end the matter. I told this fellow that I agreed that it was not proper to sing in the temple, but that after his pastor had ruled that it was all right he should not have consulted another priest. Should we, or can we be selective in obeying the decisions of a pastor?

A. We can and we should. Pastors are not infallible. Unless you have confidence in your pastor's judgment do not take your problem to him. When you have asked his advice you should respect it. But it is only the scrupulous person who should refrain from consulting someone else when doubts persist. In this case it would seem that the pastor was wrong; and evidently the missionary thought so.

Q. At a family reunion about 10 of us will be Catholics; there will be about 50 present. Should we bow our heads at the blessing, which will be asked by a Protestant, before eating? Or should we ask to say our own blessing? Or should we sign ourselves after the blessing? There are quite a few of them who openly ridicule Catholics. Would there be sin attached to just skipping through it the easy way?

98

A. I would simply bow my head and be quiet—and polite. We are permitted to join Protestants in private prayers, and this blessing is just that, even though there are 50, or several times 50 present. If you want to be really militant add the sign of the cross, without ostentation. Personally I would skip it—the easy way.

Q. *I have heard that one of our Catholic schools requires its non-Catholic students to make a retreat along with the Catholic students. Is this right?*

A. I wonder if your rumor is true. I haven't tried to check it, but it doesn't sound probable to me. They might encourage the non-Catholics to join in the retreat, to the extent of attending the conferences and reciting the prayers. They might provide some conferences on virtue and morality and fundamental Christian living which they would require the non-Catholics to attend. But I have not known of any form of pressure being put on non-Catholic students in our schools to get them to take part in Catholic religious exercises.

As a matter of fact I doubt that we would be justified in exerting such pressure on general moral principles. For one thing the presence of non-Catholics in Catholic religious services is a sort of "passive participation" frowned upon by Canon 2259; it should be permitted only for good reason. The active devotional interest of non-Catholics may constitute such reason. Herding them in would seem unreasonable.

Q. *Today I wrote to the Sisters of St. Francis in Boston, Mass., to inform them that I wouldn't continue with the Novena being sent around the world, as I didn't believe in this form of prayer. You are told to make 9 copies and send them out before the fourth day, and if you do you will receive a favor from the Virgin of Fatima; and you are warned not to permit the Novena to be broken in your house. The alternative was to write to the Sisters, and since*

99

they are no doubt sincere in their efforts, as was the lady who sent the letters to me, I wrote to them.

A. I have counted ten different orders of Franciscan Sisters in the Archdiocese of Boston, and they have many different houses in the city of Boston. Whichever one gets your letter will have a quick way of disposing of it. I am sure they are all too busy to be fooling with superstitious novenas. The crack-pot who starts these crazy things just dreams up that Sisters of St. Francis gimmick.

You did a good deed in breaking the chain. And your letter to the good Sisters will do no harm. They must be used to this sort of annoyance; probably the Post Office officials in Boston are even more provoked.

Best thing to do with any sort of chain letter is to tear it into bits and drop it in the waste basket—and grin right back at the demon who threatens you.

Q. During the recent Papal conclave, my child came home from school and proceeded to inform the family that according to the "prophecy" of St. Malachy, the next Pope would be someone who had "come from the East, over the water," etc., etc. My wife asked him where he got this information, and he said from his Sister in school. The same day, a friend of mine told me his boy had come from his Catholic high school with the story, from his Sister, that if Cardinal Spellman had been elected Pope the world would come to an end.

My question is this: What should parents do in situations like this? If we dismiss such talk as superstition which is what it is, then the child's respect for his teaching Sister is undermined. If we overlook these fantastic tales of the weird and the marvelous, then we are permitting the child to develop, at the minimum, an unhealthy, undiscriminating attitude towards religion and his Faith; and we are making it doubly difficult for him to distinguish between what is a

100

matter of belief and what is rank superstition, bordering on hysteria.

Is there any way that our good Sisters can be persuaded to rid themselves of this apparently Sisterly propensity for the fantastic and the marvelous and the pseudoprophetic? It seems a shame that parents and discerning educators and editors have to spend so much time in the delicate task of undoing the spurious religiosity the children are exposed to in the grade and high school.

Can you offer any suggestions as to how to put an end once and for all to this tampering with the Faith, and this highly subjective embroidery of its realities by those entrusted to teach our children the truth? I am angry.

A. That smoke which billows out of your ears is so black that the Cardinals might have used it to signal "no election"; it would have saved confusion.

And really, we might be able to make that "prophecy of Malachy" stand up. Of course Venice is not really east of Rome, geographically—but everyone always thinks it is. After all it is on the eastern coast, while Rome is on the western shore of Italy; and traditionally Venice has always looked toward the East for much of its trade and culture. Cardinal Roncalli's patriarchal cathedral was definitely Byzantine. So in a figurative sense we might say he came from the East; and he certainly had to cross water! How else would he get by those canals of Venice?

But even if you won't admit that the "prophecy" stands up, you will certainly have to bow to the vindication of the "superstition of the R." Those familiar with this venerable and well-proven theory might have told you that Cardinal Roncalli had an excellant chance of being elected. The new Pope just had to have an R in his name. Popes alternate between those who have the R and those who lack it. There was obviously no R in Pacelli; so there had to be one in the name of his successor. And there is.

(N.B. My research assistants find that the alternations of

101

the R hold good since Pius IX; Gregory XVI breaks the rhythm.)

Honestly, my fuming friend, I do not know the answer to your problem. But I am sure it does you good to lower your pent-up pressure, and maybe your strong words will make tiny dents in the thick surface of superstitious minds. But I doubt it.

Q. Our religion teacher has stunned my belief that St. Joseph was chosen as spouse of the Blessed Virgin by the sign of lilies growing from his staff. We have been taught this story since first grade and have been taught this all through grammar school; but now that we have reached high school our instructor says it is not true. Could you please clear up this doubt for us. If the story is not true could you tell me from whence it originated?

A. Come cry on my shoulder, little girl; it is time you knew the facts of life: there ain't no Santa Claus!

This is the second querulous question I have had in two weeks about the fabulous method of teaching religion, which is apparently current in some of our Catholic schools. If this keeps up I shall be spurred to abandon my normal restraint and start railing against those pious educators who flavor facts with fancy, mix marvels with mysteries, and mingle fairies with the choirs of angels.

Modesty does not cause my restraint in this matter; relative ignorance of juvenile pedagogy would not halt my expression of opinion. It is rather that I hesitate to take firmly the side of those dusty factualists who would drive from life all its poetry, imagination, and fantastic coloring. Most children outlive the legend of Santa Claus without losing faith in parental veracity. Of course the stork is in total disrepute, and he deserved no better fate. He was awkward and ungainly at his best. But fairies still have their fanciful place. Pixies, elves, and sprites need not be restrained in their dance; even spooks and goblins should have room to roam;

and I would not be the one guilty of driving the fatal stake through the heart of the vampire.

It would not be wise to cram into the trusting mind of the child all of the stark realities of life, just because they are true. He would be scared to hysteria. It is better that he learn unpleasant truths gradually after he has learned to love life and understand total values. It is painful to have illusions destroyed; but it were sheer tragedy never to have had them at all.

Yet when it comes to the faith, if I must take sides, I would favor the stark realities—especially when a priest or religious is doing the teaching. Fairies are fine if you keep them on the moor or in the hedges; but they are confusing when they dance on the altar. Myths are amusing on Mt. Olympus; they are misleading on Mt. Calvary.

Your story about the flowering staff of St. Joseph had its origin in the apocryphal writings of the early Christian centuries, especially one called the Protoevangelium of James, which pretends to be a Gospel written by James, the Brother of the Lord. Like all the apocryphal writings it is full of imaginings. After all, the inspired Gospels tell us precious little about Joseph, the man closest to Jesus. Read the first two chapters of Luke, and you have it; A confusing genealogy, the fact of his espousal to Mary, the various messages of the angels, his retiring faithfulness at Bethlehem, on the way to Egypt, and in his artisan's work at Nazareth. Nothing about his age, appearance, birth, or death. He is there when he is needed and then no more is heard of him.

The early Christian people were as curious as you and I. They were not satisfied with the inspiring sparcity of these details. There was not enough glamor in the simple facts. So they put their imaginations to work and let them run riot. The results appear in the Apocryphals: mostly fantastic; some fairly reasonable; but all unreliable as sources of historical fact.

Many of the stories from these Apocryphal writings made their way into the popular traditions of the Middle Ages, and while some of them were silly and all were fanciful they had a wide influence on art, poetry, the mystery plays, and writings both pious and profane. And they often livened up the dull instructions of doctrine. Then like yourself, those who heard the facts and fancies mingled, failed to distinguish between them; and later when the fancies withered they tended to infect the facts with their blight also.

Apocryphal accounts are often contradictory; so we have various stories of Joseph. But he is generally presented as an old man in his dotage, often as a widower, and frequently as the father of other children. From the Protoevangelium of James we get the story that Mary was raised in the Temple, and when it came time for her to choose a spouse, the High Priest Zachary, acting with divine counsel, prepared for the nuptials in a big way. He sent trumpeters up and down the valleys of Palestine to call all widowers before him. They came, each with his staff; but the staff of Joseph burst into bloom, and a dove flew out from the flower and lit on the head of Zachary. That was enough for the High Priest, and he proclaimed Joseph the chosen one—in spite of his humble and senile protests.

It is a story worthy of a poet; but it makes little claim to prosaic accuracy.

7. *The Second and Third Commandments*

God's Name in Vain. Using "Hell." ·
Cursing and Swearing. Private
Vows. Why Not the Sabbath? Sun-
day Closing. Servile Work. Missing
Mass. Shopping on Holy Days.
Work on Holy Days.

Q. *Is it a mortal sin to use God's name vainly?*

A. Hardly ever! If you did it maliciously, out of profound
irreverence for God's sacred name it would be. Or if you did
it so shockingly as to cause grave scandal to young people
it might be. Or if you deliberately developed a habit of
profanity it probably would be. Or if you recognize that you
have a vicious habit of swearing and cursing, and simply
refuse to try to do anything about it, you would probably be
guilty of mortal sin.

But the misuse of God's name is mostly a careless, thoughtless habit, without malice or intentional irreverence. It represents laziness of thought and poverty of vocabulary. There
are many good English words—and some of them four-letter
ones—which would express your idea precisely, but instead
of making the effort to learn and use them you throw out
the name of God thoughtlessly and without meaning.

105

Often the misuse of God's name shows puerile vanity. As a boy you thought it sounded big and manly to swear like a trooper. Now you are a great big overgrown hulk of a man, still motivated by the little boy's retarded vanity.

It indicates a failure to fully appreciate God's sacred goodness, his supreme dominion over us, and his sacrificing love for us. The ancient Jewish people, who were fearfully aware of God's immediate power and presence, did not dare pronounce his name, even with reverence. And any decent one of us will speak honorably of the person we really love—and the one we know loves us.

Q. Is it wrong to say, "Oh, hell," or "damn it" around friends who think it is wrong? Is it a mortal sin?

A. It is certainly not a mortal sin. You cannot always be concerned about the excessive sensitivity of your scrupulous friends. It is not charitable to shock them too much. But the frequent use of such petty exclamations shows a defect of forceful English rather than delinquency in morals.

Q. In our study club I have been assigned the topic, "The Second Commandment." As you well know, this deals with cursing and swearing, and I would like you to advise me on several points which I have often heard debated:

First, I have heard it said that if you direct your oath or curse at an inanimate object, it isn't considered truly swearing, and consequently is not a sin—such as damning the hammer for striking your thumb instead of the nail.

Secondly, what about those of us who use "Oh, Lord," "My God," and such, as expressions of surprise or horror, as a matter of course or habit, without even thinking (our priest does this quite often).

Last, I have also heard it argued that "Oh, hell" and "damn it" are not considered swearing as God's name isn't used.

106

I realize that I am really getting technical, but to make our lessons truly helpful and understandable we have to try to apply them directly to the members of our club.

A. First of all, I would urge that in preparing your talk you accentuate the positive: Out of love and veneration and zeal for God's glory we should be reverent always toward his Holy Name and towards all things closely associated with him—holy things in general.

Though you do not mention it, I am sure that you know that the sin most directly forbidden by the words of the Second Commandment is perjury—swearing falsely—as when we take a false oath or break a sincere oath. It is really calling upon God's name in vain to ask him to witness by his supreme truthfulness something which we know to be false and insincere.

Right off it shocks us a bit to realize that swearing is an act of religion, something good, pleasing to God and meritorious to ourselves, when it is done properly. Of course I am speaking of swearing in its original sense: appealing to God in solemn manner to witness the truth of my declaration or the sincerity of my promise. There is also careless swearing, by which we take an oath—call upon God's name—without particular concern about the truthfulness or importance of the statement we ask God to witness. This is irreverent. Then worst of all, there is that deliberately false swearing, which is perjury—always a mortal sin.

"To swear" also means to use profane language, to curse, and to use God's name in anger or for emphasis, or from poverty of vocabulary—because we don't know enough good forceful English words to express our ideas. This sort of thing is usually a venial sin of irreverence, if it is done deliberately or with some measure of awareness. It is contrary to the virtue of religion which prompts us to worship God. By showing disrespect for Him we "un-worship" Him.

When we curse a person we commit a sin against two virtues: religion, as I have just explained, and charity, which prompts us to love our neighbor as ourselves. Love of neighbor should inspire us to pray for him. A curse is a prayer in reverse. We do speak to God about our neighbor but we ask God to do sundry evil things to him—even to damn his soul for all eternity. If it were serious and malicious a curse could be a mortal sin against charity. In ordinary daily usage it doesn't get that bad.

You see now why it is not nearly so bad to "damn" the hammer as to curse the wielder of the hammer. You are not obliged to have charity towards the hammer. So you have only the sin of irreverence—even if you were deliberate about it. (Incidentally, did you ever try damning the nail for dodging the hammer? It makes quite as much sense.)

Much of our habitual profanity—vulgar, careless, passionate, or slovenly use of God's name—is relieved of sin because it is a habit and consequently is done without direct action of the will. Coddling the habit is a sin—and it might be a serious one. But acting from established habit is merely slavish.

Sometimes our daily profanity, may be delivered of sin, too, by force of custom. Words have the meaning that social acceptance gives to them. The little old lady who is shocked into an exclamation of "Oh, my goodness" is actually swearing by divine attribute. It might be a little hard to tell whether her words are prayer or profanity—but surely no one would accuse her of sin. When the German says "Mein Gott," or the Frenchman says "Mon Dieu" he means little more of irreverence than the little old lady, and creates no greater shock. The same is true when you exclaim, "Oh, Lord."

A complete presentation of the Second Commandment requires a consideration of vows: the prudent taking of them, the obligations which result from them, and the faithful keeping of them.

We have not yet mentioned the most serious of all sins forbidden by the Second Commandment: blasphemy. It is an expression of contempt for God Himself, usually inspired by hate, despair, or rebellion. It is an intentional effort to dishonor God—the direct opposite of worshipping him. Often it implies a denial of God's existence, or His mercy, or His

108

justice. Fortunately a person of faith rarely indulges in it with serious deliberation.

Q. How binding are private vows? Say, for instance, one promised to say a rosary each day for the rest of one's life and over the last 25 years one has forgotten how many rosaries were said. Could one have Masses said in honor of the Blessed Virgin to make up some of the rosaries, and if so about how many rosaries are equal to a Mass?

A. First of all, let me say that I am personally prejudiced against private vows. They are often made by scrupulous people and serve only to increase their scruples. Or they are made in surges of fervor and enthusiasm which soon die out and leave the votary bound to a galling burden, which may be resented or neglected, to spiritual damage.

Private vows should be made only with deliberate care, spiritual calmness and prudent consultation. Nearly always it is unwise to take a vow like yours for life without first trying it out for a period of years. In her public vows, in convent life, the Church requires a postulancy, a novitiate and at least three years in temporary vows before she will permit a person to take vows for life. We should imitate her prudence.

A vow is a free and deliberate promise made to God to do something good, and when it is seriously made it imposes an obligation on the votary, under pain of sin. It is a sort of personal law.

A vow prevents a licit and effective change of mind. Once it has been made the votary cannot get out of it on his own authority. He can commute or change it into something better, but only the proper Church authority can terminate it by dispensation. In a vow like yours this authority is your bishop. He can terminate your vow if he finds good reason to do so—if he judges that it is for your spiritual welfare.

If you really took a serious vow, with the intention of imposing an obligation on yourself, and if you have been fail-

109

ing frequently in it, so that it has become a barren burden to you, I recommend that you talk to your confessor, or some other priest, about the advisability of asking the bishop for a dispensation.

I doubt that you have any obligation of making up the rosaries you have missed. The harm has been done—the obligation is not cumulative, unless you definitely intended it that way. You obliged yourself to say a rosary each day. Once a day is past you cannot go back and make up the obligation in which you failed. That day is gone forever.

There is no way of answering your final question. All the rosaries on earth would not equal in essence the value of a Mass. A rosary is a prayer and takes its spiritual value from your love and fervor in saying it, from the gracious goodness of Almighty God in accepting it, and from the spiritual generosity of the Church in granting indulgence for it. But the Mass is a continuation of the Sacrifice of Jesus Christ on Calvary; so it shares directly in the infinite merits of that Sacrifice. There is no measuring its value.

However, the effect on your soul or mine is another question. We might be made saints by one rosary said with faith and fervor. And the unlimited graces of a dozen Masses might run off our hardened souls like rain on the roof.

Q. I would appreciate it very much if you would tell me why the Sabbath, the seventh day of the week, is no longer observed as the day of rest. Since Jesus taught that He did not come to change the law, I wonder by what authority this has been done. I have not been able to find any evidence in the Bible which would indicate the Sabbath should be relinquished, even though Jesus arose on the first day of the week.

A. Many of the laws of the Old Testament were ceremonial, prescribing details of Jewish worship and religious practice; for example, the dietary laws, circumcision, and various sacrifices. The Jewish religion was the true and proper wor-

110

ship of God up to the time of Christ, but it was only temporary. Its purpose was to prepare the people for the coming of the Redeemer; and once he had come and preached his Gospel its purpose was fulfilled. It was no longer the true religion; it was replaced by Christianity.

Once Judaism was replaced its ceremonial laws no longer had purpose. The Apostles were all Jews and had been accustomed to observe these ceremonial laws all their life. So they were a bit confused about their obligation of continuing to observe them. I would suggest that you read the Acts of the Apostles, Chapters 10, 11, and 15, and St. Paul's Epistle to the Galatians about their disputes and final decisions on some of these laws. It finally became clear to them that if they were going to spread Christianity among non-Jewish people they would have to gradually eliminate most of these ceremonial laws. And they realized that they had authority from Christ to do it.

Generally the Ten Commandments were not mere ceremonial laws. They were firm statements of moral obligations which arose from the natural law. For that reason—in their essence, if not in their form—they oblige all people of all time, not merely the Jews of Old Testament times. It is wrong for anyone to steal or commit murder anywhere at any time.

However, the Third Commandment is an exception. In its actual form it is ceremonial. It is based on the natural law, in that we all have a natural obligation of worshipping God, and we should set some time aside for that purpose. But the actual setting aside of the Sabbath—the seventh day of the week—and the details of its observance are strictly for the Jews, like the circumcision and abstaining from pork.

Just how long those Christians who had been Jews continued to observe the Sabbath we do not know. Probably for a generation at least, since life-long habits are not quickly unlearned. However we have evidence that during the time of the Apostles the custom developed of meeting for the Eucharistic Sacrifice on the first day of the week—Sunday—which was called the Lord's day (Apoc. 1, 10). St Paul literally talked a man to death at Troas, "on the first day of the

111

week, when we had met for the breaking of bread" (Acts 20, 7). Of course he undid the harm by reviving him.

The Didache—Doctrine of the Twelve Apostles—is about the oldest Christian document we have apart from the New Testament. It was written about the year 100. In it we have this direction: "On the Lord's Day come together and break bread. And give thanks (i.e. offer the Eucharist) after confessing your sins that your sacrifice may be pure."

St. Ignatius was the second successor of St. Peter as Bishop of Antioch. He became a martyr under the Emperor Trajan at Rome, probably about 110. Shortly before that he had written an Epistle to the Magnesians in which he mentioned that Christians were "no longer observing the Sabbath, but living in the observance of the Lord's Day, on which also our Lord rose again."

So apparently within a century from the time of Christ there was a complete change from Sabbath observance to keeping Sunday holy as the Lord's day.

Q. It was with great interest that I read an article in your paper, in regard to Sunday business. As a Protestant I am very concerned about it, because I am employed in a supermarket and have to take my turn every fourth Sunday. We also have Catholics working there every Sunday. Also Protestants and Catholics alike make their purchases on Sunday.

Our ministers have tried to bring about Sunday closing for the last few years. All merchants are willing to close but one; so everybody stays open.

I have tried to contact the local priest in town, but he never was home. Two of my letters have never been answered.

At present another large supermarket is about to be opened across from the Catholic church . . .

Can you advise me, what your stand is and what can be done in regard to Sunday legislation in our legislature?

Would your Church be willing to support such a move?

112

A. Our priests and Catholic people are becoming increasingly concerned about the trend toward Sunday business. We would all be in agreement that only necessity or proven public good should permit business to be conducted on Sunday.

The law of our Church is quite definite on this matter. Canon 1248 of the Code of Canon Law says that servile work should not be performed on Sunday and that in general, unless established customs are to the contrary, public markets and buying and selling should not be conducted on Sunday. We have no legitimate custom in this country which would permit supermarkets and the like to stay open on Sunday and do business as usual.

In general you can count on Catholic support for any efforts to keep ordinary stores and business houses closed on Sunday. However, I think we should be cautious about legislation in the matter, unless the competition becomes so great that it definitely interferes with the rights of employees in this business. In other words, legislation should not be on the basis of blue laws, but rather as a protection for workers.

Q. I am very much confused as to what is servile work, forbidden on Sunday. In one pamphlet I read that knitting was servile work, but crocheting was not. This seems ridiculous to me.

A. The law of the Church making Sunday a day of rest is expressed in Canon 1248, of which this is an approximate translation:

On Sundays and holy days of obligation the people must hear Mass and refrain from servile work, from judicial proceedings, and also from public trading, auctions, and other public buying and selling. An exception is noted for such business as may be sanctioned by custom or indult.

Several of our bishops have recently attracted nationwide attention by strong pastoral letters condemning various apparent and growing abuses of Sunday rest in our country.

113

The super-market has come in for particular attention because it is leading the way to business-as-usual on the Lord's day. But the private and personal activities of all people, Catholic and non-Catholic, give evidence that Sunday is losing its meaning as a day of rest—and even more as a day specially dedicated to the service of God. On the farms of the midwest, at certain seasons, Sunday sees almost as many tractors and implements in the fields as any other day. And in the towns you will see people working on the lawns, putting on storm windows, toiling in the garden, or painting the garage.

Regarding the increasing tendency to personal labor on Sunday I wrote an article some time ago, indicating my belief that an outmoded concept of servile work was a contributing factor. The inspiration for my article came from a review of recent literature on the subject published by Father Gerald Kelly, S.J., in the March, 1948, issue of *Theological Studies,* and if anyone is interested in further study of the subject I would refer him to the sources mentioned there. (Vol. IV No. 1, pp. 105-108).

Of course I realize that a modern, reasonable and practical concept of what type of work is forbidden on Sunday will not cure all abuses or dam a swelling tide. We must remember that Catholics are only a minority factor in the growth and direction of national popular trends. Throughout the centuries in most Christian countries the Sunday rest was popular with the common people, often a definite social boon, strongly reinforced by civil law. In our own country our Puritan and Protestant ancestry saw to the general enactment of civil laws which often exceeded in rigor the precept of the Church. Today, in many parts of the United States, there are signs that civil support is weakening, and that the spurs of competition may urge even the scrupulous and the lazy into Sunday business.

Anyway my article aroused some interesting letters. I was roundly condemned by traditionalists for contributing to the regrettable trend, but here are examples of some replies I found more pleasant:

"I was shocked when I read in a Catholic national maga-

114

zine that it is a sin for one to knit or work for an hour in one's garden for pleasure on Sunday, but is all right to type or paint for profit on the Sabbath. This is gross class legislation, a hang-over from feudal law. This medieval custom should be kept only as a relic of the dead past . . ."

"You can't possibly imagine my joy in reading your views. Women cannot sit around twirling their thumbs—and how many of us paint lovely pictures or do needlepoint? I am the mother of seven and also have a sister and nephew to take care of in a 13-room house. My week days are full of children and hard work. I have always loved sewing, knitting and crocheting, but if these were wrong that left me with reading— too much of which would be a waste of time . . ."

And this was best of all—the penmanship was precious: "I am an old lady and I still observe the rules laid down for us in childhood. The traditional list is well given. But . . . Thank God for your messing up the rules; for Satan still finds plenty work for idle hands to do."

Another lady asked that I discuss "working on Sunday at our church socials, chicken dinners," etc.: "I never work harder or am more tired . . . but some of our priests say it is all right, because we are doing the work for God's Church."

Until the past few years our Catholics, both priests and laity, were generally uncertain about the law of fasting. Traditionalists were waging a rear-guard action, splitting ounces and making menus. Then most of the bishops of the country adopted a relative norm—a common-sense, practical norm adapted to modern American customs of living and eating, and far more people are making a generous gesture of fasting than ever before.

I have never been quite sure of the legal basis on which the bishops made this adoption. Presumably they considered that general practice had already induced the relative norm of fasting, or that they were able, by reason of their office, to declare and stabilize the prevailing custom in the face of various interpretations. At any rate, it is now an accomplished fact. And if it can be done for fasting it can be done in like manner for servile works, if the bishops are interested. Certainly the confusion is equal, both in theory and practice.

And after all, the law does define fasting (Can. 1251); it only names servile works.

My contention is that the traditional notion of servile work, as handed down from the Middle Ages with little change, simply does not fit modern conditions of working and living. According to the traditional moral books, servile work is determined by its own intrinsic nature. It is a type of work—period. It is the work once done by slaves and servants, whence it gets its name. It is the work done in overalls, with a plow or an axe or a shovel. It is the work done in an apron (or more recently in slacks) with a scrub brush, and some smudge, and a bit of sweat.

By contrast, the works which are liberal, or not servile, are those of the scholar, the artist, and the gentleman—the works of mind and imagination—creative efforts.

To the traditional moralist the presence or absence of the profit motive has nothing to do with the question. If it is servile by its nature, it is servile—period. The fact that you may do it for pleasure or recreation makes no difference. If it is liberal by nature then you may earn a liberal stipend by laboring at it all day Sunday and not break the law of the Church.

Generally speaking, the traditional moralist is not the least interested in your intention or the effort you expend. Servile work remains servile no matter how charitable or generous your intention in doing it; but you can paint dirty pictures all Sunday long and only break the sixth commandment. Knitting is servile work even though it is your favorite pastime and tires you little; but you can walk twenty miles with a full hunter's pack, blister your feet, and come home half dead, and not a lick of servile work have you done.

It should be apparent to anyone that the application of medieval norms to modern life and work is quite arbitrary. We have many thousands of different kinds of work today which were never dreamed of in past centuries. Who is going to say whether the work of a laboratory technician is servile or liberal? Your guess is as good as mine. But who lays down the law that such a technician cannot work on Sunday, under pain of mortal sin? Some arbitrary moralist?

116

Many modern jobs are half brain-work and half manual labor. But you can't say that they are half-permitted on Sunday and half-forbidden. They must be either servile or liberal—though some moralists have designated these inbetween jobs as *opera communia,* which they hold not to be forbidden, because not entirely servile.

If you follow this opinion the work of the stenographer, bookkeeper, accountant or business executive is not servile. So by the word of the law it is not forbidden on Sunday. Consequently, if we were to follow the old traditional norms literally, we would have to tell the entire personnel of a big insurance office that it would be perfectly all right for them to work on Sunday, full force. What law are they violating? They are doing no servile work. There is no public marketing in the traditional sense of Canon 1248. They are just a building full of people engaged in liberal work, for pay— same as any other day of the week.

Fortunately for Sunday observance the good sense of our people is more strict than the unrealistic logic of the traditional moralist. Custom is the real determinant of what is servile work, and custom is not stagnant. It changes with the times. St. Thomas Aquinas, after firmly establishing the intrinsic norm for determining servile work, left a loop-hole for this change of custom: time and place may change the classification of various works. (Secunda Secundae, Q. 122, art. 4, ad quartum, in fine.)

Actually I believe that if we were to take the arguments of St. Thomas and apply them understandingly to the modern world we would have to come to the conclusion that many types of work he called liberal would today be called servile, and vice versa, because of changes in types and manner of servitude. Works of sin he calls servile because they are done in the service of the devil. Works of the body are servile because they are done in service of the human master. Work of the mind is liberal, because no one can enslave your mind.

Today in America no man is another's servant in the manner of the thirteenth century, but most men work for a boss, and half of them slave by mental labor rather than

117

bodily exertion. Without hinting that a man's mind can be enslaved (except by brainwashing), we would have to be blind to the facts of modern life not to see that modern man's servitude is often in works of the intellect, creative, artistic, scientific, and "liberal."

And likewise, in modern life, there are works of the body by which a man expresses his personal freedom. He knows no better method of getting away from the boss than to retire to his garden and putter there. He finds complete relief from the mental servitude of his job by tinkering with his car.

In many respects custom has already established some relative norms for determining what work is servile; and even some traditional manualists have taken it into account. My edition of Noldin's Moral Theology dates from 1923; it lists the use of the typewriter as liberal work, unless it is the kind of typing one does at his job during the week. But then the author goes on to distinguish between *acu pingere* (which I translate as embroider) and *acu texere* (to knit, or crochet). The former is liberal, allowed on Sunday; the latter is servile and sinful. How arbitrary can you get?

What do I mean by relative? The nature of the work is determined by its relation to the person doing the work, his motive, his pay, and his usual occupation. People are convinced today that it does make a difference whether you work for pay or for fun on Sunday; whether you work hard, with fatigue, or relaxed, for exercise; and whether you disturb your neighbors with your lawn-mower or putter quietly in your basement. There is a growing tendency to consider licit that work which is done as a hobby, or for a pious or charitable cause, and without pay—especially if it doesn't demand great effort or tire you excessively.

Of course some of the old categories of servile work have not changed, and probably never will, e.g., ploughing your field, or laying bricks, or stoking a furnace. Others will always remain liberal, like reading and creative writing. But the classification of others must depend on common estimation and custom—that custom which results from the Catho-

118

lic conscience, and from the common sense of priests and people.

This common sense norm would define servile work as that labor which you put out during the week to earn a living or make a profit. It is your weekday work, the exercise of your trade, or profession. If you are a doctor you do servile work in your office and at the hospital. If you are a scientist you do servile work juggling atoms or equations. And if you are a stenographer it is servile work for you to make those little hooks and curls in your notebook.

Sunday is the day of rest, and if you do your regular weekday work on Sunday you are not resting. You are making Sunday a workday, just like any other day. You are defeating the purpose of the Lord's day, even though your work be entirely liberal, mental, and imaginative. The purpose of the precept is to set you free from your routine, daily cares of the world, that you may devote yourself to divine things.

On the other hand, if puttering with your roses is your favorite recreation from the mental drudgery and fatigue of your week in the office, then common sense and growing custom are apt to tell you to go ahead. Your Sunday recreation should not be hard menial labor; but on what other day are you going to get any benefit out of your do-it-your-self kit?

Don't you agree that this is the idea of most good people who can be found working around lawns, gardens, automobiles, and basements on Sunday, without thought of serious sin? Modern interpretation as expressed in growing custom puts this puttering on a level with hunting, fishing, and bird-watching. It is something you do instead of playing golf: recreation, not servile work. Your servile work is keeping books, selling insurance, or handling radioactive isotopes.

And women can putter too. Who considers knitting work today? It is a diversion. Something you do with your hands while you talk, or watch TV.

Q. A person "misses" Mass if he lets himself be distracted

119

deliberately on Sunday or a holy day. Is any sin involved in being similarly distracted during daily Mass?

A. You are a very rigorous moralist, my friend—so rigorous in fact that your supposition is all wrong. A person does not "miss" Mass by being distracted, even voluntarily, during Mass.

We are obliged by a law of the Church to attend Mass on Sunday. The law requires:

(1) that we be present physically,

(2) at a Mass celebrated in any Catholic rite,

(3) in a church, or a public or semi-public oratory, or a cemetery chapel, or out in the open—at a field Mass;

(4) that we be present for the entire Mass from the prayers at the foot of the altar to the last Gospel, and

(5) that we maintain *external* attention. This means that we cannot fulfill our obligation of hearing Mass while we are asleep, or reading some secular book or newspaper with concentrated attention, or carrying on an animated conversation.

The law of the Church does not command *internal* attention. Voluntary distractions at Mass or prayer are sins in their own right—venial sins—but they are probably not much worse on Sunday than on a week-day, unless we are distracted out of intentional disrespect for the law of the Church.

Q. *We are a farm family and do not work on holy days. Would it be a sin for us to go shopping on those days, after attending Mass?*

A. I would like to tell you that it would be a sin, just to keep you from doing it. But actually, it isn't. Our American custom of doing business on holy days has established itself so thoroughly that it gives us exemption from the general law of the Church in this regard.

Canon 1248 commands us to go to Mass on Sundays and holy days, and to abstain from servile work on those days.

120

It also forbids court (judicial) procedures on those days; and then it adds that public markets, auctions, and other public buying and selling are prohibited, unless legitimate customs permit them.

We have a legitimately established general custom in the United States that stores remain open and business be carried on as usual on those holy days which are not also civil holidays. This custom affects only four days a year: the Ascension, the Assumption, All Saints, and the Immaculate Conception—and very often one of them falls on a Sunday, when the custom does not apply. Our other two holy days, Christmas and New Year's, are not subject to this custom.

Here is a fact worthy of note: Custom permits public buying and selling on these four holy days; it does not excuse us from the law which forbids servile work. Of course our custom of general business as usual makes it necessary for many people to work on these days in order to keep their jobs or maintain their business—but it is only the necessity which excuses them. As regards servile work, holy days are just like Sundays. It is forbidden and custom alone does not excuse from the law. But established custom may make the work necessary—and necessity excuses.

The fact that you may shop on holy days does not mean that you can extend the privilege to Sunday. There is a growing abuse in this regard. The greedy owners of a big chain-store or super-market decide to stay open on Sunday to grab more business; and then the other merchants of the community feel that they must do business as usual, in self-defense.

It is one thing to follow an established custom which the law recognizes (like our American custom of business on holy days) and quite a different thing to contribute to the growth of an abuse (like keeping stores open on Sunday).

Our American custom permits a bit of casual shopping on Sunday—e.g. drug store products, gasoline, and the Sunday paper. But shopping tours are strictly forbidden.

You can do private buying or selling on Sunday—e.g. sell that old nag to your neighbor, or trade your heap for his jalopy. But there should be no servile work involved and of

121

course you are not allowed to gyp him. It is *public* merchandizing which is forbidden on Sunday.

Q. Your answer about shopping on holy days made me wonder how a farm family should regard such a day. It has never seemed right to me to hurry to an early Mass and then rush home again to carry on the day's work as though it were an ordinary day. But on the other hand, if you are in the midst of corn-picking are you obliged to stop for that day? If we are exchanging work with a non-Catholic neighbor he isn't likely to take a kindly attitude towards continuing alone, or celebrating the holy day too.

A. The farm family, in ordinary circumstances, should consider a holy day exactly like Sunday. They should do no more work on the holy day than they do on Sunday. In other words, they should do only that servile work which is necessary, e.g., the daily chores.

I say in ordinary circumstances because it may be that changing work, or other neighborhood customs, will make it necessary for you to work on a holy day when they would not require you to work on Sunday. In the days of the big neighborhood threshing crews it was often necessary to work on the feast of the Assumption. Otherwise you let the neighbors down and seemed to shirk your fair share. This should not be true, however, when you are exchanging work with only one neighbor or another. A prior understanding could be reached on this matter, and unless there were real urgency in the work the day off should be acceptable. Failure to attempt such arrangements indicates that we do not appreciate the seriousness of the Church law—which binds under pain of mortal sin.

When there is urgency, in time of harvest, the work may become necessary. The Church law forbids unnecessary servile work. Before you decide that it is necessary to work on a holy day, ask yourself this question: would I think it neces-

122

sary to do this work on Sunday? If not, then don't do it on a holy day either.

Much laxity has developed regarding farm work on both Sundays and holy days. In the old days when corn was picked by hand and took many weeks or months, it was very rare that farmers believed it necessary to shuck corn on Sunday. Now when the whole job could be done between two Sundays we see moving tractors in every field on the Lord's day. And the same goes for plowing, planting, and combining. It is an abuse.

8. *The Fourth and Fifth Commandments*

Over-indulging Children. Meddle-
some Mothers. Fostering Vocations.
Teenagers and Money. Girls and
Smoking. Catholic Education. Duty
to Educate Children. Capital Pun-
ishment. Suicide. Mother or Child?
Suicidal Military Actions. A Just
War. Nuclear Tests. Removal of
Reproductive Organs. Hypnosis.
Ethics of Hypnotism. Blood Trans-
fusions. Anger. Anger of Christ.
Nagging. Resentment. Forgiveness.

*Q. Is it not equally sinful for a parent to be over-indulgent
with his children as for him to be negligent?*

A. In most things virtue stands in the middle, between two
vices. You may sin by either excess or defect; and it is hard
to tell which sin is the worse.

It is possible that the over-indulgent parent is less aware
of sin than the negligent parent. But it is doubtful that
spoiled brats are more desirable products than rejected neurotics.

*Q. I would like to know why doesn't the Catholic Church
preach more often about mothers who wreck their children's*

124

marriages. Isn't that a sin? Marriage is a sacrament created by God; so why should a mother go against God's law—especially if she is a good Catholic in other matters?

A. Evidently you have mother-in-law trouble. I hear it is not a rare disease. Mothers should frequently meditate the scriptural monition that a man must leave father and mother and cling to his wife, that their union may be complete. And when mommy refuses to let sonny get away from her—and is secretly jealous of the little wench who is stealing him from her—or still wants to run sonny's life as she has always done, then there is sure to be trouble.

Q. God has blessed us with 11 children so far, and since we are in our thirties we no doubt will be blessed some more; so I feel that He has a real purpose in giving us this big family and I want to do my best to cooperate. Of course I realize that vocations come from God and not from mothers, but what is the best way for us to work with Him and still not give the children the impression that we are trying to push them into the religious life? Naturally I pray for this intention, but I think there must be something more that I can do; I have never found any reading matter related to the parents' part in fostering vocations.

We have acquired a home directly across from our church and school, and so our little ones are growing up well acquainted with the Sisters and priests, and I think this should be a real good influence in their choice of a career. I have felt more than ever since I have seen the Sisters a little closer in everyday living that they live a wonderfully happy life, and I could ask nothing better for my own.

Perhaps I should not worry so much and just trust in God to work things out, but I would feel better if I could help a little; but I still don't want to go about it the wrong way and maybe discourage my children by being too enthusiastic.

125

A. I publish your question not because I can be of much help to you, but that your words may serve as an inspiration to other parents who may lack a little of your faith and generosity.

You have suggested some of the answers: you pray, and that is the main thing; you put your children under the best religious influences; and you give them splendid example. That is about all you can do, and all you should try to do, except to restrain yourself: do not let your ardent personal wishes impose themselves on your children. As you say, God gives vocations; mothers should not try to play the role of God. Follow your own suggestion: do not worry so much and just trust in God—and watch that enthusiasm of yours.

My personal advice to you is this: Really want your children to be free in their choice of vocation. It is their life; you can never lead it for them; you should guard against trying to make their decisions for them. You can pray, instruct factually and inspiringly, provide environmental influences, answer questions, and give advice when it is wanted. But avoid the propaganda. It might influence unduly, and it might easily become nagging, with distasteful recoil.

Q. Should teen-agers keep the money they earn?

A. Yes, unless there are serious family needs to which each one must contribute his share. Of course, they should not just hoard the stuff. They should learn to use it wisely for personal needs, or to save it systematically to take care of future plans. Good money habits and a sensible attitude towards the "root of all evil" should be learned early. Misers are made in miniature, spendthrifts are unchanged from their youth, and the honest man succeeds the honest boy.

Q. Is it a sin for a girl in high school to smoke?

A. In itself, smoking is not a sin for anyone. However, various circumstances might make it a sin for you, as a high school girl.

126

1. Maybe your parents forbid it. Of course, like most parents, they are old-fashioned, narrow-minded, and prejudiced; and apparently they were never young themselves, and so don't understand young people at all. But still they are your parents, and they do love you, in their own strange way; and maybe because they are so awfully old they have acquired some wisdom. Anyway you do have an obligation to obey their reasonable commands.

2. Maybe you sadden your parents and worry them. They don't forbid you to smoke, but they ardently wish you wouldn't. By ignoring their wishes you fail in your love and respect for them.

3. Maybe your smoking is a waste of money badly needed for better purpose. It might even lead you into petty dishonesties: chiseling, evasions, and misappropriations.

4. Maybe your smoking is a vanity, a pretense, an effort to create an impression slightly artificial—showing off and "being smart."

5. Maybe you are injuring or endangering your health. Lung cancer is less frequent in the female of the species, but there may be other ill effects.

6. Maybe you create a fire hazard. Many feminine smokers your age do.

7. Possibly your smoking lines you up with a clique or a "set" which may not be helpful to either your studies or your decorum—to make no mention of morals.

Most of these circumstances may be foreign to your case, and none of them should lead to mortal sin. But venial sin is the second worst evil in the world.

I don't believe the question here is so much one of sin as it is of propriety or desirability. Do you really think you should smoke? What good will it do you? You are simply developing a needless and expensive habit which will stain your fingers, taint your breath and litter your wake with ashes and butts-still-glowing.

Q. Can Catholic parents receive the Sacraments if they

do not send their children to the Catholic schools? (There is a parochial school in the city.)

A. Unless your diocese has a penalty to deprive them of the sacraments, your question reduces itself to this: Are these parents guilty of mortal sin? If they are, and intend to keep right on committing it, they cannot receive the sacraments. A person guilty of mortal sin cannot make a good confession until he is honestly sorry for his sin and sincere about avoiding it in the future. He cannot receive Holy Communion until he makes a good confession and is in the state of grace.

But are these parents guilty of mortal sin? That question involves so many factors that it is impossible to give a general answer to fit all cases. But we can consider the principles:

1. Parents have a grave responsibility for the proper education of their children: physical, intellectual, and spiritual. That should be written in reverse order for their first and most important duty is to see that the children are trained for proper religious and moral living, to prepare them for heaven.

2. Since parents usually cannot give this education themselves they turn over their duty to schools. By the very nature of things public schools cannot give religious education, and there is room for question about the thoroughness of their moral education. Who then is going to give this education? The parents? Can they? Will they? They are gravely bound to give it, and Sunday school alone does not fulfill that obligation.

3. Parents are gravely bound to protect their children from unnecessary dangers to faith and morals. They must examine their conscience carefully on this point—without rationalizing.

4. We must all avoid scandal. Even when parents honestly judge that they are justified, by special reason, in sending their children to public schools, they must consider whether their example may not lead others less justified to imitate them, and thus be guilty of sin.

5. There is always danger in sending children to public school—danger to the youngsters themselves and danger of

scandal. So if we are to encounter these dangers there are two things we must do (a) make the danger remote—be careful that the harm never happens, and (b) have sufficient reason to justify the danger.

To make the danger remote the parents must really be on the ball in moral training and example.

There is no need for me to list the reasons; parents find them readily enough:—distance, poor equipment, overcrowding, restricted curriculum, etc. Sometimes there are good sound reasons worthy of careful consideration. More often there are excuses contrived to salve consciences.

The entire question is summed up in Canon 1374: "Catholic youngsters must not attend non-Catholic, neutral, or mixed schools" (Our public schools are certainly in that class). "Only the Bishop can decide, on the basis of instructions from the Holy See, what circumstances may permit us to tolerate such attendance and what care we must take to prevent harm and danger to the children."

My translation is not entirely literal, but is pretty exact as to meaning. Parents should often meditate on that law when excuses crowd in on them: when fine buildings invite, with industrial arts, domestic science, social advantages, and a good football team; when they are on the outs with the pastor, or Johnny gripes about Sister. Holy Mother Church is severe only for the good of her children; and she is certainly not very lenient in Canon 1374.

Q. What does the Church teach in regard to the duty of parents to educate their offspring? Specifically, what is expected of us as parents in this regard?

A. The most important duty of parents—after a child is born—is to educate it in such manner that it can live happily and well in this life and prepare itself for eternal life in heaven. The law of the Church calls this duty most serious— *gravissima* (Can. 1372).

The right and duty of educating children is given to the parents directly by God—with whom they share in creating

129

a new human life and forming it for eternal living. If they perform their duty well their children will join them before the throne of God. If they fail their children may curse them forever in hell.

Maybe my answer will be more useful to you if I take note of that word "specifically" which begins your second question:

1. *Parents must love their children,* and let the children know that they are loved. Probably no one thing is more important in child education. You can get by with many mistakes in educational methods if you love your children honestly and thoroughly and rightly. But even the most careful scientific methods will produce neurotic adolescents with various behavior problems if true love is lacking in the early years—or if the youngsters are fouled up by the wrong kind of love.

The right kind of parental love has much warmth in it, and expresses that warmth frequently, regularly, and reliably to the child; but it is not sentimental and selfish and emotional. Its constancy and orderliness give the child a feeling of security. It is understanding of childish vagaries, yet predictable in firmness; tolerant and gentle, but strong. It is never possessive, or demanding; never harsh and rigid; never fussy, or nervously anxious. It must be a deep and spontaneous love which is very real, because you can't fool a child—not for long.

2. *Parents must give their children good example.* No amount of teaching or correcting or telling can do much good without this parental example. Children are so constantly with their parents in early years that they absorb without knowing; and the love which they have for their parents lets this example imprint itself deeply. An ounce of good example is worth a pound of fine words, or a ton of nagging corrections. An erg of bad example develops force sufficient to destroy a character.

3. *Parents must provide a happy home for their children,* with security and order and love in it. Otherwise, their straining efforts at education will be ineffective. Turmoil and tempests, dirt and disarray, anxieties and tensions can

rob teaching of all its point and purpose. Nothing is so important to the child's life and character as the home. Nothing can substitute for the home environment, or replace it, or entirely compensate for its failings.

4. *Parents must exercise authority.* It must be constant and firm, but gentle and relaxed; not fussy or blustery, not frightening and threatening, not mercurial and emotional, and above all not angry. It must not be foolishly indulgent, pampering, spoiling, always giving in. And especially it must not be fluctuating, now stern and irritable, now weak and lenient. Its firmness should be nearly equal from both parents; papa should not be made the tyrant to enforce mamma's threats, or mamma the loving refuge from dad's harshness.

The ideal parental authority is heroic in its patience, loving in its firmness, tolerant in its understanding, and sparing in the frequency of its exercise. It should combine the modern tenets of self-expression with a gentle measure of self-denial. It should give childhood natural freedom of range without forgetting Proverbs, 22, 15—"Folly is bound up in the heart of the child and the rod of correction will drive it away."

5. *Parents must teach* children of all ages a variety of details which I can only vaguely imagine. Basically education is a matter of training in good habits—of body, mind, will and emotions. It begins with the tiny baby, continues with the toddler and the pre-school youngster, and continues without interruption from kindergarten to eighth grade, on through high school, and just as importantly with the college student, or the post-school adolescent.

I would never dare try to indicate the things to be taught, the habits to be formed, or the methods to be used. But I do know a good book which can give you a helpful start towards knowing: "Christopher's Talks to Catholic Parents," by Greenstock (Templegate, Springfield, Ill., price $3.75).

As in all teaching you should try to accentuate the positive —teach good habits rather than constantly correct bad ones. You must be patient, and you must persevere through al-

131

most endless repetition, which is the unpleasant secret of learning.

6. *Parents must teach religion.* It can't be left to the schools, not even the Catholic schools. It must begin in simple ways long before school years. There must be casual arousing of interest, gradual imparting of knowledge, early habits of simple prayer.

The law of the Church emphasizes the necessity of special instruction in religion in preparation for first Confession, first Holy Communion, and Confirmation, and for a continuation of these instructions after these sacraments have been received (Can. 1330-1331). While the law is directed to pastors, it imposes its obligations on parents also, because theirs is the primary duty in this as in all education of their children. And we all know how little a pastor, or Sisters, can accomplish without the encouragement and help of parents.

7. *Parents must give sex-education* to their children. Gradually, carefully, reverently they must respond to growing curiosity. Gently, understandingly, lovingly they must be ready with guidance, correction, and encouragement. They must inspire confidence, avoid tensions and prudery, and encourage frankness. And above all they must, by word and example, inspire proper attitudes of reverence and modesty. These duties belong almost exclusively to the parents. They cannot be successfully delegated to others. Defects can hardly be supplied. Mistakes can be tragic.

8. *Parents must train and prepare themselves* by learning the meaning and methods of education. They should know the purpose and goal of education: the training of the individual for good and happy living; the child to fit into the family, the gang and the school; the citizen for society; the worker for his job; the Catholic for his part in the Mystical Body; but with all these things as intermediate goals, and steps to the ultimate end: eternal happiness. They should know the methods of education. We train our teachers well, demand that they have degrees and certificates, require that they pass examinations and be subject to inspection. The educational work of parents is much more important. Yet they often start on it cold, accomplish it by hit or miss, and

132

learn it by trial and error, batting immortal souls from here to eternity in the process.

9. *Parents must send their children to Catholic schools,* when that is possible. Can. 1374 says that Catholic children may not attend non-Catholic, nonsectarian, or public schools, and the bishop alone may decide the circumstances which permit exception to this law. Education is a complete and integral process. It must train and develop the entire human personality. It is lopsided if it only trains the body or the mind—if it imparts good walking habits and good thinking habits but neglects good praying habits—if it teaches how to be learned but not how to be good.

10. *Parents must support Catholic schools.* Canon 1379 is very explicit in stating that all the faithful are obliged to lend their assistance, in accordance with their means, for the establishment and maintenance of these schools.

11. *Parents have a double duty* of teaching religion in those cases in which they must send their children to the public school. They have to supply the daily work and influence of the Sisters by their own efforts and example. And they have to counteract errors, indifference, and bad example at the same time.

12. *Parents must somehow compensate* by guidance and example for the worldy, materialistic and immoral tendencies which challenge the youngsters of our day: at the movies, on radio and TV, in comic books, newspapers, and books, on the street and playground, sometimes in the school, and frequently in social customs. In a world which tends to push religion aside and ignore morality, children must somehow be trained to live and think and act like Catholics—to make religion an integral part of their everyday life.

13. *Parents must pray.* It is evident from the above list that they are expected to be saints. You can only become a saint by prayer. And if you aren't trying to be a saint you will do a poor job of educating your children.

In summary, parents are obliged to give their children the best education which it is within their means to provide. And it must be physical and mental education as well as spiritual. Nothing in life is more important to them. That doesn't mean that every child should get a Ph.D. It is quality that counts. And sometimes the eighth-grade graduate is better trained for life and eternity than the erudite man of the world—this world.

Q. How does the Catholic Church justify her tacit approval of the legalized killing of human beings as a penalty for certain crimes? If there is one principle of natural law which transcends all others, it is that God is the author of life and that He alone has the right to terminate it. This the Church rigidly espouses in her uncompromising condemnation of abortion, suicide, and "mercy killing."

In view of the absolutism with which this position is held, I find it impossible to understand how ANY exception can possibly be made (except, of course, as death may result from an act of self-defense). Yet I have never heard the Church raise her voice in objection to the vengeful killing of criminals. (Vengeful is the correct adjective, since it is the only plausible rational reason for such killing.)

This question cannot be answered by a simple restatement of "expert" opinions without rational justification. Nor is the contention that the State has the right to legalize killing at all satisfactory. What do you mean by "State"? Isn't Russia a "State"? Does she have such a right? And if a State has this right does it not follow that the State may enforce abortion and "mercy killing"?

A. I just looked up the word absolute in my dictionary. It means unqualified. But if you want to be a good moralist you should not make absolute statements until you carefully qualify them. Otherwise you have to start out making exceptions—as you just did for killing in self-defense.

The true principle is this: no person or power on earth has the right to take directly the life of an innocent person. Note two limitations to my absolute: *directly* and *innocent*. It is sometimes permissible to take innocent life indirectly—

134

when we do something proper and legitimate, for a good purpose, and death results from it. And it is sometimes permissible to kill directly the unjust aggressor, as in your own case of self-defense.

It is true that God is the author of life, and that he retains ownership and control of human life. But it is possible for God to delegate his rights. We cannot presume such delegation, however; especially where something so precious and irreparable as life is concerned.

As you admit, God certainly delegates to us, as individuals, his divine right of terminating life when we are violently and unjustly attacked and have no way of protecting our own life except by killing. The attacker has surrendered his right to life by unjustly seeking mine; and God relinquishes his right, that I may protect mine.

Actually, God is not extravagantly jealous of his supreme right over human life. He uses it mostly to protect man's right to his own life—and when man forfeits his right, God may relinquish the divine right. About the only case in which God insists strongly on his right is against the suicide. Man violates God's right if he kills himself; and he may not voluntarily give up his own right to life, because God's right interferes.

Apart from suicide, we can solve most problems of killing on the basis of man's own right to his life, without special consideration of God's supreme right. Except for the case of the unjust aggressor, whom you kill in self-defense, man does not forfeit his right of life to another individual man. But what of society? We know that God instituted society: He made man a social being; created him to live with his fellow man in harmony, dependence and helpfulness. Such living requires authority and the security which only organized power can furnish. So God created the State. And in creating it He gave it the rights and powers necessary to perform its functions.

By divine plan the State exists for the common welfare of its members. It must protect its people both from outside attack and from internal crime. Either can destroy the people and despoil them of their rights. So, when absolutely neces-

135

sary, the State can wage war, in common self-defense against an unjust aggressor. And in similar manner the State can punish criminals, with such punishment as may be necessary to curb crime—again in common self-defense against the unjust aggressor.

Your statement that vengeance is the only plausible reason for capital punishment is hardly correct. It is true that modern penologists design their punishments to reform the criminal; and hanging is hardly so designed. But the deterrence of crime is still society's main purpose in punishment; and some people still maintain that nothing deters the criminal so effectively as a dangling noose, a sizzling chair, or a clammy gas chamber.

The State may not use punishments more severe and cruel than necessary. Today there are many penologists who hold capital punishment unnecessary for any crime. So we may profitably consider the question:

Is capital punishment licit in our modern advanced society? Do we need it to protect us from crime? Is it effective as a deterrent to the criminal? Should it be abolished?

A few years ago the discussion of this subject became intense when a reprieve from the governor of California arrived at the prison two minutes late. Those two minutes meant eternity for the victim in the gas chamber. And the world was impressed with the unalterable finality of capital punishment. No discovery of new evidence, no change of official attitude or public sentiment can be of any help once the trap has been sprung or the switch closed.

Most of us still feel indignant about the sentimental propaganda which produced demonstrations throughout the world a few years ago when our own nation executed the Rosenbergs as proven traitors.

In London not long ago a blond model was hanged for shooting her unfaithful lover. Criticism was world-wide; much of it was sentimental, but it was bitter, and it ultimately led to a caustic debate in Parliament and to the practical abolition of capital punishment in England.

More recently public indignation was inflamed when a Negro in Alabama was under sentence of death for stealing

136

$1.69, or some such miserly amount. Not only was it a cause of national shame, but it also pointed out forcibly that the death penalty can result in terribly unequal justice by reason of race, locality, time, popular mood, or prejudice. Can we call it justice when we have different standards for different races?

Still more recently we heard sharp arguments about those executions in Cuba, which seemed to us to be shockingly numerous and altogether too summary. Most of us know little about the factual guilt of the men who were shot, or about the flagrant atrocities which inflamed popular feeling. But the point is apparent that the death penalty may be subject to vindictive abuse. Whatever the facts in Cuba, brisk trials, uncritical evidence, and biased courts may offer little sound protection to man's inviolable rights. Revolutionary tempers may later cool and new evidence be brought to light, but tardy remorse can bring only one benefit to men who are dead: prayer for their souls.

While the Church has never condemned capital punishment in principle, it is not necessary to conclude that she is positively in favor of its retention in our modern society. The Church is traditional and conservative, but she does not close her eyes to profound social developments. Methods which suited medieval needs are not necessarily appropriate today.

The Church's history should give her little sympathy with the death penalty. Our religion had its origin in capital punishment; our divine Founder was the victim of an execution which was expeditious, arbitrary, and unjust. His death brought great benefits to us, and we prize them above all else in life. But no Christian would want to be identified, even remotely, with Pontius Pilate. When we inflict the death penalty we are cast vaguely in his role.

The sad and glorious days of early Christianity were marked by frequent atrocities of capital punishment. We are proud of our early martyrs, inspired by their courage, stimulated by the avid zeal with which they suffered death for Christ. But none of us would want to have part with the vicious emperors, corrupt judges, and brutal executioners

137

who tortured and dismembered God's chosen ones and fed the saints to the lions.

The entire history of the Church has been glorified by intrepid missionaries and valiant fighters for the faith, who have been executed by their enemies in various vicious ways —often with the legal trappings of formal punishment. Barbarian tribes, medieval Saracens, and early American Indians have recently been succeeded as executioners by communist persecutors in various countries of Europe and Asia.

St. Joan of Arc is a glorious example of those many saints of the Church who have been victims of capital punishment. Her later vindication is evidence that human justice is fallible, and that the death sentence is irreformable.

The Church has never exacted the death penalty by her own authority. Her theologians have long debated whether or not she would have the right to impose it, since it does not seem necessary or useful to her spiritual purpose: the salvation of souls. But even as we say this we know that those who cherish the corpse of the Inquisition will lift an accusing finger: the Church has certainly cooperated very closely with the state in imposing capital punishment, and has watched its execution with evident approval. Surely in those violent days no one needed to ask the attitude of the Church on this question.

Frankly I believe that even the Church's vigorous part in the Inquisition serves to emphasize by contrast the spirit of her example and doctrine. Her divine Master advocated only one kind of severity: rigorous control of self. His message was always one of forgiveness, even to 70 times seven times. He showed mercy to the adulterous woman, and gentleness to the repentant sinner. He preached love for the prodigal son. He brought people back to life on various occasions, but he never put anyone to death—or recommended that anyone be executed. Only his own forceful action in driving the money-changers from the Temple warns us against sentimentality in handling offenders.

Christianity has its roots deep in the ancient law of Moses, which provided firmly for vengeance and retribution. It imposed the death penalty for murder and kidnaping, for blasphemy and sacrificing to false gods, for sorcery and sodomy, and even for false witness in some cases. In general, punishment for injury was by law of the talion: "You will give life for life, eye for eye, tooth for tooth, hand for hand."

But Jesus changed the law of the talion completely: "You have heard that it was said, 'An eye for an eye' and 'A tooth for a tooth.' But I say to you not to resist the evildoer; on the contrary, if someone strike thee on the right cheek, turn to him the other also; and if anyone should go to law with thee and take thy tunic, let him take thy cloak as well; and whoever forces thee to go for one mile, go with him two."

The Church has four doctrinal principles which bear directly on the question of capital punishment.

1. Man's life is sacred; God's dominion over it is supreme, and man's natural right to it is inviolable.

2. The State is an essential part of God's plan for mankind; its authority comes from God, and that authority extends to all just laws and sanctions required for the attainment of its purposes, which are the general welfare of society and the protection of the rights of the individual.

3. Man has a free will, and the normal man is morally responsible for his acts, whether they be good or evil.

4. Justice often demands retribution. God punishes sin for this reason; and the maintenance of a high sense of justice in society requires that the criminal pay for his crime.

We believe that the state is not playing the role of God but acting as a delegate of God when it justly imposes the death penalty. It is not murder because no injustice is done. The guilty man has forfeited his right to life by his crime. But we must be sure that he has forfeited it. His native right to life is certain, and we must exercise supreme care that we do not violate it. So the Church's moralists have laid down rigorous rules restricting the death penalty.

1. It may be imposed only by a lawful and sovereign state, never by a tyrannical usurper or by mob violence.

2. There must have been, before the crime, a definite, promulgated law which clearly imposed capital punishment as sanction for its violation.

3. The criminal must have a fair and impartial trial with ample opportunity for defense and appeal, as the due process of justice demands.

4. The proof of guilt must be certain, beyond any reasonable doubt.

5. The sentence must be imposed and the execution carried out by proper officials of the state, acting in lawful manner. Lynch law, in all its forms, is illegal.

We know that these restrictions are not always observed, especially when prejudices, violent emotions, and political strife are involved. Capital punishment can easily become a tool of hate and vengeance; injustice can be done, and it is so final!

Many modern penologists tend to eliminate all notions of punition and retribution from their theories of sanction. Punishment can have only two purposes for them: to reform the criminal and to deter others from crime. And since they are often dubious about the deterrent effects, their principal stress is likely to be on reform. They do not speak of punishment to fit the crime, but of a remedy to fit the criminal. And one of their strongest reasons for opposing capital punishment is that the noose is not noted for its remedial effects, though it can induce a hasty repentance.

It has often been maintained that some crimes are so shocking to the public conscience that only this supreme penalty can repair the harm. But it can also be argued that retribution can easily degenerate into vengeance and thus injure public morality still further.

Besides, no human agency can exact retribution which is minutely just and adequate; only God can do that; He alone knows the full extent of man's personal guilt. And the criminal can repay his debt to society by methods other than death. The Church would not be impressed with the pragmatic argument that society should not be burdened with the expense of maintaining a prisoner for life. If we execute him merely to be rid of him we may find our argument applied to other undesirables who are a burden on society.

Up until modern times it was simply taken for granted, by all governments and nearly all systems of political

140

thought, that capital punishment was essential to the purposes of the state. The worst criminals would never be deterred by any other punishment. And often it was believed that the public should see the blood of the criminal and share the horror of his death agony, so that the supreme penalty might have its full frightening effect. The guillotine was set up in the midst of the crowd, the scaffold was erected in a public place, and the victim at the stake was burned with crackling realism.

Today we are not so sure. In the measure that criminality is a disease, no threat or example will cure it. But even for the normal person it is probable that blood begets blood, that cruelty propagates itself, and that one who is habituated to horror comes to accept it as a normal part of life.

Maybe we are faint-hearted and squeamish, but we now try to choose methods of execution as humane and inoffensive as possible. It may be that we are less concerned with the actual pain to the victim than with the shock to ourselves. Doctor Guillotin claims that the sharp instrument named in his honor caused only a slight chill on the neck as the cold blade did its quick work. But we find it too bloody. Even hanging is considered barbaric; we prefer the electric chair or a nice quiet dose of gas.

Our modern executions are solemn, formal, and nearly private, attended by only a few witnesses. Some countries will not permit the newspapers to print any descriptions, even though they wrote up the original crime in all its piquant and gory details.

Panorama Chretien, a popular Catholic magazine of France, had a provocative discussion of capital punishment in its January, 1959, issue. Patrick Chevasson quoted the chaplain of the prison at Bristol as reporting that of 167 prisoners condemned to death, 164 had already witnessed an execution before their crimes. The horrors of exemplary punishment apparently had no effect on those men. Possibly the scenes they had witnessed had lowered their esteem for human life, had stirred resentment against brutal justice, or had provoked admiration for the criminal who went to his

141

death with jaunty defiance. Momentary terror was later dissipated in the passion of crime or in the confidence of escape.

It is generally accepted that sureness of punishment is more effective than its severity. Modern methods of crime detection have contributed largely to disuse of the death penalty. Three centuries ago the average nation prescribed death in some violent form for about 150 different crimes. Today 30 nations have discarded it completely, or practically, and the rest keep it for relatively few crimes.

The U.S. hangs on to this traditional punishment more tenaciously than any other advanced nation. Before Hawaii was admitted to the Union only eight of our states had abolished it: Maine, Michigan, Minnesota, Wisconsin, North Dakota, Rhode Island, Delaware and Alaska.

The Iowa legislature recently considered a bill for abolition of capital punishment. Studies reveal that over a number of years there have been 250 homicides in this state with only one execution, which took place nearly eight years ago. Idle threats breed contempt; even a child quickly learns to ignore a warning which is never carried out. A criminal, if he stops to think on the subject, will quickly compute his chances, trust his luck, and rely on his ingenuity. A murderer's chances are 100 to one that he will never get the noose.

In the entire U.S. there were 65 executions in 1956, one-third the number of 1936. Decline has been steady for many years. And it is worthy of note that those states which have discarded the death penalty have lower rates of capital crimes than similar states which retain the penalty.

The same can be said for the 30 nations of the world which have abolished this penalty; nearly all of them report decreases in crime. It is significant that the only great nation to restore it is the USSR. Russian leaders boasted loudly of their advanced social thinking when they discarded capital punishment in 1947. But apparently they found themselves handicapped in enforcing their socialistic ideals, because in 1950 they re-established the penalty for treason and political crimes, and then in 1954 they extended it to murder.

All the nations of Europe west of the Iron Curtain, except

142

France and Spain, have abolished the death penalty, at least for practical purposes. But in spite of all arguments and example, public opinion in the U.S. remains firmly in favor of its retention. In 1955 the American Institute of Public Opinion conducted a poll which showed 68% in favor of capital punishment, 25% opposed, and 7% with no opinion.

Panorama Chretien reports a similar poll by *Le Figaro* in France in 1953. There the majority still favored retention of the guillotine, but by a much narrower margin: 55% to 45%. It might be interesting to compare a breakdown of these percentages to our own observations of the American scene. Those definitely against capital punishment were teachers, students, labor, social workers, artists, and penologists. Those strongly for it were the liberal professions, engineers, doctors, merchants, farmers, office workers, people retired on pensions, the police, and the military. Churchmen, judges, and lawyers were evenly divided.

In general, well-founded opinion is growing in the world that our modern society does not need this extreme penalty to maintain order and protect the rights of citizens. As a deterrent from crime its effectiveness is over-estimated; it gives us a false sense of security. Lesser punishments are possibly more effective because they are more certain to be imposed. Our American juries often shy from conviction when the supreme penalty is at stake.

I am confident that the Church, with her teachings of love, mercy, and forgiveness, would not want the modern state to use punishments more severe than needed. If abolitionists would stick with her in upholding the fundamental rights of the state and the basic freedom of man, she would back them in their pleas for more humane punishment of criminals.

Q. I have heard many interpretations of the Church's views on suicide. Being a Protestant, I would like to know: first, if suicide is a mortal sin, then how is there forgiveness after death; second, would one have a Christian burial; and third, would one have the benefit of the prayers of the faithful?

143

A. I shall begin by giving direct answers to your three questions, and then explain some of the reasons for my answers.

1. Suicide is a mortal sin when it is free and deliberate; and since it is likely to be the final voluntary act of the decedent there is little possibility of forgiveness, either in this life or in the next.

2. Those who kill themselves with cold deliberation are denied Christian burial.

3. Suicides who are denied Christian burial are also deprived of a funeral Mass and of the anniversary Mass of requiem. Otherwise, prayers and Masses may be offered for the repose of their souls.

Suicide is a mortal sin because it is a rebellion of the creature against his Creator, and because it violates God's supreme right over our lives. Rebellion is the essence of sin; it is contrary to the purpose in life for which God created us. That purpose is union with God in love, union here in grace and conformity of will, and union in heaven in posssession and happiness. Mortal sin rejects God. When we love God we choose Him above all things, and our wills conform to his. When we sin we choose his creatures ahead of him, forgetting that their goodness is only twinkling tinsel reflecting his unlimited goodness.

Repentance is an act of the will opposite to sin. It rejects the creature which has been exalted to the place of God; and then turns back to God and chooses him again in first place. Thus we prepare ourselves to be enveloped by God's love and grace and restored to union with him. Without that act of our own will, which is repentance, we can never be reunited with God, because he will never force us into union.

Yet we can never repudiate sin and turn back to him by our own power. Only his grace can let us repent, but without our cooperation his grace will not be effective.

I am writing all this to explain why it is that the suicide has so little chance of forgiveness. By his last free act on earth he rejected God's love, and he never had a chance to change his mind: to repent. So he goes into eternity with his mind made up to reject God and go to hell, and he goes there immediately. There is no way out. Repentance is an act of this life; if it is not done before death it will never be done.

Some of my readers may object that venial sins may be forgiven after death, and, of course, I will agree. Their forgiveness is one of the purposes of purgatory. But they are not forgiven through our repentance; rather they are obliterated by our sufferings and burned up in the mutual love which exists between God and ourselves.

These lesser sins never did imply a rejection of God, merely a slighting of him. In our faltering human love we chose him definitely and firmly, but not a hundred per cent. We never chose evil in his place; we merely tried in a clumsy, inconsistent manner to fit a little vice into our love for Him. When we die with venial sins unrepented our wills remain essentially attached to God. We love him ninety-five per cent, and he has ways of purifying the residue.

But you may still ask, what that evil is which the suicide chooses in preference to God. His particular choice may vary, but the essential evil of his act is his defiant violation of God's right as Creator and Lord. God made us from nothing, and we depend utterly and momentarily on his provident power. We had nothing to say about the beginning of our lives; and of ourselves we cannot maintain them a moment. It is God's right to say when they will end.

God has given us our lives, but not absolutely; He retains the supreme dominion and ownership in them. They are his as well as ours. We might say that he has lent them to us to use and enjoy; and he has a purpose in lending them. He intends that we use them for his honor and glory and to attain our own eternal happiness. He wants us to use them thus, but he does not compel us. We are free to substitute our own contrary purposes.

Suicide is a sin because it violates the rights of God; but it is also a crime, because it violates the right of society to the service of its members, and because it tends to spread false doctrines regarding life and duty, death and immortality. Therefore, suicide is usually regarded as a crime by the state as well as the Church. There is no human way to punish

145

a suicide, if his act is successful, but the state has penalties for attempted suicide, and the Church finds a way of teaching others to avoid the crime, by depriving the suicide of Christian burial.

The severe discipline of the Church in this matter dates from early centuries. There is evidence that as early as 563 those who committed suicide were deprived of Christian burial. Pope Nicholas I would not permit the Sacrifice of the Mass to be offered for them. Today, Mass may be offered privately, without public announcement, on days other than the anniversary. But the body of the deceased may not be taken to the church or buried in a consecrated cemetery.

However, the Church's practice is to give every consideration to the possibility that the crime was not committed with deliberate and responsible freedom. If there is evidence of insanity or temporary derangement all the privileges of Christian burial are given; and in case of doubt the bishop is to make the judgment.

The Church keeps two things in mind in the practical enforcement of her law against suicide. 1. She wants to show kindness and sympathy to the doubly stricken family of the deceased; so she judges his action with all possible leniency; and 2. she wants to avoid that scandal to others which would result if she seemed to encourage the idea that suicide can sometimes be justified or condoned.

The Church also has penalties for attempted suicide. A person who seriously tries to kill himself is considered irregular for reception or exercise of Holy Orders. The Church does not want priests with suicidal tendencies. The young man who is irregular may not be ordained without special dispensation; and the priest who is irregular may not say Mass or hear Confessions until his irregularity has been removed by Church authority. In general, clerics who have attempted suicide are deprived of any office they hold for such time as the bishop may determine, and laymen are restricted in certain Church privileges. There is a special penalty, called interdict, for those who maliciously permit Christian burial to a suicide deprived of the right to it.

Suicide is the voluntary and intentional killing of oneself.

Accidental killing is not suicide, though sins of negligence might have caused the accident. The self-destruction of an insane person is not suicide. And it is possible to cause one's death indirectly in such a way that the act, while voluntary, is free of any sin or crime.

Determinists deny the freedom of man's will. They see our motivations as compulsive forces beyond our voluntary control. We do not imply any such error when we state the belief that many of the people who kill themselves, probably the majority of them, are not morally responsible. We insist on man's normal freedom, but admit that his voluntary choice can be overridden in certain abnormal situations. When fears and depressions become strong enough to crush our powerful instinct of self-preservation they may well obliterate also our religious convictions and distort our concepts of morality, so that we are incapable of sane, responsible judgment.

The Old Testament gives us some examples of indirect suicide. Samson prayed to the Lord for strength, grasped the columns of the temple, and shook the great structure down on himself and the Philistines. It is possible that he was justified in his act, since his purpose was to destroy the enemies of his nation, and he only permitted his own death to result from the same action.

The heroism of Eleazar might be more easily justified. He went between the feet of the elephant and put himself under it and killed it, knowing that it would fall on him and cause his death. He intended to save his people, and his act was directed to that purpose.

The Church's penalties would not apply to involuntary or indirect suicide, and her judgment of the individual is generally kind and generous. However, she must maintain a stern attitude towards suicide in general to combat a variety of errors which tend to crop up and spread widely. We find them throughout history, especially among those who doubt God's supreme power and providence, or the purposefulness of man's life.

In the world's literature suicide has often been presented as an act of great virtue, portraying strength, courage, nobility, and sacrifice. Pagan societies favor this notion and militaristic influences encourage it. You may have recently read recommendations from our own military authorities that suicide pills be standard equipment for soldiers fighting in certain areas. But as a considered philosophy the notion was the most clearly set forth by the Stoics of ancient Greece. They were discriminating: suicide was not always a virtue, but when indicated by cold pragmatic reason it might become an act of greatest heroism.

This Stoic notion was not entirely foreign to God's chosen people. The Old Testament often relates facts and portrays popular attitudes without giving dogmatic approval to all their implications. King Saul, after his defeat by the Philistines and while he was suffering bitterly from his wounds, commanded his armorbearer to kill him. He wished to rob the enemy of the satisfaction of complete triumph. Achitophel was bitterly disappointed that his advice was not followed against David; so he put his house in order and hanged himself. Razias went through a superman's series of violent efforts to end his own life, "choosing to die nobly rather than to fall into the hands of the wicked."

Christian history has many instances of martyrs who sought death ardently, ran to meet it fearlessly, and brought it directly onto themselves. In some cases they may have been acting under an extraordinary inspiration of God's grace. God can, when He wishes, relinquish his supreme right to our lives and permit them to be immolated for love of him. But in most cases these eager saints were probably acting in error and good faith, pushed to excess by their zeal. Their love, courage, and sacrifice rightly inspires us; their example is not to be imitated.

Sometimes religious fanatics have sought death as a liberation or an immolation. The Circumcellions were heretics of the 5th century who thirsted so ardently for martyrdom that they joined in mob suicides, throwing themselves off cliffs in droves, or jumping madly into water or fire. In the 12th century the Albigensians believed that the body was an evil thing from which the soul should be liberated; so death, as a means of sloughing off vile flesh, was holy and desirable.

148

They favored suicide by bleeding or poison, but especially advocated starvation.

The ancient Epicurean philosophers held suicide to be the lesser of two evils in some tough cases; they often justified it as a means of deliverance from life's pains and problems. This was consistent with their general principle that pleasure was the goal of life. When pleasure was no longer possible, life became purposeless. Basically they were pessimists.

Modern Existentialists have revived much of this Epicurean attitude on life and its aims. Their philosophy of despair is opposed by Christian hope and confidence. It is only when we have confidence in a future life that we have the purpose and strength to face the problems of this life. It is only when we have assurance of God's love and help that we have courage to persevere.

Modern morality presents two allied notions; one might be called the popular poll; the other, social utility. Both have a bearing on suicide. If the morality of an act depends on majority opinion, we may expect fluctuations of approval or condemnation, but there will surely be times when the sentimental common sense of society will approve of genteel self-destruction.

When the value of human life is measured by its social utility we may expect a period of diminishing returns and even a point where we become a hopeless, unprofitable burden. This morality provided the point of departure for Nazi practices in Germany. Since certain groups were a burden to the master race their elimination was indicated. The same basic idea has vogue amid those who favor euthanasia. It shares the common error of failing to acknowledge God's supreme right as author and provident sustainer of man's life. Once God's right is eliminated who will protect the rights of man?

Q. When a mother is giving birth to a child and medical science clearly sees that both cannot be saved, why does your faith insist that the baby be spared at the expense of the

149

mother? Even if the mother has other children who need her and a husband who needs her, he is forced to be left with still another child and no helpmate to help him with the raising of the family. This law of the Church does not make sense to me nor have I been able to find justification in the Bible for it. I should like to know on what authority or reason this law is based that gives the right to say which life should be spared.

A. Such a law would make no sense to me either. The Church has no such law. She couldn't have, because no human being has the right to say which should be spared—mother or child—if in saying it he would also decide which should die. No man has the right to say when another innocent human being must die, and no right to make him die. This is murder, and the Church is opposed to murder.

It may surprise you that I simply reject your whole dilemma and refuse to squirm between the horns of it. The false suppositions upon which your question is based are often proposed to us; evidently they are widespread. And certain bigots have done a disservice to truth by spreading them wider (cf. Blanshard, American Freedom and Catholic Power, Ch. 6, especially p. 111).

The Pope certainly is a better authority on Catholic laws and teachings than Paul Blanshard. In November, 1951, Pius XII gave a talk to the National Congress of the Family Front, in which he said: "Never and in no case has the Church taught that the life of the child must be preferred to that of the mother. It is wrong to put the question with this alternative: either the life of the child or that of the mother. No, neither the life of the mother nor that of the child can be subjected to an act of direct suppression. In the one case as in the other, there can be but one obligation, to make every effort to save the lives of both, of the mother and of the child."

Yes, you will say, but suppose it is simply not possible to save the lives of both? You can save only one. Then what? Well, save the one you can. The Church will not argue with you. She simply reminds you that you must not murder either one in order to save the other.

Catholics are not monsters. They are thoroughly human, with feelings strongly akin to your own. That goes for the hierarchy as well as the laity. It is even true of moralists. In making our judgments as Catholics we do try to keep reason paramount, not too much swayed by sentiment; and we do try to keep the supernatural in mind, so that our judgments will not be based entirely on practical worldly arguments, without regard to God and eternity. We are alerted to avoid the pragmatic easy way out, which would discard principle and stick to the expeditious.

However, that does not mean that we lose sight of human, natural values, or that our attitudes are not often influenced by emotions. A Catholic doctor treating an endangered mother, or a Catholic moralist standing by his side, will be strongly aware of the necessary place this mother holds in her family, in the love of her husband, and the needs of her children. Hers is a developed personality, with strings of attachment firm and intimate. Her death would be a great human loss, and a great spiritual loss to those who remain, as far as we can determine. Without her love and help it will be much harder for her husband and children to get to heaven.

The Catholic doctor should discard his caduceus if he does a bit less than he rightly can to save this mother. He would be trying to play the part of God if he were to decide that she should die, even to save a thousand babies. But he would be playing God with equal presumption if he were to decide that her baby must die, and then personally see that it does. A doctor may not do murder even to save life, no matter how precious the life.

It may happen that the doctor will decide in desperation that he simply cannot save them both, either because he cannot do two things at once, or because he must do things to save the mother which will result in harm to the baby. In that case, I am sure that any worthy conscientious doctor will devote himself unremittingly to the care of the mother, doing what he can for the baby, on the side. He would like

151

to save it, but he can't. He tries as much as he can, but he knows he is helpless. He lets it die. And the moralist who stands beside him, if he is sane and orthodox, will offer no criticism.

On the other hand, I cannot imagine any doctor, Catholic or pagan, deliberately neglecting the mother in order to save the baby. In the scale of human values the mother comes first, by a long way; and the Church has no argument about it. She simply reminds the doctor, in his concentrated professional devotion to the mother, not to forget the Fifth Commandment: "Thou shalt not kill." She encourages him in the use of every available proper means to save the mother and prays that he will succeed; but she advises him not to do anything morally wrong to accomplish that purpose. The end never justifies the means. You may not do evil that good may come of it. Even an enormous good result does not excuse a tiny evil done to attain it.

So far, I have concentrated on one false presumption of your question: namely, that the Church has a law requiring that mothers be destroyed to save babies. But there is another presumption which is about 99% false in these days of modern medicine. You suppose that doctors go around in daily debate over the question: mother or child, which shall it be? From what I hear, the skilled obstetrician in a modern hospital rarely sees the question in that light at all.

There are two ways in which a baby might be destroyed in order to aid or save its mother. 1. The more common, would be by abortion. 2. The other would be by a destructive procedure at time of delivery: craniotomy is the best known. Abortion is the expulsion of a living fetus from the mother's womb before it is able to live outside the womb. Sometimes this expulsion is spontaneous; we call it a miscarriage, and no question of morality is concerned. But sometimes it is intentional, brought about by some drug, physical interference, or surgical procedure.

In legal and medical thinking two kinds of intentional abortion are distinguished: criminal and therapeutic. Criminal abortion may result from homemade prescriptions or the ministrations of quacks. We are not concerned with them

152

here. Therapeutic abortions are legally performed by doctors to save the life or aid the health of the mother.

Medical science began to accept therapeutic abortions as legitimate procedures about 100 years ago, and until recently they were considered indicated and ethical in many situations, like kidney and heart diseases, tuberculosis, severe diabetes, leukemia, and anemia, in addition to sicknesses resulting directly from pregnancy, like severe vomiting and eclampsia.

At present there is a strong trend to reduce the number of therapeutic abortions. Doctors find that they sometimes produce unhappy results, and that they do nothing to improve the health of the mother. In 1951, at a meeting of the American College of Surgeons in San Francisco, Dr. Roy J. Heffernan, of Tufts Medical college, said, "Anyone who performs a therapeutic abortion is either ignorant of modern medical methods or unwilling to take the time and effort to apply them."

This same Dr. Heffernan, writing with another obstetrician, Dr. William A. Lynch, in the *Linacre Quarterly* (February, 1952) and the *American Journal of Obstetrics and Gynecology* (August, 1953), said that in the preceding 35 years there had been a great change of attitude among doctors with regard to the deliberate interruption of pregnancy. They have come to realize that no more mothers die in Catholic hospitals than in non-Catholic hospitals. "Of special interest is the fact that the maternal mortality rates in the hospitals performing therapeutic abortions, while excellent, were not better than those in the hospitals wherein no therapeutic abortions were performed. In fact, a few more mothers died in the hospitals allowing therapeutic abortions.

"Science is at last catching up, so to speak, with ethics. Following bitter experiences, the advocates of therapeutic abortion have, in the past twenty years particularly, consistently narrowed down what they felt were proper indications for this procedure."

He then goes on to show how therapeutic abortions actually increased the death rate in some cases. "As therapeutic abortion involves the direct destruction of human life, it is

153

contrary to all the rules and traditions of good medical practice. From the very beginning, the approach to the problem has been unscientific. In too many cases it was learned, after innumerable babies had been sacrificed, that interruption of the pregnancy not only caused 100% fetal loss but also increased the maternal mortality."

Margaret Hague Maternity Hospital in Jersey City, one of the best-known in the country, has less than one therapeutic abortion in 16,000 admissions; and the surgeon-in-chief of Boston City Hospital's obstetric and gynecological service reported in 1951 that his hospital had not had a therapeutic abortion since 1923, and that during those 28 years they had not had one mother die from any condition which might have been benefited by such abortion.

Dr. Joseph L. McGoldrick, writing in the *Homiletic and Pastoral Review* (February, 1948) sums up the answer to your question as follows. "The mother-or-child dilemma is a relic of the early days of obstetrics. If it is talked about today by any medical men, it is only by those whose training and experience evidently do not qualify them to perform modern obstetrics." He then goes on to tell of his own experience in one of the largest hospitals in New York City; more than 3,000 babies are delivered there in a year, and in 20 years of service there he never once encountered the problem of choosing between mother or child.

Mostly we have been talking about abortions, but much the same can be said of destructive procedures still used sometimes in deliveries. A good obstetrician in a modern hospital can avoid them all if he wishes. Some doctors think it unfair to ask a mother to undergo a Caesarean operation to deliver a hydrocephalic child which, while awaiting early death, will break the mother's heart and the father's purse with its deficiencies and needs for care. Craniotomy is easier. But even these doctors now know that there are other procedures which are ethically acceptable. And in any case, it would be most rare, if ever, that the life of the mother would be at issue, and that the child would have to be sacrificed to save her.

Until I got started on the subject, I had not intended

154

to write so much about the medical aspects of this subject. I merely want to show that the supposition upon which your question is based is mostly hypothetical, or at least old-fashioned. I am more concerned with setting forth the moral principles on which the Catholic attitude is based.

1. The dignity and sacredness of human life. We believe that each human person has an immortal soul, created directly by God, made in his own image, destined for filial adoption, and called to share God's personal love and happiness forever. This is true of any human being, no matter how young or old, whether brilliant or defective, whether happily well or hopelessly suffering. For practical purposes, we believe that the tiny human embryo in its mother's womb has this sacred spiritual life, this divinely given soul. It must be respected as God's most personal possession.

2. We believe that the individual has inviolable rights to his life. Unless I am guilty of major crime or engaged in violent unjust attack, no one has the right to kill me. Even organized society, the state, may not take the life of an innocent person directly. We believe that the unborn child has the same right to life as you and I, and that we violate his right when we intentionally terminate that life.

3. We believe that almighty God retains a supreme right and dominion over the life of each individual. You and I have a right to life, but that right is not absolute; we had no part in deciding when our lives would begin, and it is not for us to decide when they will end. We are the caretakers and custodians, with the right to enjoy life and reap its benefits; but we cannot terminate human life, even our own, without usurping the rights and powers of God. Suicide is a terrible sin; it is so final. With our last breath we refuse to submit to God's will or conform to his plan.

So anyone who takes the life of an innocent person violates two rights: that of God and that of the victim. A guilty person may sometimes forfeit his personal right to life, as in violent attack or crime or war. And in such case God may relinquish his rights, so that I may protect my own life from unjust attack, and that our country can protect itself from criminals, traitors, and warring enemies.

155

4. As already mentioned: you may not do evil even to accomplish a good purpose. So you may not kill a baby even to save its mother's life; and it does not matter how much more valuable you may esteem the mother's life, for personal reasons.

5. This principle is a rather complicated one, but very useful and reasonable: we may sometimes do a good deed to accomplish a good purpose, even though we foresee that our deed will have a bad effect as well as its good one.

Examples are better than explanations. A pregnant mother is found to have cancer of the cervix. The surgeon judges that her uterus must be removed at once if her life is to be saved. Of course, that means that the baby will die. But the surgeon does not directly kill it; he operates to save the mother, not by removing the baby, who is doing her no harm, but by removing a malignant growth which will kill her. She is not saved by the death of the baby; so the surgeon is not doing evil to accomplish good; he is doing good and it has a bad side effect.

A similar mother seems to be bleeding to death from a partially detached placenta. The doctor gives drugs to contract her blood vessels and stop the hemorrhage; but the same drugs contract the muscles of the uterus also, and an abortion results. The drug has two effects, one good and one bad. The doctor intends the good one (to stop the bleeding) and permits the bad one (the death of the baby). Such procedure is permissible when necessary.

Here is an example in another area. My buddy and I are shipwrecked. We are both trying to cling to a piece of driftwood; but it isn't big enough to keep us both afloat. I am a hero; so I leave the saving driftwood to my pal and swim off into the wild blue yonder to eventual death by drowning.

This is not suicide. I do not wish to drown; I do not directly drown myself. I simply give my driftwood to someone else, an act of love and generosity. I swim away with a faint hope that I may find another lifesaver. It is not by my death that my shipmate is saved. He would survive just as well if I found another raft, or happened to be picked up by a rescue squad.

156

This final principle, which may seem a bit complicated to the person unfamiliar with it, is very practical in situations where the lives of mother and child are in danger. Very often it is because of this principle that there is no need to choose directly between them. I may never directly kill any innocent person, either child or mother, but if I am a skilled obstetrician I may often do things which are necessary to save the mother's life, even though they greatly endanger the child's life or will certainly result in the child's death. And such procedures are fairly numerous and frequently used in Catholic hospitals and by Catholic doctors, with full approval of Catholic moralists.

So you see, the Church never sides with the child against the mother; she doesn't take sides. She just reminds us that we are not allowed to commit murder.

Now it may be that I have not explained this final principle very well. It is a bit technical and complicated, but very clear and definite to the moralist who is used to it. And it is very important. It permits a doctor to save a mother's life without violating the first four principles. It safeguards the fundamental right of an innocent man to his life, and the supreme power of God over all life. It permits us, in some extreme circumstances, to allow a child to die, when we cannot reasonably prevent it; but forbids us to kill directly.

Suppose that you were once to admit our right to kill directly in limited circumstances. Where would you place the limits? It wouldn't be long until you would be admitting abortion to save a girl's reputation or a family's financial status. Then euthanasia would creep into acceptability. And from there it isn't far to the gas chambers, genocide, and arbitrary extermination. For our own protection let us keep the principle clear and inviolate: no power on earth may directly kill an innocent person.

Q. In a recent news story, Dr. James G. Miller, a psychiatrist at the University of Michigan, who is also a civilian scientific consultant to the army, is reported to have said that American soldiers carrying high-level secrets during war-time should be "provided with a cyanide pill or other means of suicide" and should be "ordered to make use of (the pill)" in order to prevent the enemy from brainwashing them and learning the secrets. He is reported to have said that "the individual life has to go for the welfare of the country."

I realize that suicide can never be morally right. What I am wondering about is how moral theologians determine which military actions are suicidal (and therefore illicit) and which are licit. For example, when Colin Kelly of Pearl Harbor fame, dove his bombing plane into a Japanese warship, was that a suicide or a noble act of heroism? How far may soldiers, sailors and airmen go "for the welfare of the country" before their actions can be defined as "suicidal?"

A. Moralists determine the rightness or wrongness of a particular action by the application of general principles. It is not always easy. Sometimes the reasoning must be very careful. And often there are many circumstances connected with an action which can greatly change its specific nature, and if we forget to take all these circumstances into consideration our judgment may be faulty.

One of the principles we must keep in mind in this question is that we may never do something wrong—commit a sin—in order to achieve a good purpose. The end never justifies the means.

This principle alone will take care of your cyanide pill. What is the immediate and direct natural result of taking it? Death. You know that, and when you take the pill you foresee it. So you are responsible for your own death—directly. That is suicide—something morally wrong. It is true that you have a noble, lofty purpose. But that purpose is accomplished only through the suicide. You make yourself dead, and because you are dead you cannot talk, and since you cannot talk your secrets are safe, and the country's welfare is served.

With the "kamikaze" flier this principle does not apply.

158

Colin Kelly did not commit suicide. He tried to destroy an enemy ship by diving his plane into it. A desperate thing to do, certainly. But I believe his total situation was desperate at the time. In any case, it was not as a result of his death that the enemy ship was destroyed. If he had been thrown clear of the wreckage and his life saved, the destructive effects would have been the same.

In cases like this we have a different principle: theologians call it the principle of the double effect from the same cause. Very often an action of ours has more than one effect: maybe two, maybe a dozen. Some of the effects may be good, others bad. They all follow directly from the same action. We may foresee all of them. May we rightly perform the action?

The principle is this: If the action itself is good (not sinful), we must evaluate the effects. If the good effects are at least equal to the bad effects we may be justified in performing the action—provided that our purpose is to achieve the good effects, not the bad. We merely permit them, without wanting them. If we intended the bad effects we would be guilty of them.

Does that sound complicated? Apply it to the action of your "kamikaze" flier. In itself—apart from all circumstances and results—flying a plane into a ship is neither morally good nor morally bad. Two main results follow: (1) destruction of the enemy war-potential—a tremendous good effect—and (2) death of the hero—a deplorable bad effect. Do they balance each other? Apart from all circumstances, the answer would be negative. Our first obligation is to protect our own lives. And it is significant that the code of "civilized" modern warfare does not expect its heroes generally to give their own lives inevitably in destructive procedures—in the manner of human bombs. They are expected, often, to run extreme dangers. But the Japanese "kamikaze" efforts were rightly regarded as barbarian, because they are not morally justified as normal destructive procedures in warfare.

However, there may be circumstances which would make the "kamikaze" right and heroic. For instance if it were the only way of saving your fleet from destruction—or if circumstances gave you little or no hope of saving your own

159

life anyway, because of the condition of your plane. Then the good effects would equal or exceed the bad.

Q. When is a war just?

A. War is a fight between nations. A nation has the right to protect itself and its rights. When the individual citizen has need to defend his rights, he can call upon the State to protect him. But nations recognize no higher authority on earth. There is no one to settle their dispute. If they can't compromise or arbitrate, the only solution is to fight.

During the past 40 years the world has been making practical efforts to establish a higher authority which might settle the quarrels of nations. We have tried the League of Nations, and the World Court, and now we are experimenting hopefully with the UN. But so far the nations have been too jealous of their own authority to pass any sufficient measure of it on to a world government.

So wars still seem to be necessary and unavoidable. And for purpose of simplicity, we may say that no modern war is just unless it is necessary and unavoidable.

A war may be fought only for a just and grave reason. A just reason would be the protection of the lives and property of citizens against an invading or attacking enemy, or the liberation of oppressed people, or the protection of religion against persecutors. It might be a just reason to go to war to recover stolen territory, but not to gain new territory. Imperialism is a poor excuse for war. Other poor excuses are the demands of a dictator for power and glory, and the imagined destiny of a superior race or nation, not to mention the achievement of a new economic order through world conquest.

The reason for war must be grave and serious. That is doubly true for modern warfare. By its very nature war brings on many evils, not directly intended but clearly foreseen; the destruction of homes and cities; the killing and maiming and raping of innocent women, children and old people; starvation; misery; displacement of civilians; infla-

160

tionary loss of savings; brutalities; thievery; violent fear and despair; and the unknown horrors of the atomic bomb. It takes a very grave and compelling reason to justify a nation in allowing all these evils to come to earth.

Some modern moralists contend that no war is justified in our day. They maintain that there can be no cause sufficiently grave to justify all the evils of total war, known and feared, including the threat of complete destruction of our civilization or of the human race itself.

It is true that the weapons we use in war must be in some way controlled. Nothing could justify the complete destruction of mankind. But we are in a moral dilemma. No one can question the gravity of the Communist threat. And no one believes that our enemy is greatly influenced by moral considerations. If they were convinced that they could destroy us without suffering prohibitive retaliation, they would do it in a moment. Our quandary is this. We must maintain the weapons of massive retaliation, and in the face of the enemy we must show no hesitancy about using them. And all the while we remain painfully aware that their use might be immoral.

Should we fold up meekly and let the enemy take us over, obliterate our liberties, destroy the souls of future generations, and force our civilization back to the time of the Vandals and the Huns? Just how much destruction could be justified to avoid it?

I believe we must recognize our moral dilemma and pray to God that we may never be called on to make the ultimate decision. We must maintain our forces of complete destruction and use them as a constant threat to prevent attack. And then we must hope that our threat will never be challenged, that some system of mutual disarmament may be worked out and that there may be a gradual conversion of Communist thinking.

Others who contend that no modern war is justified probably mean that our modern civilization should be able to finds way of preventing war. We agree. But the way is not yet found. We hope and pray that it may be found soon.

That a war remain just, the means used in fighting must

161

not be against natural law or the international law generally accepted. Direct killing of innocent civilians is always wrong. Indiscriminate air raids on civilian targets, for moral effect, are wrong. Mistreatment of prisoners is wrong. Plunder and pillage of private property is generally wrong. On the other hand the bombing of a military target may be justified even when great destruction of civil life and property is foreseen. War is a horrible ruthless monster, even when morally and justly fought.

Q. I have been reading so many attacks on nuclear tests in the Catholic papers lately. They refer to something Pope Pius XII said in 1953. They don't quote him; they merely refer to his statements and then editorialize. Anyway, the papers say it is immoral to test nuclear weapons. Did the Holy Father really say that under any circumstances whatever it is wrong to test the bombs? I'm not just asking this to be difficult. My husband is in Nevada right now testing weapons and there are a lot of other Catholic physicists here who are concerned about this question. Their opinion is that so little radiation is given off by the test weapons compared with natural radiation and radiation from reactors and X-ray machines that it is something like getting excited because someone threw a burning match into a building that was already burning down.

A. To the best of my knowledge the Holy Father never said flatly that it is immoral to test nuclear weapons. He has certainly pleaded with the world to end the testing of these bombs, especially in his Christmas message of 1955, but if I may quote my Jesuit namesake, the Rev. Edward A. Conway, whose article appeared in the Messenger for June 20, 1957, he did not ask that the testing be ended "as a separate measure, independent of any overall arms control agreement. What the Pope called for . . . was a three-part package including: (1) renunciation of the testing of nuclear weapons; (2) renunciation of the use of nuclear weapons; and (3) ef-

162

fective air and ground observation to ensure compliance with the first two agreements."

To quote the Pope's own words, "The sum total of those three measures as an object of international agreement is an obligation in conscience of nations and of their leaders."

The Holy Father did not suggest that we are under obligation unilaterally, and without any firm, enforceable international agreement, to discontinue our testing of nuclear weapons. He would not ask us to commit national suicide. He rather insists that "equal security must be established for all." And he even discourages an end to experimentation apart from the three-part package deal: "There would be sufficient reason to doubt the sincere desire to put into effect the other two agreements."

The Pope has expressed concern with the dangers of radioactive fallout from nuclear energy tests. In his Easter message, in 1954, he spoke of "new destructive arms of unprecedented violence" which "are now capable, with artificially radio-active isotopes of extended average life, of polluting in a lasting manner the atmosphere, the land, and also the oceans, even where those areas are very distant from the ones directly stricken and contaminated by the nuclear explosions . . . Before the eyes of a terrified world, there is presented a preview of gigantic destruction, of extensive territories rendered uninhabitable and unfit for human use— over and above the biological consequences that can result, either by the changes brought about by germs and microorganisms, or through the uncertain effect which a prolonged radio-active stimulus can have upon greater organisms, including man, and upon their future offspring."

Of course the Holy Father was here referring to the "dirty" bomb, and speaking primarily of its possible use in warfare. Your people are using the "clean" bomb. But from my casual reading I doubt that all scientists are as ready to shrug off its possible deleterious effects as are those whom you quote.

During the past 15 years His Holiness has spoken many times on the dangers of atomic warfare. As early as 1943, more than two years before the first atom-bomb was exploded at Alamagordo, and while atomic experiments were super-

163

secret, the Pope outlined to the Pontifical Academy of Science the nature of a self-sustaining nuclear reaction, and urged that this "tempestuous process" should not be used to cause an explosion, lest there follow "throughout our entire planet a dangerous catastrophe."

Probably the 1953 statement to which you refer was the one made to a group of military doctors. On that occasion the Pope said that the only justification for war "is defense against an injustice of the utmost gravity which strikes the entire community and which cannot be coped with by any other means." And he insists that many injustices must be tolerated rather than resort to war, especially when the losses expected from the war are out of proportion to the injustice. Then he continues: "This is particularly applicable to the A.B.C. war (atomic, biological, chemical)." And he asks: "Is it not possible, though international agreement to outlaw and efficaciously avoid A.B.C. warfare?

"After the horrors of the two world wars, We can only repeat that any kind of glorification of war must be condemned as an aberration of the intellect and the heart . . ."

The Holy Father concluded this address with a question and answer directly pertinent to your problem: "May the doctor place his science and activity in the service of A.B.C. war? He must never give support to an injustice, even in the service of his own country; and when this type of war constitutes an injustice, this doctor cannot take part in it."

In my own opinion, anyone who editorializes that statement so that it would stigmatize your husband and his fellow scientists as being engaged in immoral activities is going entirely beyond the words and meaning of the Holy Father. They must first establish the injustice of our national effort at preparedness. It is true that the Holy Father has condemned the "costly relationship of reciprocal terror" as a means of peace (Easter Message, 1954) but his three-part package program, quoted above, implies with clarity that a unilateral cessation of preparedness cannot be considered. We know that it would play abjectly into the Communist strategy, and lead directly to our total destruction.

So my advice would be that your husband stick to his

dangerous job valiantly until firm and enforceable international agreements take the job—and the need for it—away from him. And we hope that such day will come sooner than we think it will.

Q. I am bearing my fifth baby and have just celebrated my fifth wedding anniversary. My doctor has told me that he thinks I will not be able to carry many more children, because of damage done during labor and delivery. He also says that unless I have surgery that may include removing my reproductive organs, I will probably develop cancer in a few years. I know that this type of surgery is permitted if the organs involved are diseased, but is it also permitted as a means of preventing the development of cancer? I should hate to wait too long and leave my husband and five children without wife and mother.

A. And such a wife and mother! I am sure that the Lord loves you, even as your husband and children do.

I have a sneaking suspicion that your doctor would like to have you sterilized, and is trying to find an excuse that will permit you to accede to his wishes. But don't pay too much attention to my suspicions. If there is real, special danger of cancer, you are certainly permitted to have the operation your doctor recommends. You don't have to wait until the cancer develops—which might be too late.

I say special danger, because there is danger that anyone will develop cancer. Cigarette-smoking men are particularly worried about cancer of the lungs; and women, especially those who have several babies, are suspicious of cancer of the cervix. But that general danger is not enough to permit you to have this operation. It has to be something special: more immediate and threatening indications—and frankly I have no idea what those might be.

The general rule is this: if the operation is needed for your general health, then have it, by all means. If it merely keeps

165

you from becoming pregnant, and consequently saves you troubles, dangers and worries, then it is not permitted.

Ask your doctor to be honest with you, and then ask him this question: Would he recommend this operation even if you were now sterile? If his answer is affirmative, then the operation is licit.

Q. Being a recent convert I was surprised when a friend told me a Catholic should not be hypnotized. How should a Catholic feel about hypnotism?

A. It seems that hypnosis can be used in certain cases as an effective means of anesthesia or as a means of treatment in mental and emotional problems. In such cases, at the hands of a competent and responsible doctor, its use would be permitted for a Catholic. It is not a plaything. It is wrong to use it lightly, as a means of entertainment or an experiment of curiosity.

Q. While I was in the service I learned to hynotize, and I entertained with it quite a bit until I heard that it was wrong to hypnotize. So I stopped it until I could find out if it was really wrong. That was six years ago, and I still do not have a definite, concise yes or no, and proof why. Some answers I have read say "No," under any circumstances—not even to permit a dentist to fill a tooth, or to allow a doctor to facilitate a delivery.

Other sources say yes, even by a layman for entertainment, provided the subject agrees to it, and there is no intent to cause sin.

One strong reason it is sinful to hypnotize—some sources say—is that it controls another's free will and weakens it. I don't quite agree with this, because a person under hypnosis can still resist doing anything against his morals—if he truly wants to do so.

166

A. The truth lies neatly between the two extreme answers you have been given. When medical reasons indicate its use, and a capable and conscientious practitioner is handling it, hypnosis can be justified, just like any other form of suggestion or anesthesia. But it is not a plaything to be used for amusement and curiosity—any more than surgery should be used on the stage.

A few weeks ago I read in THE CATHOLIC MESSENGER (Nov. 20, 1958), a splendid interview on this subject with Doctor Otto Berdach, clinical director and practicing neuro-psychiatrist of East Moline State Hospital, in Illinois. He summed it up in these words:

"Hypnosis, therefore, is a medical procedure which should be done only by fully qualified doctors of medicine."

As regards the effect of this procedure on the will, Doctor Berdach says: "Hypnosis is a phenomenon by which a person concentrates exclusively on the words of the hypnotist just like you may be concentrating so much on your work you don't realize you have cut your finger until the next day, when you feel the pain.

"Hypnosis makes use of the power of concentration. If I told you that you will have no pain and if I suggest to you that you feel very pleasant and relaxed then by concentrating on this you have to disregard the fact that I may be pulling your tooth . . . The opposite would be that you would concentrate on the pulling of the tooth and would feel the excruciating pain.

"We are very susceptible to negative suggestions. So what does the physician do but replace these with positive suggestion? He doesn't diminish your will-power or make your actions involuntary. But you rely on him and you believe it is absolutely true when he says that 'it can be done.' And in this way you have eliminated your negative suggestions. What happens is that the will is diverted from its concentration on the negative and is led to concentrate on the positive. This does not harm the will; it helps it."

Doctor Berdach also points out that doctors and nurses are professional people who have a high code of ethics and honor; and that "it is assumed, from our present store of

167

knowledge, that a person will not do things under hypnotic suggestion that he would not do under normal conditions."

Q. What is the best way to explain to a Protestant why we do not consider it a sin to accept blood transfusions, even though the Bible says: Do not partake of any blood.

A. I don't believe you will have to explain this to a Protestant—only to a Jehovah's Witness. Protestants generally agree with us in a common-sense interpretation of the dietary laws of the Old Testament:

1. They were a part of the Old Law; they were rules to be obeyed by the Jewish people up until the time of Christ. They do not form a part of the New Law. It is true that the Apostles made a temporary regulation at the council of Jerusalem that the new Christians should abstain from blood (Acts 15, 29), but it is evident that this was done as a compromise, to pacify the Jewish Christians and to keep from scandalizing them. The early Christians did not long continue to observe it. St. Paul frequently and forcefully taught that Christians are not bound by the Law of Moses; the whole Epistle to the Galatians is devoted to an exposition of this teaching.

2. Even for the Jewish people of the Old Law, these were dietary laws. It is one thing to drink the blood of an animal, or to eat meat that has blood in it, and quite a different thing to receive a blood transfusion. Typical texts quoted by Jehovah's Witnesses are Leviticus 17, 10; and 17, 14: "And if anyone . . . partakes of any blood, I will set myself against that one who partakes of blood and will cut him off from among his people." "Since the life of every living body is its blood, I have told the Israelites: You shall not partake of the blood of any meat."

It is evident that "to partake" here meant "to eat." I have used the new Confraternity translation. The Douay Bible reads simply: "If any man . . . eats blood, I will set my face against his soul, etc." "You shall not eat the blood of any

168

flesh at all, etc." It is stretching the meaning out of all sense to make it forbid blood transfusions.

Q. Is anger a sin when you get mad at the children, when they won't mind?

A. Anger is a sin in the measure that it is voluntary, or when we are aware of it and make no reasonable effort to control or restrain it. Anger of the type you describe would not be a mortal sin. Often it would be no sin at all, because it is simply the frustrated, exasperated response of frayed nerves and weary bones, more physical than voluntary. But it is the type of thing which merits study and watchfulness. It produces unhappy situations, and is disturbing to children.

Q. During Advent I read the Gospels of St. Matthew and St. Mark. When our Lord was teaching he frequently admonished, rebuked and corrected the public, his followers, and the Scribes and Pharisees. Yet in the evil time, during his Passion, he did not defend himself, and spoke little. What example does this give us? Was it not anger and lack of charity, especially since he sort of blew his top, once or twice?

A. You delight me with the informality of your expression, especially since there is no evidence of irreverence.

I believe our Lord's example might teach us many lessons:

(1) That anger is not always a vice. It can be controlled and righteous and just. We often see it out of control, aroused unreasonably, inflamed by frenzy, prolonged by peevishness, stirred by jealousy, and inclined to strike out wickedly. So we forget that it is a good normal emotion intended to arouse us from lethargy and inflame us with zeal for things that are good and true. Our Lord became angry only at evil and at those errors of teaching which misled the people he loved.

(2) Charity can sometimes mean severity. Softness is not

169

always love. The stern parent often seeks only the good of his son. The rigid law is meant to protect the people, and the sharp punishment can sometimes be for their good.

Charity has a proper order of values. The love of God comes first. On that one occasion when Jesus "blew his top" it was love for the house of his Father which inflamed him. And his sharp whip taught a needed lesson which long out-lasted the mark of its lash.

(3) It is the placidity of Jesus in his own sufferings which teaches us the greatest lesson. When do you and I become angry? When someone crosses us or foils our plans. When someone scorns us or seems to lord it over us. Yet those were precisely the times when Jesus offered no complaint. His anger was aroused for the glory of God and the good of his people—never for himself.

Q. My wife and I go to Holy Communion almost daily. My wife is a religious woman, but has a hot temper. We barely get back from church and she starts (most of the time) to argue about this and that. It is either work or the weather or the neighbors, or I did this and that—and there is no end to it. Now for my side: I may not be an angel, but I won't accuse her of anything until it is too much for me, then I either protect myself, or I just don't agree with her. What happens then? Argument. But if I don't say anything, it looks like I am being mad; and that is no good either.

I often doubt that our going to church and to Holy Communion has much value, if any; and other times I think it is a sin to receive the sacraments.

A. Oh, how like a serpent's tooth . . .

You have a cross to bear, my friend; and you have my deep sympathy and prayers. But I know of nothing else to give you. Who can change a nagging woman? Even the sacraments won't do it, unless she somehow gets wise to herself. And you know from experience how useless it is to try to tell her. It is probably an illness of some nervous or emotional sort.

170

Isn't it too bad that we have to spoil the happiness of a day which comes only once in our lifetime: every day! Isn't it too bad that we undo so quickly the merits of our religious zeal, and lose so foolishly the graces the sacraments give us! Some sins may have some fun in them; this type has only frustration.

Keep on receiving the sacraments! You need them to strengthen your virtue of patience. God help you!

Q. Is it sinful on the part of parishioners to be resentful towards their pastor because of his manner of preaching to them? If it is a sin, how serious is it—mortal or venial? My dictionary says that resentment has to do with anger. Is it possible that this feeling of resentment hinders or delays wholehearted, active and harmonious participation in parish activities?

A. I am confident that your final question can be answered in the affirmative. About the others I am not so sure. We can sometimes be hurt, irritated, and offended without sin. But I doubt that it is possible to let resentment linger without some measure of sin. Patience and charity should stamp out loitering anger before it becomes chronic.

Resentment is apt to harm the person who harbors it much worse than the person resented. It rankles and gnaws; it irritates the spleen and the gastric lining; it raises the blood pressure and creases the brow. And when it does seek to strike out, it is often ineffective and frustrating—as well as sinful. It berates, or maligns; it carps and digs; it rips reputations and exaggerates the truth. Listeners are startled, embarrassed, and sometimes offended; and the speaker is left with a feeling of guilt—after the momentary relief which his pressure valve brought him.

One of the problems each of us has—with the help of God's grace—is to understand and control our lingering feelings. Why are we angry? What offended us? Why do we remain resentful? We will usually find much of ourselves in the

171

answers. We are irritated largely by things inside ourselves; the irritator merely comes into conflict with these inner feelings. So when we can't change the irritator we had best try to change ourselves—for our own happiness, as well as our virtue.

And I will wager that all your inner fuming will not change your pastor's oratory by a single inflection.

Q. Can a person forgive another who is and remains without sorrow for deliberately hurting you, like a thief who is caught but does not make amends?

A. Almighty God in his love and mercy will not forgive the unrepentant sinner. But he does not hold hatred or resentment towards him; only pity, love, patience, and the proffer of grace.

It may be that we sometimes prevent people from repenting their injuries to us; we so prolong the evidence of our hurt that we call forth their defenses against a sense of guilt. Furrows of resentment on the brow or stains of grieving on the cheeks do not always hasten remorse in the person who touched the fuse of hurt to them.

It is a strain, but if you remain loving long enough—without selfishness—you will be loved in return, by anyone worthy of your love.

9. *The Sixth and Ninth Commandments*

Rules for Courtship and Dating.
Juvenile Love-Making. Modern
Dating Customs. The Good-night
Kiss. Dancing Cheek-to-Cheek. Is
Going Steady a Mortal Sin? What
about Going Steady? Modesty of
Dress. Low Back Dresses. Sleeveless
Dresses. Modesty for Men. Bermu-
da Shorts. Beauty Contests. Occa-
sions of Sin. Parking. Dirty Stories.
Confession Magazines. Vatican Col-
lection. Bad Thoughts. Impure
Thoughts. Reading. C Movies. Le-
gion of Decency Pledge. Artificial
Insemination of Livestock. Dating
Divorcees. Company Keeping. Sex
Deviation.

Q. You have written a great deal on the moral problems involved in courtship and dating, and have indicated realistically that these problems are indeed formidable for young unmarried people. What practical, specific steps can these young people and/or their parents and advisors take to help keep these problems within manageable proportions? The passions are pretty powerful; what can young people do to keep them from getting out of hand? Prayer, and what else?

A. Prudence is the word you are looking for: prayer and prudence. This sensible virtue will remind young people often that the basic rule for sane courtship is the same as that for safe driving: Don't rely too much on your brake.

Prudence will determine details of activities and conduct, but it cannot be effective without an honest good intention. The young person who sets out on a date to get all the sensation he safely can has already tied prudence hand and foot; he has reduced a beautiful virtue to calculating sense and restraining fear, which may keep him out of serious trouble, but hardly diminish his sin.

So the first step for both youngsters and parents is prayer: that honest, deep prayer which brings our wills into line with God's will, and makes us really want to do what is right. That takes a lot of prayer, augmented by Mass and the Sacraments.

After that, for parents and advisors, I recommend the following practical, specific steps:

1. Sound instruction on the nature of the problems involved; on the force of human passions, their normality and natural goodness; and the sound reasons, both moral and practical, for restraining them. Let young people be wisely forewarned, lest they learn blunderingly by trial and error. It is evident that this instruction cannot begin an hour before the first date. It must be a long, wise sympathetic training of concept and attitude.

2. Sane, calm information on the morality of sexual activities and pleasures, so that the young people may know clearly what is right and what is wrong. Rare is the youngster who has such clear and certain knowledge. Most of them are mixed up. And why not? Their parents, who should do most of the teaching, are confused. Religious teachers often impart shining ideals which are impractical; and companions inculcate laxity by their boasting and ridicule. Frankly, we live in a world which holds up no high ideal of chastity, and decries in all its publicity any rigorous efforts at modesty.

3. A definite aim in all instruction and formation of attitudes is to eliminate two conflicting forces which agitate the magnetic field in which prudence must operate, namely:

174

curiosity and fear. A calm understanding of facts can do much to eliminate curiosity; and sound moral knowledge should help eliminate scrupulous fears. The confessor knows that fears in sexual matters do not make a person good; they merely shred vices into uncertainties and make them indistinguishable from virtue. And fears so concentrate attention in anxious indecision that they make the acute moral problems of sex chronic.

4. Parents should try in every way possible to keep the confidence—and confidences—of their children. They will have to be hep—keep posted and patient—show interest and enthusiasm. They will have to take a positive attitude of encouragement and cooperation—reduce the "Don'ts" to a minimum—help plan parties and entertainment—keep the home an interesting and inviting place. And above all they must show interest in the dated one.

5. Keep the automobile in the garage as much as possible.

And for the young people themselves I suggest the following practical, specific steps:

1. Plan your dates. Have something to do: movies, dances, parties, games, concerts, TV. Maybe even books and arguments—as long as they are animated. But if you want to avoid danger beware of two alone with time on your hands.

2. Cultivate foursomes. Don't be afraid of chaperones—or parents. Don't be afraid of the light. Don't shun the public.

3. When you start going steady, and as occasion demands, have a mutual understanding on things—on attitudes and behavior—on ideals and wishes. Be respectful, considerate, and mutually helpful. Being virtuous in company-keeping is a two-person job; only a team pulling together can do it.

4. Delay that steady company-keeping. Its dangers are inherent. Very few boys and girls can keep steady company over a long period of time without some serious problems.

5. Affectionate caresses are nice little things; but just like harmless bunnies they increase and multiply.

6. Drinking and dating combine to form dynamite.

7. Be careful of imitation. The fact that others do it

175

doesn't make it right. And besides, don't believe all you hear, either in gossip or boasting.

8. Develop interests—individual and mutual. Be good at conversation, athletics, and games that are played in the light.

9. Aim at maturity. Look forward to happiness; be willing to sacrifice present thrills for it. Be responsible; when young people are trusted alone without supervision, they are expected to use their own good judgment, exercise their own self-control, and not confuse their freedom with license.

10. Remember that an automobile is a vehicle for locomotion.

11. General modesty in dress and behavior—and in conversation—prevents the first sparks which enkindle fires.

12. Don't stay out too late.

13. In the presence of parents it is not necessary to clam up about your dates as though you were invoking the Fifth Amendment.

14. The two of you might pray together—and receive the Sacraments in unity of intention.

These rules are mostly for teenagers, dating or going steady. For those who are engaged problems intensify. My general advice would be: don't get engaged until there is really some prospect of marriage.

Q. Please give me a thorough and exact definition of a hug, prolonged kissing, necking and petting, respectively. I know that a hug is wrong because it arouses the passions. But what is meant by a hug? The boy having his arms around you as when he kisses you? Is an instantaneous embrace as a sign of affection a sin? How long is a prolonged kiss? As you can guess, I am a teenager trying to live by the Church's views on these things and not sure what is meant.

A. My dear young lady, you have my sympathy, praise and good will; but I have put off answering your letter for weeks —hoping it would go away. My own dallying makes me more

176

tolerant of your mother. Why hasn't she told you some of these answers? She should have started several years ago, so that she would have your confidence by this time; so that there would be no tension between you in talking over these matters.

However, you should have no resentment against your mother. She is like most other parents, who are prudes before their children, afraid of this important subject. Their tenseness makes their children self-conscious with them and tints the whole subject with a shade of shame.

I hesitate to give you precise definitions of the words you list, because it is not the touch or embrace which creates sin, but rather the intention and the will. You cannot define sins with a tape measure or a stop-watch. Your mother or father might hug you tighter than your boy friend would, and there would be no sin in it. But when you are tightly embraced by the boy friend your imagination starts working, you breathe faster, and your blood pressure rises. Emotions are stirred up. And then the will finds them enjoyable and accepts them—and that is sin.

And then you are aware that the young man is reacting in similar manner and you encourage him in it, and that is another sin.

Now I doubt that anything like that would happen in your instantaneous embrace, but I certainly cannot tell you how many instants it can be prolonged without sin's intrusion. That depends on many factors of intention, personality, reason and circumstance.

Something similar can be said for your prolonged kiss. My stop-watch can time you, but it cannot tell you how much sin you commit. But I think it might waver with suspicion after the first few seconds. Long kisses are by nature a preparation for something teenagers must avoid.

My dictionary doesn't help me much in making distinction between necking and petting, and my moral books are not familiar with the terms. But I understand that necking is that moderate show of affection which is socially acceptable—a thrill within limits. Petting goes much farther, demands privacy, and is much more intense and purposeful.

177

Its limits are only vaguely defined; it is passion on a tread-mill.

It is quite evident that serious petting is for husband and wife. And anything more than playful or affectionate necking is not indicated for teenagers.

When I encounter sensitive and serious young people like you I am hesitant to give advice on this subject for fear of two extremes. I do not want to make you nervous and fearful about sexual things; and I would not encourage you to laxity and compromise.

I know many young people who have let their fears and doubts about sexual sins become habits and develop into real anxieties which then spread out into other areas of life and become nagging disturbances. I do not know how all these fears and doubts can be avoided, but I am confident that it would help greatly if parents were ready with sympathetic information when it is needed and if children were helped by frank word and calm example to develop the right attitude towards sex.

Even when we are in violent fight with temptation we should keep in mind that sex is in itself, something morally good, socially acceptable, and frankly desirable—as long as it is kept reasonable, in accord with God's purpose. If young people are made to think that sex is nasty and dirty and shameful, they can readily develop fears of it, because they are sure to find a conflict between their normal instincts and their repressive shame.

Often the dark and dreadful things we fear hold no terror for us when we see them calmly in the light of day. Sex should not frighten us unduly if we understand it. Too often it creeps up on young people and takes them by surprise before they know what it is all about. Doubts are there before knowledge; and by the time understanding comes fears have grown into habits and refuse to go away.

So do not be afraid, my trusting friend; you will be often tempted, but you should learn with God's grace to direct your own life, choose your own pleasures, control your own emotions, and handle the boy friend happily, so that you restrain him but do not estrange him. It is a big job for a little girl—but you are fast becoming a young lady; and no one else can handle it for you.

The big problem of modern youth is not their own personal passions, but the demands of modern customs. Necking is accepted pastime. Late hours and lonely places are routine. Automobiles are easily parked. Your boy friend has been conditioned to expect some juvenile love-making. And your girl friends will brag of their escapades.

Do you have the courage to be different from the herd? And do you have the ability? You cannot be successfully different by sulking prudery or rigid coldness. You want the boy to like you and ask you for another date. But you must not bribe him. He can get his petting from various cheap girls. You can flash on him the total worth of your personality: your interests, animation, honesty, happiness, beauty, conversation, dancing and various skills.

Any moron knows how to pet, or can quickly learn. You have other things to offer which promise a full life of happiness, and all the while you can quietly tantalize him with a hidden promise and a restrained hope of exquisite intimacy in its proper time.

Q. I am just beginning to date and I am puzzled about a couple of standards. After how many dates with a boy should a good night kiss be allowed? I have heard that if there is a kiss, it should be no longer than I would kiss my brother, and I wonder if this is true. What does the Church say about holding hands?

A. Answering last questions first: To the best of my knowledge the Church has never made a formal pronouncement on the subject of holding hands. I doubt that this practice will lead you far astray; and maybe it is to be recommended if you are holding his hands to keep them from going astray.

Your suggested standard of measurement of the length of a kiss represents a virtuous ideal. I suspect it is occasionally exceeded even in modest practice. Remember, though, that

179

it doesn't legitimize a torrid clinch to terminate by gasping: "Oh, Brother!"

Do I seem facetious? Frankly, I am just trying to evade your questions. I don't know the answers. I believe that most good girls, like yourself, will get the best practical advice on these subjects from their mothers; and if mothers have done their duty in earlier stages of education, it should not be too difficult or embarrassing for daughters to ask these questions now.

If I were you, I would rather trust mother's advice in these matters than that of some old celibate like myself who has a lot of pat theories but little practical knowledge of modern dating customs and conventions. Probably mother won't know the exact answers either, but your frankness with her will develop confidence and rightness in your own decisions; and if you continue to take growing questions to her I am sure you will avoid serious trouble.

Mother will be perplexed, of course. She remembers some answers she found, and is probably only half-satisfied with them. She will be anxious that her daughter avoid some of the mistakes she made herself, as well as the ones she avoided; and yet she will be concerned that her little girl be popular and a target for frequent dates. The advice will not be easy for her to give; but if she will relax, no one can do it better.

Another reason I refer you to your mother is that I do not want to answer your question in a book. A few hundred teenagers will be looking for my answer, and not all will be as honest and conscientious as you are. They will grab onto any laxity I manifest as authority for their deviations, and they will repudiate my strictness as the opinions of an old square who doesn't understand modern youth. That is why I tried to beat them to the draw by modestly protesting my incompetence.

As you may know, I have written quite a bit on this subject, incompetent as I proclaim myself to be. Modern dating customs present serious problems to youthful modesty; and if those problems are not rightly and firmly solved they will quickly grow into problems of chastity . . . problems which can have a profound influence on happiness throughout this life and eternity. And there is apt to be a wide divergence between the popular ideas of youth and the strict monitions of moralists as to the proper solution of these problems. Maybe mother can form a bridge of understanding between these extremes. Ask her, anyway.

And now, just one practical question for you, little lady. Do you think you are old enough to be dating any one boy often enough for your first question to be immediately practical? Steady dating at your age may have eventual problems much bigger than that of whether to kiss him as you would your brother.

Q. Is it a sin, or an occasion of sin, when you go out with a boy, say to a show or something, if you stay in the car after you get to your home and kiss the boy three or four times? I know that to go parking is a sin, but I didn't think this was considered as parking, with the intention of arousing the passions. I am very confused on this subject.

A. I have a suspicion that most of your young friends and contemporaries are very confused, too, about the same subject, just as their fathers and mothers were confused in their day.

I am confident from your manner of writing that you yourself are not guilty of direct sin against chastity in these little good-night incidents. As you say, you have no intention of arousing the passions. But what about the boy who is kissing you? What are his intentions? What are the effects of these kisses upon him? Is he simply expressing sincere love and proper affection? Or just what is he doing?

As far as your own personal reactions are concerned, I doubt that you are guilty of serious sin against modesty; you are probably not putting yourself in serious danger of consenting to that pleasure which comes from aroused passions. But again, what about him?

The virtue of chastity requires that we must not intentionally lead another person into sin against chastity. And the

181

virtue of modesty requires that we must not provide another person with occasion or a temptation to sin against chastity.

I make a distinction between the virtues of chastity and modesty because I believe it will help clear up confusion such as yours if we understand the nature of each, and the difference between them. Chastity is the virtue which keeps us from seeking unlawful sex pleasure, intentionally, or from consenting deliberately to such pleasure when it comes along unsought. A deliberate sin against chastity is always a serious sin. But remember that it deals with sex pleasure, as such, and not with those various sense pleasures, warm feelings, and romantic thrills which may easily and quickly lead to sex pleasure. These are controlled by the virtue of modesty. It is the duty of modesty to keep you from the danger of sinning against chastity. So it is a prudent, flexible, vigilant virtue, which evaluates reasons and dangers and comes up with common-sense answers as to what to do in a particular case.

Your problem is in the realm of modesty. If you went out parking, to arouse your passions and his, there would be no question: it would be a mortal sin right from the beginning. There would be confusion between shame and desire, between a guilty conscience and demanding passions, but there would be no uncertainty about the kind of sin you committed, or how serious it was.

It is not possible to avoid all confusion in the realm of modesty. Reasons must be weighed, dangers estimated, circumstances evaluated, and judgments made. You can't draw clear definite lines which never waver. The only general advice I can give you is to try to make your decisions with confidence and honesty. Be sure you are not kidding yourself. And try to keep fear and the emotional feeling of guilt from clouding up your judgment. These are the things which cause scruples.

Your own special confusion results from an established social conflict between modern American dating customs and safe-and-sound principles of morality. Our society throws teenagers happily into danger, encourages them to skirt the precipitous edges of sin, but warns them not to go too far, without giving them any clear or right measure of distance.

182

In the midst of this confusion, I am confident that you must be stricter than average if you are to avoid sin. So here are my suggestions:

If it is a casual date, bid him good-night without any kiss—just a promising smile, which will keep him hopeful and interested.

If it is a very dear boy friend, make the kisses few and sweet, and non-lingering.

If it is your fiancé, then kiss him firmly enough to let him know that you love him, but briefly and cautiously enough to remind him that you are not yet his wife.

My favorite moralist in this field is Father Vermeersch, and he sums it all up in one short rule: *don't do any more than you could do before other people, particularly your parents.* That doesn't mean that you want others watching you; you might still blush rosy with confusion if you were caught. But you wouldn't really be ashamed or sorry.

Q. I have had a problem for some time now and I hope you will answer it for me. It is about dancing. I have been wondering whether light cheek-to-cheek dancing is all right. Of course I don't let boys try the ape-like technique on me, but I should think that light cheek-to-cheek (really not the intense kind) would be all right. I asked my mother about this and she agreed with me. Sometimes I think it is all right; and other times I wonder. Maybe it is the devil plaguing me with scruples. I don't know, but I hope you can help me.

A. I am going to duck this. I can expound the theories for you, but I am out of touch with the techniques. I presume that the ape-like technique has some monkey business connected with it. Since you rightly avoid that it is evident that your problem is not immediately concerned with the virtue of chastity. Your conflict is between the modesty of a nice little girl and the desire for popularity and conventionality which we all share. How far should you go in pleasing the

183

boys and doing what they expect—and want? That is the specific problem I leave to your mother; and I am confident that if you continue to consult her frankly and follow her advice confidently you will steer a safe and happy course between the shoals of immodesty and the whirlpools of scrupulosity. God bless you.

Q. I have been told that going steady is a mortal sin. I would like to know if this is true, and how it could be if nothing sinful is done?

A. I would judge that you are a very young person; and I think it might be a sin for you to go steady at your age; however, I would want to talk to you personally and find out all the factors involved before I would say definitely that it is a sin, or how much of a sin it is.

For two young people of reasonable maturity who are falling in love and hoping to be married, going steady may be a good and virtuous and beautiful thing, pleasing to God and sanctifying to their souls. They have respect for each other and for God's laws; they conduct themselves properly, and yet manage to give expression to their love and to encourage love in return. They encounter dangers, but handle them prudently. Their good intentions and the happy home they hope to establish give them good sound reasons to encounter dangers. They go steady without any guilt at all.

The picture is quite different for two little brats—or angels —just entering their teens. It would be ridiculous for them to think seriously of marriage for six or eight years yet. Are they going to go steady all that time? And if they do, what will be the moral results? Intimacy increases with time and familiarity. Or will they break it up, and each start over anew with someone else? And if such are their plans and prospects, do they have sufficient reason to encounter present passing dangers?

This teenage dating business is a real problem. Generally Catholic moralists, educators, and parents are opposed to "going steady" during high school years; but there are some

184

exceptions whose prudence and experience can hardly be ignored. And many teenagers are quite in favor of it—especially the girls. They will tell you of the security and confidence it gives them—social security. I have even heard them claim that it keeps them from being boy-crazy, giggly, and self-conscious.

So there are some reasons for it; but I am confident that the reasons against are much more important. Youngsters should grow up with the crowd, keep interests and activities befitting their age, extend their friendships and acquaintance, and above all avoid those moral dangers which are very likely to result when two immature youngsters are much together and trying to impress each other that they are quite grown up.

So, whoever you are, and whatever your age, don't let anyone tell you flatly and indiscriminately that you are guilty of mortal sin if you go steady. But I would advise you seriously to follow the counsel of your parents and your confessor—so that you will not run foolishly into dangers you do not surmise.

Q. What about going steady? I am fifteen, going on sixteen, and I don't think I know too much about it. Everyone I ask gives me a different answer. One priest in my parish is very strict and says definitely, "No!" Another one gave permission to my girl friend. My mother, who loves me very much, does not see anything wrong with it, as long as we do not do the "wrong things." Some of my nuns at school will say, "no, never!" While others will say, "Yes, if you do not see him all the time, alone."

Most of the kids around here are going steady and they are certainly not bad Catholics; so I think that I could, if I had the right intentions; but then some priest will come out and say it is a mortal sin and throw me into a turmoil again. I want to do the right thing, of course, but I certainly don't want to be an outcast.

I am not sure, but maybe going steady has something to

do with age. The older you get the wiser you become. Maybe it is all right for the older groups to go steady while the younger groups should not.

A. You are on the trail of the answer yourself. I am not sure that we all get wiser as we grow older, but age does have much to do with the propriety of going steady. Exclusive and regular company keeping should be a remote and contingent preparation for marriage. Such preparation for marriage is rightly the business of people old enough for it—at least past the high school age. Youngsters of 15, like yourself, should have many other things on their minds, good, healthy, lovely interests in youthful fads, fashions, fun and fantasies.

This going steady business is really a serious problem, especially for Catholics. Social customs and attitudes have undergone sweeping changes in the past few generations and some of them have gone far out of line from the firm, unchanging principles of morality. Divorce and birth control are two familiar examples. Going steady seems to be the latest. Our Catholic youngsters are growing up in a society which finds a couple of eighth-graders real cute when they are going steady, and so affectionate towards each other—and so faithful! And as you say, our Catholic young people don't want to be outcasts. So what are they to do?

I don't think that anyone can rightly say that going steady is a mortal sin—period! And I am sure that no one can say that it is all right for a couple of 15-year-olds to go steady —period! The problem is complicated and that is why you get so many different answers. Much depends on intentions, circumstances, reasons, and personalities. And these various elements are hard to evaluate precisely.

Like many other things in life, going steady may well be an occasion of sin, and becomes a bigger occasion the longer two people go steady. It is hard to imagine a normal young couple going steady for years, seeing each other frequently, and being much alone together, without their falling into habits of sin, increasingly serious.

It might be helpful for us to review the moral rules about

186

the occasions of sin. You know that occasions of sin are persons, places or things which offer a real danger of sin to us, because they invite and entice us to sin, or make sinning easy. Some occasions are very near to sin; they are the ones which usually lead us into sin; they are serious. Other occasions are remote or minor. They offer some opportunity for sin and a certain invitation or temptation, but with reasonable effort they can be resisted.

Now you may not go around putting yourself into any kind of occasion of sin without good reason; and the more serious the occasion the more important your reason must be. You learned in catechism that if you seriously intend to avoid sin you must avoid the occasions of sin, or else make them quit being occasions of sin to you. In this life it is not possible to avoid all occasions or opportunities of sin. Some of them we have to learn to handle. But there are others so serious and powerful that we can never hope to handle them, and we kid ourselves sinfully if we think we can. These we must avoid.

Sometimes we may have very good reason for putting ourselves in an occasion of sin. We have to study this suggestive book to learn to be a doctor. Or young people have to get acquainted so that they can decide whether to marry each other or not, and they must encourage their mutual love for each other and yet avoid sin.

The more serious the danger in which we put ourselves the more serious must be our reason. My old book of moral theology say that the only reason which justifies steady company keeping is the hope of future marriage, and it may not be simply a long-range, indefinite, possible future hope, but something reasonably close and probable.

Now, young people in their late teens may be thinking seriously about getting married, not in the immediate future, and not necessarily with any certain person; but in accordance with the courtship and marriage customs of our society it is time for them to be getting acquainted and to lay the foundations for future definite plans. So boy and girl start seeing each other regularly and frequently. That involves some moral dangers. But marriage is one of the most impor-

187

tant things in life, and preparations for it provide sufficient reason to encounter the dangers. These young people must simply keep in mind that no reason, however good, can justify sin. So they must see to it that the dangers become no more than that, and never actually become the sins they threaten. Then their company keeping is good and right.

On the other hand, take your case and that of the 16-year-old boy who thrills you. What reasons do you have for keeping steady company? About the only really good reasons I have been able to learn are: (1) social security: that you may have dates for parties and events; (2) emotional security, which comes from knowing that you are wanted and have an assured place where comfort and intimacy may be found; and (3) the assurance that you are not a social outcast, as you say, yourself.

Now these are not bad reasons, in themselves, and they certainly receive rather general acceptance in our modern society. However, it is quite probable that when you bolster your self-confidence by a going-steady arrangement you are simply using a crutch which prevents your proper maturing in the area of self-sufficiency. And if our homes were what they should be the family circle should provide to youngsters like yourself that assured place of comfort and intimacy which you need. Furthermore, I think that it is possible to counter every reason for going steady, at your age, with an equally good reason for not doing it. For instance: (1) you narrow your field of acquaintance, so that you develop no sound norms of comparison, to see if your man (or boy) measures up; (2) you shortcut your emotional development, leaving out those gregarious years of polygamous tendencies and romantic dreams; and (3) you make your choice of partner with immature judgment, and he may become a habit.

So as these reasons cancel each other out I think that my old moral book is just about right even today. It was written long before steady company keeping became an established juvenile custom. But it still seems to be basically true that the only reason which justifies steady company keeping is some hope of marriage in the reasonably near future. I suppose a modern book might consider the established custom as a partial reason in itself—a cause for tolerance and moderation in dealing with the compulsion of our Catholic youngsters to conform. On the other hand, maybe this established custom is reason to be more forceful and vehement than ever, simply to combat the trend. At least many people seem to think so. My only worry is that they create some false consciences by their vehemence.

We old-timers should be careful not to make everything black and white by contrast. Certainly we fail to see sense in the juvenile fidelity of modern teenagers. We know that this steady company keeping is dangerous. But not all was purity and holiness in the old days either, when youth played the field and sought its rapid conquests. Occasions of sin are not necessarily made remote by variety.

As you suggest, yourself, more depends on intention than on anything else. If a young fellow sets out for a thrill his sin is no greater if he seeks it with his steady date than with a casual one. But what of the moral condition of the girl who dates young Lothario steadily? And what of the moral condition of two young people who, in spite of good intentions, find themselves drawn by the tide of normal desire into turmoil beyond their depth?

Q. This problem has troubled me and I imagine, many other young girls for a long time. What is modesty of dress? How do we know what is pleasing to God in this matter? I know God is reasonable and does not expect us all to go around dressed like nuns in this day and age. I think the human body is beautiful and should not be completely hidden, but I also know that too much exposure can be dangerous to others. Where do you draw the line?

A. Your question is so honest I can't resist it. And yet I know that I should. Many of my answers get me in trouble, but none so deeply as those about women's fashions. People feel strongly on this subject and differ widely. There are some rigorists who insist you should dress like a nun, even

189

these hot days. And they are countered by laxists who think you need little more than a sun tan to be acceptable. No wonder a good little girl is in doubt.

The good little girl never has the deliberate intention of exposing herself in such way as to arouse men and incite them to sin. But on the other hand, if she is pretty and well formed and vivacious, she is probably going to put some of them in a dither however she dresses.

The only answer I can give you is that you should use prudence and modesty, and these are virtues for which we cannot draw definite lines. Some crusaders try it. Every time I write on this subject I get letters and papers telling me that any dress which is cut two inches lower than the Adam's apple is immodest; and sleeves must come below the elbows and skirts within so many inches of the ankle.

My only answer is: bunk—sometimes prefixed by a strong adjective. Moralists are not stylists, modesty is not measured with a tape, and prudence is seldom gauged in inches. Besides, much depends on whether you are dressing for church, the beach, the street, a picnic, or a formal party.

You evidently have a sense of modesty, but you are not sure of your judgment on the subject. For you personally I would recommend that you must not be fearful, merely sensible. Scruples are the enemy of prudence. Observe and use good judgment; no one else can do it for you. I would like to simply refer you to your mother and tell you to trust her judgment while your own is being formed. But I hesitate; some mothers have so much pride in their daughters' charm that they encourage the display of it, even at a risk of modesty.

You want to be modest; so I am sure you will be, most all the time. The person who is inspired by vanity, levity or lust to push modesty aside will hardly be pulled back into line by the tape-measure boys.

Q. Are all low back dresses immodest, or just the ones which go to extremes?

A. Where are the extremes?

190

Apparently it is my levity which gets me into trouble on this subject; some people seem to think that the cut of a woman's dress is dead serious business, and that an inch of margin here and there makes the difference between virtue and vice. Personally I don't think you should hew the line that closely; and I think a good Catholic woman should have a native sense of modesty and propriety which will guide her in making her own measurements—or leave them to a competent couturier. It is not an area for amateurs, especially clerical ones.

Q. There is a difference of opinion among us as to whether it is proper to wear a sleeveless dress to Mass when one intends to receive Holy Communion. What is the Church's teaching on this?

A. There are many pronouncements of Church authorities which are quite strict on this subject. There are some countries—and some parishes in this country—in which you would be refused Communion if you went to the altar railing in a sleeveless dress. But there are many other parishes where such manner of dress is taken for granted in the hot summer time.

You should be modest at all times—and particularly in church—and above all at the Communion railing. But, when it comes to a matter of sleeves or no-sleeves, local custom and acceptance largely determine what is modest.

Q. Every time I have heard a sermon or a retreat conference on virtue, the virtue of modesty was always directed to be practiced by the woman. What about the man? Yes, a woman must be careful how she walks, sits and dresses, and I am in a hundred per cent agreement with this.

Now that summer is almost here, why not protect the woman on the beach? Girls are told to select their bathing suits to be of modest fashion. It disgusts me no end to see some of the scanty attire worn by our men on the beach.

191

A. You know, young lady, you might have something there. At least your gripe is worth a few inches of space and a bit of meditation. No one has ever openly advocated a double standard. It is simply that we take it for granted that the feminine form is better adapted for display; and that male eyes are more roving and voracious. After all, who could get much of a thrill from the scrawny legs and sunken chest of the average male.

But still there are those bronzed imitations of the divine Adonis who delight in the gorgeous display of their biceps and bulges, in the fond hope that the girls are looking. Modesty certainly applies to them in all its vigor. And modesty applies to many other things besides dress and bearing. It guards our thoughts and reading, our touches and sensations. And in these various areas it certainly applies to men as thoroughly as to women.

Q. Isn't it all right to wear Bermuda shorts around the house? How far around, other than home, would you say it would be all right to wear them?

A. I have had my ears beaten down so often for my answers on subjects like this that I became defensively frightened when I opened your letter. There seems to be violent disagreement on the subject of women's dress in general. I can only give you my own opinion, which I believe is based on sound moral principles.

Modesty consists as much in the manner in which clothes are worn as in clothes themselves. It is manifested in conduct and attitude as much as in measurement and pattern. And, my critics to the contrary, custom does have much to do in determining the modesty of a garment. If properly worn—by a person adapted to wear them—I cannot see that there is anything immodest about Bermuda shorts in your own home. They should be much more modest than other types of warm weather deshabille to which you might be tempted.

I will have to trust your own good feminine judgment as to the propriety of wearing Bermuda shorts in various places outside the home. Personally I have not found them quite appropriate on city streets, or down-town in our midwestern villages. Yet I think they may not be out of place in the supermarket, if you go there in the car. They should be quite all right for sports and picnics (unless the mosquitoes are bad), but I believe they are distracting in classrooms, unacceptable in offices, and completely out of place in church.

Q. I am rather confused about this beauty contest business. The reason for my confusion is an argument between Catholics. One maintained that beauty contests indicated a lack of true Christian values and that they involved the sin of vanity, at least. Another insisted that because these contests were a part of the American way of life, and because they involved a "cultural" as well as a beauty test, the contests would be justified. Please tell me, is there a Catholic attitude towards beauty contests?

A. I am pleased to see that you put "cultural" in quotation marks.

The Catholic Church has official teachings on various principles of doctrine and morality which may apply to beauty contests, and occasionally some Church dignitary may speak out in condemnation of a particular notorious contest (I have never heard one speak out in praise), but I don't think it can be said that the Church has an official teaching on beauty contests, as such. Much depends on the contest, its methods and its purposes.

The Church has a high appreciation of beauty; it is a form of goodness, a perfection of being, a reflection in tinsel of God's eternal beauty. But while earthly beauty may be tinsel in comparison with God's infinite perfection, it must still remain true and genuine in its own order or it fades into ugliness. Artificiality is a contradiction of beauty; and exploitation for publicity purposes smacks of artificiality.

The beauty of a woman is divinely designed. It is good, and if used for good purpose it becomes virtuous. But like

193

all good things it can be abused, and if used for evil purpose it becomes vicious. What is the purpose of the vulgar display of beauty which features most beauty contests?

Even when our purpose is good we must often consider the circumstances of our acts. Modesty is an important virtue. Is it carefully observed in beauty contests? And giving scandal is worse than having a mill-stone tied around your neck as you flounder in the sea (Matt. 18, 6). Scandal leads other people into sin; beauty can sometimes do this.

The cheap and shoddy are a negation of real beauty. These features are seldom absent from beauty contests, even when the publicity is opulent and the rewards are golden.

Sentimentality distorts beauty by exaggerated emphasis on some of its features while completely obscuring others. In spite of its "cultural" clap-trap, a beauty contest emphasizes the physical out of due proportion—even while stressing proportions. It contributes to our false sense of values in American society.

Vanity is a vice. Beauty contests exploit it shamelessly.

So it looks like the scales of morality are rather heavily weighed against the highly publicized exploitation of beauty for profit. And we say it with respect and admiration for some recent contest winners.

Q. Am I right in believing that conversations and jokes with double meanings and dealing with sex are not a serious sin as long as they do not cause impure thoughts, and one does not dwell on them?

A. You are right; these things are not serious sins unless there is grave danger that they set some of your hearers off on a process of sinful thinking.

Q. It seems to me that students at Catholic high schools and colleges do the same amount of parking and necking that other U.S. youths do, and that everyone knows it: parents,

194

chaperones, house mothers and the students. Do you moral-
ists take the firm stand that you do (no couple not planning
marriage can ever kiss for the sheer pleasure of it), knowing
that the majority won't take your advice, but that at least
you scare them from getting into serious trouble morally?

A. We have no schemes or ulterior motives; we simply expound the moral law and let the hardships fall where they
may.

Incidentally, I think that, amid your implied protests, you
are rather rugged in your own statement of moral principle.
I would disguise your bald statement with a few confusing
distinctions.

Q. I have been troubled concerning a past confession. At
one time I worked with a group of women who liked to tell
off-color stories. I did not enjoy listening to them, but
laughed with the others. I confessed these sins and honestly
intended to avoid listening again, but knew I could not get
away from them, and would laugh with them again. I would
put off going to confession until I thought things were not
so bad. Do you think I had the intention or sincere desire
to avoid sin, or would I have to make a general confession
from that time?

A. Forget the whole thing, please. Your confessions were
good. You admit that you are a scrupulous person; so don't
even think of making a general confession. Just try to develop
more confidence in the love and goodness of God; and trust
your confessor when he advises you as I have. You worry that
he did not understand you; scrupulous people always do.

Actually you magnify mightily your original guilt in listening to those stories. You admit that you took no personal
pleasure in them; and anyway you are a married woman to
whom reasonable pleasure of that kind might be permitted.
And I am sure that your hesitant, guilty laugh gave no encouragement to the story tellers, anyway. The only way to

avoid dirty stories is to become deaf—and even then you would probably learn lip-reading.

Q. How would you rate confession-type magazines? Is continued reading of such magazines sinful?

A. I would rate them in the same class with garbage, trash, offal and vomitus. They stink, with a putrid, fetid, decaying odor. They distort life, entice morbid curiosity and invert a sound sense of values.

The continuous reading of them is not only a sin, it stultifies the intellect, perverts the imagination, befuddles conscience, and blunts all sense of taste.

Q. Recently my husband overheard a man say, "Indiana University has the largest collection of pornography next to the Catholic Church." Is there such a collection at the Vatican? If so, why?

A. Kinsey's studies on sexual behavior might account for the reputation of Indiana U. I have no idea why the Catholic Church was brought into the comparison. We have a well established reputation (through the Legion of Decency, the National Office for Decent Literature, and the censorship of books) for fighting this sort of thing. We are accused of being puritanical and authoritarian on the subject. Maybe some people think we make a great show of fighting it in public to hide our secret treasuring of it. We cannot prevent their thinking.

The Vatican has a museum, an art gallery, and a library. The museum has some of the most valuable works of sculpture in existence, and most of them are quite nude, in the classic manner. The art gallery has a typical collection of precious paintings, not all of them fitting decorations for a convent. And I presume the library—one of the most famous in the world—has a number of historic manuscripts which are not recommended for children. I am sure that none of it

196

could be called pornographic or obscene, even by the "old lady from Dubuque"; but some of the books might need to be handled with care and reserved for competent scholars.

Q. I am many times bothered with bad thoughts, and sometimes I wonder if I get them out of my mind quickly enough; so just to make sure I always confess them and add that I am sorry to any extent I am guilty of dwelling on them or taking pleasure in them. I am a married woman.

A. I am confident that the thoughts you have are not "bad" for a married woman, and they need not "bother" you at all. Just let them come and go. The only way you might commit a serious sin would be to deliberately entertain yourself with desirous fantasies of some one other than your husband.

The general rule for married people in matters of this kind is that thoughts which serve to bring husband and wife more closely together and make their marital life more complete are perfectly good—even though they might be seriously sinful for single people.

Q. Would you tell me what constitutes an impure thought? The catechism defines it as a thought about an impure subject, but that is using in the definition the same term we want defined. I skip so many Communions for fear some question or idea that comes to mind might be a sin.

A. You can think on any subject without committing a sin. And I suppose you might be able to commit a sin by thinking on almost any subject. The "impure thoughts" which are sinful are not really thoughts at all, in the strict intellectual or abstract sense of the word. They are imaginings: pictures drawn by the imagination. Sometimes they become very vivid, and when they do they produce physical effects: glandular secretions, changes of breathing and blood flow, muscular movements and sensory responses. Abstract thinking

197

will never produce these physical changes directly—only by arousing images which are closely attached to certain thoughts. So thinking is neither good nor bad, in itself— though it is usually much better to think than not to think.

But what about the morality of these piquant pictures which have the power to shake you up a bit? That is your question. You imply that they are frequently going through your mind. My advice is: let them go through—all the way through and out the other side and give them only casual, unperturbed attention as they pass. That way they will do no harm at all. Worrying about them merely concentrates attention on them and perversely invites them to linger.

Even vivid images are not bad in themselves—only dangerous. And the sin comes from flirting with the danger needlessly. With a bit of timing and selectivity married people can dally with these images sinlessly; no danger involved, only closer marital union. A conscientious medical student may have a veritable gallery of such pictures in his mind and commit no sin. He has reason to think on such subjects and let his thinking call up assorted images. He need only keep his purpose serious and studious—not sexual.

Letting your imagination linger on suggestive, sex-colored pictures may be sinful for one of two reasons:

(1) You are using them as a means of getting forbidden sexual pleasure; you are seeking sensations and savoring them. This sin is mortal; it violates chastity. Your motive is bad from the beginning. But this is not the type of sin which worries your anxious conscience, my questioner; you have no conscious intention of seeking sexual pleasure—only those repressed desires which trigger your anxieties at the same time they arouse your mental images.

(2) You are putting yourself needlessly in danger of giving voluntary consent to the sexual pleasures which accompany the sensations aroused by your mental images. That sounds like a chain reaction, doesn't it? Well, it is; and like an atomic reaction it may be suddenly explosive.

Remember that if the sexual pleasure is licit for you—as a married person—you are putting yourself in no danger, and the "impure thoughts" are not sinful.

198

Note that you are putting yourself in this danger needlessly. You have no good sound reason which will justify the danger—as the medical student has.

Sins committed for this second reason may be slight or serious—depending on the degree of danger. For good reason you can run a lot of danger and commit no sin. Calming your anxieties might be such a reason. For a minor reason you can run ordinary dangers and commit no sin. For no reason, except curiosity or inertia, you can dally with thoughts which produce considerable danger and still be guilty of only venial sin. But once you get yourself in real serious danger without real serious reason you are guilty of mortal sin.

Now what does that do to your anxieties? Well, let me calm them with some soft but sound words: Don't be skipping those Communions. You are certainly not guilty of any mortal sin; and I feel reasonably certain that you are guilty of very few venial sins by your "impure thoughts." As I indicated before, the calming of your scruples may well be sufficient reason to justify some casual dallying while those perturbing thoughts find their own unagitated way into the fringe areas of attention; and you calmly turn your thoughts to less vivid subjects. For people who worry I advocate an easy, relaxed method of crowding "impure thoughts" out of the mind. Remember that you can't drive them out by tension; you have to push them out with better thoughts. And remember, too, that you can't commit a mortal sin without knowing it; and unless you know it definitely you may receive Holy Communion.

Q. The Legion of Decency publishes a movie rating. I have often wondered what is done in regard to books. I go to a public school and there is a reading contest. We are supposed to read the "better things" such as the old classics, and others. In some there are many impure things. I do not understand whether or not it is a mortal sin to read books which have bad parts in them. Even if it were not a sin are you supposed to read such books? We were told not to read

199

them for the impurity, but for what is good in them. I know
from experience that they would be an occasion of sin to me.

A. Your final statement probably indicates the answer to your question. If a certain book is an immediate occasion of sin to us then we may not read it. An immediate occasion is one which invariably leads us into sin. For the average, fairly mature person the "better books" are not an immediate occasion of sin. They are suggestive and exciting and may very well lead to sin—but they need not do so. The moralist would say that they are remote occasions of sin. Usually we are permitted to read books of this kind, under the following conditions:

1. We have very good reason to read them. We have to learn what is in them, or they have notable educational or literary value.

2. We read them with the right intention, as you say: not for the impurity but for what is good in them.

3. We take precautions, including prayer, to see that they do not lead us into sin.

4. We have assurance, from past experience, that we will be able to avoid the sin.

We need not be prudes; we must not confuse temptations and suggestions with sin. On the other hand we must not over-rate our strength, or run foolish, needless dangers.

And let it be noted that none of this discussion applies to trashy pulps of the pocket-book type which have suggestion and titillation as their principal theme and purpose. It would be hard to find sufficient reason to justify sloshing through their filth.

Q. A girl who attends a Catholic college maintains it is not a mortal sin—only a venial sin by reason of scandal—to attend a "C" movie. Is this correct?

A. I doubt that this girl has learned her lessons well at college. In the mature and careful judgment of those who rated the movie for the Legion of Decency it would be a grave danger of sin against chastity—or some other virtue—for the average person to attend this movie. A Catholic college girl is probably above average in many respects, but it would be well for her to get some sound impartial advice before she rates herself above average in immunity from temptation.

Besides, even if it were ONLY a sin of scandal I am not sure it would be ONLY a venial sin. The bad example of a Catholic college girl can be a powerful influence: "Woe to the man through whom scandal does come." Your college girl would look funny with a millstone for a necklace.

Very few movies are put on the C list any more. They have to be really bad to get that rating.

Q. If you have taken the Legion of Decency pledge are you committing a serious sin by going to a B movie or watching an objectionable TV program?

A. You commit the same sin you would be committing by the same action if you had never taken the pledge. Figure that out!

Q. I wonder if you would explain the position of the Church in regard to the artificial insemination of livestock and other animals?

A. To the best of my knowledge and belief the Church has not found it necessary to assume any position on the subject. It is a problem for the veterinarian and the breeder. In normal practice there should be no question of faith or morals involved.

Q. We have four or five men in our parish, all "good" Catholics apparently, attending services regularly and receiving the sacraments frequently, who are doing something which

201

I cannot condone. Whether it is through ignorance on their part or not I do not know. All of these men are keeping regular company with Catholic women who have been divorced. One of them even brings his date to church with him. I contend that these Catholic men and women are committing two sins: one of scandal, and the other of not avoiding the proximate occasion of sin. Actually, I do not think that any of them are doing anything wrong morally, but . . .

A. In your last statement you are more charitable than I would be; and surely more charitable than many of the fruity gossips of the parish. What you mean is that they are not engaging in acts against chastity; and we may hope that your surmise is true. But they are doing things morally wrong, and we know it without any rash judgment. You have given the reasons yourself: scandal and the occasion of sin. And there is strong probability that more than one of them will end up in an invalid marriage where they can no longer salve their consciences with the sacraments.

Q. In a recent Question Box you stated that a girl commits a sin (venial) if she dates a divorced person, because she puts herself in an occasion of sin. I can understand that, but I was also taught, in my twelve years of religion, that two or more venial sins combined do not make a mortal sin. Of course it is very poor judgment that a Catholic should keep company with a divorced person, but how does the sin of this Catholic differ from that of two single persons who are keeping company without marriage? The occasion of sin is there for them also. Please explain.

A. First of all, I don't think I ever used the word venial in writing about company-keeping with a divorced person. I said that it was a sin because it was an occasion of sin—but our wallowing in the occasion of sin is very often a mortal sin. And I don't think we should mince words: keeping company with a divorced person is a mortal sin—unless it is positively known that this person is free to marry in the Church.

The occasion of sin differs from sin in this: we may often put ourselves in the occasion of sin without sin. Sometimes the occasion is necessary and unavoidable. Sometimes there is excellent and sufficient reason for running the danger of sin—which we are reasonably sure we can avoid. Sometimes the occasion of sin is very remote and then we don't need a very serious reason to permit us to encounter it without sin.

By the mere fact of living we are in some occasion of sin. But a reasonable amount of prayer and precaution will permit us to live in the midst of life's ordinary occasions without committing sin.

Company-keeping between a young unmarried couple presents a special occasion of sin, which becomes more dangerous as affection and familiarity increases between them. But the prospect of love and marriage may provide sufficient reason to justify their running these dangers of sin—as long as they honestly avoid sin itself.

But what good reason could possibly justify a young girl's keeping company with a divorced man? The thing is dangerous and it can come to no good end. It is scandalous too, because she is really hanging around with another woman's husband.

True there is danger of sin in ordinary company keeping; but with good intentions and God's grace that company-keeping can be made a holy and beautiful thing, as pleasing to God as it is to the young couple in love. But what good intentions can ever motivate dangerous and scandalous dalliance with a married man—who happens to be divorced.

The real danger lies in the ultimate outcome. Ordinary company-keeping may lead to occasional sin—transitory, we might call it, because quickly repented. But keeping company with a divorced man may lead to permanent sin—a state and habit of sin, which brings sorrow without repentance.

Q. I recently read an article by a priest on the problem of "sex deviationism," or in plainer language, homosexuality.

I could understand his point that people should be charitable and sympathetic towards such people (he says that most of the deviationism springs from loneliness and the friendless existence in our big cities). My question is whether homosexuality can ever be a purely physical ailment, or whether there is always moral guilt involved in each person. In other words, is sex deviationism something which can occur and grow involuntarily in certain persons? Is it ever just a physical affliction which can only be controlled or reduced in its expression, but can never be completely eradicated?

A. Certainly we should be charitable towards sex deviates. All of us who are sinners need charity; and only to those who are without sin did our Lord give permission to cast stones. He knew that He was safe in giving that permission. So few would qualify, and those few would be too charitable to use their privilege.

We should also be sympathetic, but only in the true and better sense of that word. We should try to understand. But we should not permit our sympathy to become sentimentality. There is a tendency, today, originating amongst advocates of determinism and a-morality, to be fairly maudlin about the unfortunate weakness of these poor perverts. And that drippy sentimentality is just the treatment they want. It accepts them as they are and relieves them of the arduous duty of trying to change. It coddles them warmly as mamma used to do. It makes them feel secure and bolsters their wavering feelings of inferiority. Like all immature people they are disinclined to grow up and accept responsibilities. The benign attitude of sentimentalists accepts them as bumbling children, and they are content.

We must be understanding. These people are afflicted; they are sick. Their condition is not too much different from that of the alcoholic. A compulsion seems to drive them. Maybe this compulsion derives from factors of native temperament: a jumbling of genes, goofy gonads, or hebetudinous hormones. More probably there were unfortunate influences in

204

their early environment, in the home or the neighborhood: emotional conflicts, psychic injuries, a possessive mother, or freakish friends.

These things are true only of genuine homosexuals. Just as alcoholics constitute only a percentage of drunks, so genuine homosexuals are only a part of those who sometimes engage in perverted sexual activities. There are many others, with fairly normal desires and interests, who are led on by circumstances or curiosity or plain concupiscence to the delights of deviation, simply for the sexual thrill. They are just plain sinners, and deserve less sympathy than an adulterer.

The traditional attitudes of society, which have been generally inconsiderate of alcoholics, are likewise unfair to deviates. Suspicion, scorn, and contempt are their lot. And their unique social value is to be the butt of vulgar jokes. Hostility and severity serve to increase the feelings of inferiority from which they usually suffer, in spite of their brazen refinements.

On the other hand society must protect itself and particularly its minors and its children. The activities of these deviates are often antisocial, sometimes violently so. Sympathy becomes sentimentality if it vests all its concern in the weakness of the deviate and forgets the harm or danger to others. Such sentimentality would excuse him from all moral guilt—lest he develop a guilt complex—and would give him a sympathetic slap on the wrist for his sex crimes.

Sympathy becomes sentimentality when it tends to destroy basic moral concepts and relieve these people entirely of responsibility. The fact that they have an urge does not confer on them the right of giving in to their urge. A normal, heterosexual person is often strongly urged to sexual sins. That urge does not justify his philandering. He must restrain himself and control his urge, violent though it be.

It may be true that an abnormal urge is sometimes stronger than a normal desire; and a real compulsion can reduce freedom of will and moral responsibility. But the basic moral rule must be kept in mind—to ward off the fuzzy errors of determinism—that any deliberate action or desire contrary to the sixth commandment is a mortal sin for these deviates

205

just like it is for the rest of us. Very rare and psychopathic is the case in which compulsion so reduces freedom as to excuse the pervert from mortal sin.

If the deviate is to avoid sin he must, like everyone else, avoid the occasion of sin. And for him those occasions are apt to be doubly dangerous. If he cannot correct his abnormal tendencies—and it is the general opinion that many true deviates cannot correct them—then he must simply learn to resist those tendencies, with the aid of divine grace, and sublimate his desires and energies into legitimate interests and activities. Such sublimation has produced some of our greatest art and literature.

The pervert is not much different in this respect from the normal person who does not marry. Both must avoid sexual pleasures. It is a hard task for both. And if it should be a bit harder for the pervert, then God will give him more grace, and he will have to try harder. If either one or the other is to be well adjusted he must fill his life with strong interests other than sex.

Trying to counsel these deviates is one of the most difficult tasks of the priest who acts as counselor or confessor. He must be truly charitable and sympathetic, patient, persevering, and resigned to disappointment. Trying to cure these same people is one of the most discouraging jobs of the psychiatrist. Some do claim cures after long effort. But others believe that no genuine deviate is ever cured. Most are agreed that the biggest obstacle to cure is the fact that they don't really want to be cured.

10. *Marital Morality*

*Q. It seems to me that American Catholics today have a
hard time living up to the teachings of the Church in various fields of sex and marriage. We are opposed to steady
company-keeping for youngsters, but they all do it. We say
it is a sin to neck and pet, but it is common practice. We
won't allow divorce, but many of our friends and neighbors
get them. The Church keeps warning us against birth control, but it has become a national practice, and we are told
that our old-fashioned ideas contribute to the population
explosion.*

A. We Catholics in the United States are a minority group
in a culture dominated by ideals, doctrines, and practices
which are divergent from our own, and often in direct con-

207

flict. Yet for the most part we are not isolated or insulated from this dominant culture. From the days of our immigrant forefathers we have striven towards equality and uniformity. The strong urge of Catholics to fit into the community and become indistinguishable from the majority has its good aspects; it contributes to the harmony of our American life and inspires us with zeal for advancement. But it makes it more difficult for us to maintain our beliefs, ideals, and practices which are essentially different from those of the dominant culture.

It cannot be said that our differences are inconsequential. They are both profound and practical. They have a bearing on eternity; and they touch upon vital areas of daily action. The entire secularism of our materialistic age is foreign to the Catholic ideal which would entertwine religion thoroughly into the fabric of daily living. But it is particularly in that vast area of courtship, marriage, and family life that our differences are accentuated.

We as Catholics have some very firm convictions and principles in these matters which are not shared by our non-Catholic neighbors.

First of all, we hold that the reproductive powers of man and woman—their sexual instincts and pleasures—beautiful and good as they are in the plan of God, are not to be used outside of marriage. They have a divinely given purpose, and are to be used in conformity with that purpose.

Secondly, we believe that marriage is sacred—that it was established by Almighty God, and elevated by Jesus Christ to the sanctity of a sacrament.

Thirdly, we believe that marriage is by nature permanent and indissoluble.

Fourth, we hold that the primary purpose of marriage is the procreation of children; and that this purpose must not be directly and maliciously foiled.

And fifth, we believe that the primary objective of the family is religious: to worship God, to raise children in the knowledge and love of God, and to achieve the salvation of all its members.

Let us see now how these five doctrines, and the practice
208

of them, may fare in the atmosphere and example of American living.

1. *General attitude towards sex: chastity and modesty.*

There is no doubt that our present civilization in America has a strong tendency—even a frank, conscious tendency—to accentuate the sexual. It has been called a sensate civilization. This tendency manifests itself in every phase of our modern living: in dress, manners, talk, songs, entertainment, advertisements, and especially in the movies, in our books, and on the stage—to say nothing of night clubs. Exhibitionism is openly accepted and publicly advertised. Routines of suggestion and excitation have even reached TV.

All of us have a tendency to imitate—to succumb to our environment. The customary does not shock. We tend to adopt the mass attitude—to accept the daily habits of those with whom we live. And this we do even though it be entirely foreign to our Catholic ideals or contradictory to our Catholic principles. We can't accept all these sensate customs and attitudes without conflict, but we sign an uneasy truce; in compromise we shuttle between opposing conformities, and try to live with our resulting anxieties.

Our modern American society has not only developed customs contrary to our Catholic ideals, it has gradually formulated principles to justify its customs. It is a process of rationalization. Nowadays, when we talk to sociologists, psychiatrists, or counsellors, we run into a startling attitude which might be expressed in the general principle that there is nothing morally wrong with any sex gratification unless it becomes antisocial, i.e. harmful or offensive to others. Oh, of course, excesses are undesirable; they may be harmful and upsetting to the practitioner. But they are merely undesirable, not morally wrong. These people are sincere, and they propound their theory with apostolic zeal. They have not formulated it to justify actions of their own, but to help others. They want to avoid the harmful effects of repression, feelings of guilt, and anxieties in the people they treat or counsel. They feel that this result can best be achieved by assuring people that there is no moral guilt attached to

209

thoughts, desires, or efforts at self-gratification. They urge reasonableness and moderation. They caution against abnormalities. And they encourage a mature, balanced attitude, with reasonable restraints—and always, of course, consideration for the rights and desires of other people.

This same process of rationalization—of developing principles to justify customs—extends into preparation for marriage, into marital life itself, into family life, divorce, etc. We will note them in contrast with each of our basic Catholic doctrines. The point is that our whole moral code on sexual morality has been changed by spokesmen for the dominant element of our American society. Their theories may not have seeped down into the popular areas in explicit form; but the popular practices generally invite the theories, and the public is gradually adopting them.

As previously indicated there is conflict in our public life; it is particularly emphasized in the whole field of entertainment, publicity, and advertising. If we are not careful our sensitivities, which result from Catholic principles and ideals, can be blunted. We come to take for granted smut, vulgarity, suggestion, display, and even open solicitation.

However, the conflict is specially acute in the area of dating, company keeping, and engagement—in the personal relations of the sexes outside of marriage and in preparation for marriage:

The first problem of dating concerns its early inception, the second concerns the frequency with which it continues, and the third the manner in which it is conducted.

Twelve years seems to be the acceptable age to begin dating. I suppose there wouldn't be any violent objection to this infantile association if it were kept strictly casual and occasional. But the tendency quickly grows towards regular and frequent dating: once, twice, three times a week. And on these dates the youngsters are alone and unsupervised. They have grown up on movies and romance, and have been indoctrinated by the bragging of their companions. So there is apt to be early experimentation in the art of juvenile love-making.

In its process of rationalization, our dominant society finds

210

good and convincing reasons for this early dating. It develops self-confidence, gives ease and assurance, and relieves that gawky curiosity of adolescence about the opposite sex. Many of these things are true, of course, and an easy early acquaintance is a desirable thing; but it should be carefully done lest the seed be planted for bigger problems than those remedied.

Much more serious than dating are the problems of steady company-keeping. This too begins early. In non-Catholic communities it is not at all uncommon for youngsters to keep steady company during their first year in high school. In accordance with Catholic moral principles this is clearly an unjustifiable occasion of sin. But here too there is a definite tendency to imitate. Catholic parents do not want to be old fogies. They are often as anxious as their children that their beloved offspring should not be left behind in the race for social security.

Still more dangerous is the manner of this company-keeping. Our society accepts it as entirely right and proper that teenagers with passions, potentially violent, should be alone together, in dark secluded places, for long periods of time, while familiarity and affection develop, and a measure of physical contact is sanctioned. About the only warning given these youngsters is that they must not go too far, but there is no clear determination of just when the brakes should be applied, and certainly no guarantee that the brakes will work when applied. Our society gives these youngsters every opportunity to make mistakes—even encourages them to make minor mistakes—but woe to them if they make any big mistakes. Our intolerance resembles that of the Puritans once a girl becomes pregnant.

And all this encouraged familiarity is not for engaged couples planning marriage, but for the casual courtship of teenagers, in love with love, intrigued by adventure, thrilled by romance, and often deeply moved by normal desire.

We get so accustomed to these social customs that we think they are normal. Foreigners coming to our country are often shocked. Last year at our University we had a

211

young European student from a good Catholic family. He was simply astounded at our American dating customs. For him, he told me frankly, it would be a matter for confession if he went out on the most casual American date; and in his own country, if he were to take a young girl out like that, alone and unchaperoned, he would be expected to marry her. No decent girl's parents would permit that sort of dating until the couple were engaged.

In our dominant American society there is an increasing philosophy which would exclude all notions of morality from the problems of courtship and engagement and substitute common sense, mature judgment, and fairness to one's partner as norms of conduct. Young people should be taught that certain things are just not smart—that in some matters greater happiness will be attained by a measure of restraint—that we must be careful in calculating the risks—that we must look out for frustrations, and not forget later problems of remorse. And a real gentleman will realize that these things can be more serious for the woman than for the man.

I have a very fine non-Catholic book on marriage and its preparations. It enumerates and discusses eleven good sound natural reasons why excessive petting is undesirable, and never once mentions the word sin. It gives fourteen weighty reasons against sexual relations before marriage without any intimation of moral guilt.

These are the modern principles which our Catholic morality must meet, and the practices which constitute a strong current of custom against which our Catholic young people must swim. It is not surprising that these young people usually end up with a compromise between conscience and custom: a split theory of morality, which holds that sins against chastity are measured by how far you go physically—that a measure of sexual pleasure is all right, but an excess of it is definitely wrong. And there is considerable doubt and disturbance as to when excess begins. Actually, Catholic morality holds that deliberate seeking or accepting of sexual pleasure outside of marriage is a mortal sin—no matter how serious the physical contacts.

212

2. *Marriage is sacred.*

However, in spite of the seriousness of all these pre-marital problems, it is when we come to marriage itself that we find the real basic conflicts between Catholic ideals and principles and the practice of our dominant American society.

We Catholics believe that marriage is sacred. American society may hold it important, beautiful, sentimental and a tremendous social event. But basically it is only a civil contract which may receive an incidental blessing from a minister who happens to officiate in place of the justice of the peace, who might do it just as well except that his office isn't very clean. No idea of a sacrament which gives God's grace. Little concept of a solemn contract entered into before God and with God. And we do not have to look carefully to find many of our Catholic people sharing these ideas—finding it perfectly all right, for instance, that the State regulate this sacrament of Jesus Christ.

3. *Marriage is permanent.*

We Catholics believe that marriage is by nature permanent and indissoluble. But in our American society hardly three marriages out of four happen to turn out that way. The others are considered merely unfortunate. And what is the result? In practice Catholics are following right along in the example set for them by their neighbors. We may not agree in principle, but when trouble comes our people get a divorce almost as quickly as the next fellow. They may promise the bishop that they will never marry again—that they need the divorce merely to protect their civil rights. But how many of them remember their promise after a few years of lonely celibacy?

There are two bad effects of this prevalence of divorce— other than the divorces themselves: (1) Since divorce is a dimly admitted possibility in the back of the mind, quarrelling husbands and wives may not give the all-out effort to make things work in their marriage that they would if they knew there were no way out. And (2) There are so many divorced people running around with seeming freedom that they constitute an ever threatening danger to our young

Catholic people, particularly since our society seems to find it acceptable that these divorced unfortunates keep company like single people. They must not be denied another chance for happiness—or a chance to blight the happiness of another person. It is very discouraging to see how frequently our Catholic young people date divorced persons, keep steady company with them, and seek to marry them. Sometimes, of course, there can be a declaration of nullity, or a Pauline Privilege, but more often nothing can be done to permit the marriage. And what is the result? In almost every case, attempted marriage outside the Church and loss of faith, or at least an abandonment of the practice of religion. A generation or two ago it would have been scandalous and shameful to have the first date with a divorced person. Now it is quite acceptable to the majority of the society with which we live.

4. *Marriage has a purpose.*

One of the most difficult problems of all is that of maintaining the Catholic concept of marital morality. Birth control is a generally accepted practice in the dominant portion of our society. It has long since been rationalized into moral acceptability. It is piously urged by planned-parenthood groups. Not only is it advised for eugenic reasons, but for economic, social, and educational reasons. We are told that it isn't fair to deprive children of the comforts and conveniences of a good home and fine food that they may share with more brothers and sisters. Better have a few and give them everything, than many who have to pinch a little. And it is so much easier to raise a small family; they can have more of mother's and father's personal attention. And of course they can receive a better education. The large family is ridiculed. Its parents are accused of moral dereliction—of depriving their children of the luxuries and advantages of the good life.

In the best of circumstances it takes strength of character, unselfishness, and a bit of heroism to raise a large family. But when the mother finds herself receiving sympathy from her friends—"Oh, you poor thing!"—she must be a fortified

214

saint not to rebel. And when father and mother are both pointed at with ridicule their hard task becomes seemingly thankless.

The result of all this is that Catholics incline to adopt not only the practices, but also the ideas, of their neighbors. There are people who still retain the name of Catholic who state that the Church is simply wrong on this matter of birth control. There are others who habituate themselves to sin. And there are still others who lead a divided life on the subject: alternating between sin and sanctity, or receiving the sacraments with half-hearted resolution.

There are physical and economic facts which make the Catholic ideal of marital morality doubly difficult. Homes are built today for small families. It is hard to find a house with more than one or two bedrooms, impossible for the average family to afford a bigger home if they found one. Our wage scales are adjusted to the small family. The father of two can make it easily. The father of seven will find it tough on exactly the same salary. Our life today is urbanized; large families fit better in the country. Many city apartments will not even take children at all.

5. Marriage is religious.

It would be hard enough for the Catholic minority to adjust to these basic differences even if the divergent principles and practices were definite, clear-cut, and permanent. But they are actually fluctuating. To defend against them is like shooting at a moving target. Our social customs of dating and company-keeping have been undergoing extensive change these past two generations. Divorce has acquired acceptability in fifty years; and birth-control would hardly have been talked about openly in the days of Queen Victoria. So the American Catholic minority must not only guard against opposing principles and customs; it must be wary of the shifting position of these same principles and customs.

And it can all be summed up by the word secularism. Our American way of life is the way of the world: big, generous and abundant, but entirely practical and immediate, with only sentimental respect for the spiritual and eternal. It is

215

this spirit which develops our customs of courtship, our manner of marrying, and the size of our families. And it is this same spirit which urges our American families to their immediate goals: comfort, convenience, respectability, security, education, social position, and entertainment. These can easily become the goals of the Catholic family too, even though our Catholic faith tells us that they should be quite different. The purpose of the family is to produce souls in the image of God. It educates souls to the love and service of God. It forms young personalities in the image of Jesus Christ. It is a nucleus for the worship of God and for the sanctification of its members. It should make the father and mother saints through their love and sacrifice for each other and for their children. And it should lead the children on to sanctity, that their eternal happiness may be assured. In a secular society these goals of the family become badly blurred.

Q. You recently had a question in your column as to whether a husband committed a mortal sin in looking at his wife's breast while she was feeding the baby. You answered it with a curt "No." I felt this answer was a bit inadequate. It seems to me such a diseased concept of evil might be pointed out to the poor fellow.

A. Maybe you are right. I thought the question so ridiculous as not to deserve an answer. But I do realize that there are many people who are confused on the subject of marital morality. They have a lurking feeling that sex is dirty. They know that certain basic relationships between husband and wife are a necessary part of marriage, but they are almost afraid to enjoy them fully; and as for the fringe benefits of their intimacy, these can hardly be right unless they contribute to regeneration!

Husbands and wives should remember that they gave themselves to each other completely—for the thorough enjoyment of each other: in thought, desire, sight, touch, embrace and every kind of tenderness, allurement, provocation and solici-
216

tation. Apart from solitary sin, no husband can do wrong by looking at his wife too intimately, or desiring her too ardently, or imagining her embrace too vividly. And likewise no wife can commit sin by dreams, hopes, images, longings or sensations which are reasonably associated with her husband—even when he is miles away. And when they are together only a sense of decency and mutual respect need limit their intimacy.

The sexual relations of husband and wife are virtuous, a means of expressing and enkindling their love for each other, and a means of showing their love for God by cooperating with Him in the creation of a new person to love him eternally. Thoughts, desires, looks, words, feelings and emotions are an integral part of their sexual relations, not only at the times of their complete physical union, but at any moment of their daily living, whether they are together or apart. As long as these sex-tinted activities form a reasonable part of happy married living they partake of the virtue of married love.

Man's emotional life is an integral thing. You cannot cut it down the middle and expect it to function normally. Love and desire can not be turned on and off at will. If he does not think of his wife and desire her intensely when he is away from her, there will be something lacking from his physical union with her. His joy in watching his wife nurse their baby might well contribute to his love for both of them almost as much as his begetting of that baby did.

The diseased concept to which you refer arises not only from those psychopathic fears of sex resulting from early trauma, but also from the failure of normal persons to make proper transition from celibate modesty to marital morality. Sex is good as long as it is sensible—as long as it obeys right reason and conforms to its natural purposes. Single people find it arduous to be sensible. Sex finds its reasonable purpose only in marriage; so deliberate sex pleasure is forbidden to the single. But their normal desires are strong and their reactions alert. So they have to be careful constantly: thoughts, reading, words, looks and touches can quickly pull triggers and lead to sinful satisfaction.

217

In married life that is changed: the same thoughts, reading, words, looks and touches may lead a man to more ardent love of his wife, to complete union with her, and the virtuous satisfaction of his own normal desires. Some people fail to understand this change, or if they grasp it intellectually they fail to adjust their emotions to it, and thus come up with restraints, inhibitions, and feelings of guilt—things which are apt to undermine married happiness.

Generous love and mutual consideration are the keynotes to marital morality. There will never be serious sexual sin in married life unless it pull husband and wife apart into selfish, solitary, or disloyal satisfactions. Even those things, like birth control, which defeat the primary purpose of marriage fit technically into this divisive pattern.

To put it more explicitly, only two kinds of relationship are seriously wrong between husband and wife: (1) wilful efforts to prevent conception by artificial means, and (2) unnatural acts or perversions, which would include intentional pollution.

Apart from these two classes of sinful acts there are others which might be venial sins because they are excessive, or morose, or inconsiderate, or dangerous as temptations. It is important that both husband and wife avoid those things which might lead them to adulterous desires, or create immediate danger of solitary sin. But there should be no false modesty in marriage; it detracts from the warmth and spontaneity of marital response, and from the peace and security with which mutual love and pleasures are embraced. Fears, doubts and inhibitions should be kept out of the marriage relationship. A husband is virtuous when he seeks to make his wife happy while enjoying every enticement she offers; and a wife is virtuous when she gives herself to her husband with love and abandon.

Q. I would like to know what rule married people can follow in regard to the deliberate acceptance of sex pleasure in non-physical things, such as conversation, looking at pictures, and thoughts. I believe that such pleasures between
218

husband and wife are lawful, providing they are not car-ried to the brink of the sex climax. For instance, it would be lawful to think of a past marital act, or anticipate a future one.

However, I would like a clarification of the following:

1. Suppose a person gained pleasure from the sight of a photograph of some person other than his wife, in a scanty bathing suit. It would seem to me that this is sinful—and seriously so if it is wilful and deliberate.

2. Suppose a husband gained pleasure from the sight of his own wife in a bathing suit. This it would seem would be sinless and within his rights—though for some mysterious reason it might not be so thrilling as the sight of someone else.

3. Suppose a married man gained pleasure from a comical drawing (of no woman in particular). I would have thought, from earlier reading, that this would be sinful.

4. And what about telling stories with a sexual cast to them? Are they sinful for married people?

I would like a definite "safety point" which a married person can follow in determining just what wilful pleasure is sinful in matters of this kind.

A. It will help us to think clearly on this subject if we keep in mind the two purposes of marriage: union and produc-tivity. The direct and intentional violation of either purpose is a serious sin. But in general married people need not worry about serious sin unless their activities actually violate one of these purposes, or tend violently and unreasonably towards the violation of them.

Generally, anything is morally good in marriage if it brings husband and wife closer together, increases their mutual love, sharpens their need for each other, and intensifies their pleasure in each other—it is good as long as it does not wrongly frustrate the other purpose of marriage: produc-tivity.

The detailed question which you have presented, as a

219

good conscientious husband, illustrates rather well the moral problem of married people. Their consciences are often confused by the need to make transition from the concepts and attitudes of single morality to the norms and notions of marital goodness. All of us are trained from childhood to live modestly and chastely as single people. In this state sexual activities and pleasures are not legitimate; so we may not deliberately encourage, desire, or dawdle with them. Our thinking, reading, looking and conversing on sexual subjects are activities to be carefully curtailed lest they lead us into sin.

Then after years of conscientious care in avoiding these things they suddenly acquire sound and delightful purpose. They contribute to the joy, love and fulfilment of marriage. The intellectual part of us may readily see the difference; but our attitudes and feelings do not quickly readjust. Guilt feelings long associated with "bad thoughts" or suggestive conversation do not disappear over night. Ingrained sensibilities linger and may inhibit the freedom of a wife's response or the pleasure of a husband's day dreams.

No human being can engage in marital activity with his whole heart and never think about it before or after. He would have to split his body neatly from his soul. No husband can enter into sexual activity with a natural enthusiasm satisfying to himself and his partner unless he ardently desires it at times when it is not available. He cannot divide his life into compartments: never think of food except at table, never enjoy his golf except on the course, and never love his wife except when he is sleeping with her. Man is not built that way. Life is integral. The perfect husband enjoys his wife at all hours of the day; whenever he thinks of her he gets a thrill; and the more he thinks of her the better.

That part of the question you have already answered for yourself: "it would be lawful to think of a past marital act, or anticipate a future one." But these same principles also give us the key to other types of thoughts, reading, looking and desiring. Do these things contribute to the unity, harmony and completeness of married life? Or do they lead a husband away from his wife: to self-sufficiency, or a feeling of need for some other woman, or to a lack of concern for the emotional needs of his partner?

Remember what we said earlier: things which make marital union more perfect are good for both husband and wife; things which jangle harmony or reduce mutual need are bad. So if a man moons around, thinking, looking and day-dreaming about some other woman he is apt to be guilty of sin, and if he lets his desires become strong and explicit his sin will be mortal.

On the other hand, a certain amount of casual wool-gathering and smooth-as-silk feelings are not necessarily wrong; they may merely make a man want his wife the more. And they should be judged on that basis. A married man's idle thoughts are seldom serious unless they become positively morose—a means of solitary stimulation so exaggerated that it separates a segment of his sexual life and pleasure from his wife.

A good practical question might be this: What would his wife think of such thoughts? Would she be happy that he has them? Or would she resent them as a foreign intrusion into the intimacy of their life together?

This is not a complete norm, because many wives are jealous and unreasonable. And I would not advise that the average husband communicate to his wife every fanciful thought which gives him passing pleasure. Harmony might suffer. But the notion may help as a general guide. For instance, it readily shows why explicit desires are so much worse than dreamy thoughts: no wife wants her husband panting after some other woman. So such desire, if ardent, definite and voluntary, would be a serious sin. It interferes with a man's desire for exclusive union with his wife.

Now to apply these principles to your questions, one by one:

1. Casual pleasure from a bathing beauty's photograph would not be seriously sinful, unless it were to lead to explicit desire of some person other than the wife. Exaggerated seeking of pleasure from such sources would hardly contribute to a man's exclusive love, union and need for his wife. So

it would be wrong by reason of its exaggeration, and seriously wrong if it tended to lead him astray.

2. If a man doesn't gain pleasure from the sight of his own wife in a bathing suit, then he should buy her a new suit—and never give her hint of his coolness.

3. I doubt that a married man would be guilty of serious sin in any reasonable enjoyment of a cartoon—unless he were to use it as a spring-board to roving desires.

4. The same is true of stories. Some moralists may be a bit more rigorous, but I believe that seldom would a group of married people be guilty of serious sin in the telling and enjoying of ordinary vulgar or suggestive stories—unless they become a spur to foreign desires, or a wedge to split open modest reserve. Evidently these stories are less indicated by proper modesty when the company is mixed, and should be carefully avoided when young single people are present. But a bunch of ditch-diggers or cat-wollopers, stopping for a coffee break, can get pretty rough before being guilty of serious sin. And a chatty group of women at tea might do less harm with some witty jokes than with gossip about their neighbors.

The same principles may be applied to reading and movies. Generally speaking married people are guilty of serious sin in only two circumstances:

1. The thing they do, or intensely desire, leads them apart from each other, diverts their love or their yearning, and tends to violate their mutual faith and fidelity. Such things might be: solitary sin, desire of another woman, or dallying with another person.

2. The thing they do directly vitiates their marital act by defeating its primary purpose of conception: this would include birth control and various forms of perversion.

In general, the relationship between husband and wife should be one of generous love: thoughtfulness and consideration of the needs, desires, tastes and feelings of each other. Self-seeking tends to violate marital love and unity. So the practical "safety point" I would give you is this: Neither husband nor wife should engage in thoughts, talk, desires or activities which the other would rightly resent. But as a

222

general rule, those thoughts, desires and feelings which are good for them when they are together are also good when each is alone—provided they are not carried (in your own words) "to the brink of the sex climax."

Q. Those book reviews which you wrote recently in The Catholic Messenger *have got me and my wife all mixed up on the subject of rhythm. Can you help us out?*

A. If you are confused on this subject you are thoroughly normal. Doctors seem to be confused, or at least their answers are often diverse. And as you have observed, moralists view the problem from divergent angles.

I can readily understand the confusion of medical men. First, in earlier days, there were theories on the subject of rhythm which were entirely false; so doctors became suspicious. Then when true theories were advanced, exaggerated claims were often made for them; so doctors became disgusted. And after all false ideas are cleared up this business of counting days, keeping charts, and taking temperatures requires time and effort, and many doctors feel that they have more important things to do. And finally, even after the most thorough observation, there still remain so many variables that some practitioners consider it hardly worth while; and only Catholic doctors can be expected to appreciate the reason for so much fuss when more secure and practical methods are temptingly available.

It is more difficult to understand the confusion of moralists. They all operate on the same set of principles. It seems to me that the differences in their attitudes and conclusions arise from their diverse evaluation of the reasons or causes for practicing rhythm—those things which the Holy Father calls "indications": medical, eugenical, economic and social.

All moralists agree that as an act—apart from all motives and circumstances—rhythm is morally indifferent, neither good nor bad. Certainly it is not wrong for husband and wife to have sexual relations at times when there is no possibility of conception. With equal certainty there is nothing wrong

223

with their abstaining from sexual relations at any time when they both wish to do so and are able to do so. And there, in that periodic use and abstention, you have the essentials of rhythm.

However, it is evident that when any couple takes elaborate care and precautions in such periodic use and abstention they have some purpose in mind, and generally the essential morality of their activity will be determined by that purpose. If their motive is right and good the practice will be good. If their intentions are bad the practice will be a sin.

Of course we cannot forget the circumstances of their action either. The manner of their procedure or unintended results from it may make their action all wrong regardless of their good purposes. There are two basic requirements essential to the licit practice of periodic abstinence:

1. Both husband and wife must agree thoroughly on the practice. Otherwise one might be guilty of depriving the other of rights mutually given when they contracted marriage.

2. Both husband and wife must be able to stand the sacrifices involved in this practice without immediate danger of sin, and they must be able to carry it on without those tensions and resentments which might endanger their mutual love and happiness.

So far, I believe all moralists are in agreement, but then come a couple of points more difficult to evaluate:

1. Married couples who are fertile and make use of their marriage rights have a general obligation of producing some offspring for the good of the race and to fit their lives into the plan of God. The precise determination of this general obligation in a particular case is very difficult, and the wisest theologians may well be in disagreement about it.

2. Children are one of the greatest blessings of married life; marriage is incomplete without them, and the married partners do not entirely fulfill their purpose in life, attain their own complete and mutual happiness, or achieve their highest destiny as spouses unless their union is fruitful. They must never disdain the glory given to God by a new soul made in His own image and destined to eternal happiness

224

with Him in His own home, nor belittle the privilege they have of helping God create a new personality which will be able to know and love and live forever.

All moralists are aware that the practice of rhythm may have bad effects in eliminating or limiting these great blessings and purposes of marriage, and consequently that it must have good effects equally important to justify its use. Of course when there are already several children in the family the bad effects are not so pronounced, and the justifying reasons may be less. But no moralist, however lax, would advise a couple in ideal or normal circumstances to practice rhythm. It would be a selfish shirking of the ordinary obligations of their state in life. It would be morally wrong, because their intentions and purposes would not be good.

However, there are many young couples today who find themselves in circumstances which are far from ideal and normal, and I do believe that it is difficult for the priest who is not a sympathetic pastor or confessor to appreciate the reality and gravity of their problems. Here are a few typical examples:

People marry young today. It is the trend and you would fight vainly against it. It might not be advisable so to fight, because our modern social customs of dating and courtship may well make early marriage morally advisable. But in any case, early marriage lengthens out the child-bearing period to problem proportions.

After marriage today there are often studies to complete or military service to perform. Maybe you find such situations deplorable, but deploring them will not change their reality nor lessen the acuity of the problems which result.

Young people today do not always have financial security. They usually have to start from scratch, and are often quite on their own. When wages are high the cost of living is equally high. And sometimes they must both work in order to eat and pay the rent.

Young families frequently live in tiny apartments, little adapted to the raising of families. Most of them live in cities where children cost much and earn little.

Modern education is an expensive thing, especially Catholic education—but it is a thing of increasing necessity.

Social status and living standards must be maintained, or there may be emotional revolt, with dire marital results.

Problems of health are frequent. Occasionally the mother's life is endangered by future pregnancies. More often she is simply worn out by frequent child-bearing and constant child-rearing. Sometimes the children present the health problem, and occasionally it is the father who is unable to do the work of supporting a larger family.

Sometimes there are inadquacies of character and personality: the mother who can't stand the emotional strain; the father who can't get away from his bottle.

Friends and neighbors of our young Catholic couples find an easy solution to these problems and dozens of similar ones; and they laugh openly or sympathize patronizingly with the repeated pregnancies of the young Catholic wife.

Some people are stronger than others, more able to face life's problems and take its hard knocks, more capable of sacrifice. Consequently the same set of reasons has different values for different people. And most of us are poor judges in our own complicated cases; we are apt to rationalize with ourselves and find excuses to do the things we want to do; or we may feel guilty about things which are quite all right. So many couples find it advisable to consult their confessor or spiritual director before deciding that they are justified in practicing rhythm.

I would be deeply regretful if anything I wrote were to detract from the honor and praise due those courageous and self-sacrificing couples who face a thousand problems of life with confidence in God and happily raise their large families for his honor and glory, without serious thought of any methods of restriction. But as a pastor I do have a deep sympathy for those couples who are maybe less courageous but still conscientious, who are more oppressed by life's problems but sincere enough to avoid the easy and sinful practices of their neighbors; and who are willing to take the trouble, exercise the self-control, and make the sacrifices required in the practice of rhythm—sometimes with disappointing results.

226

They may not be heroic saints, but they are a good, struggling lay variety of saint.

Q. *A priest in my parish states it is a mortal sin to practice the rhythm method of birth control without the consent of a priest. As a result a number of mothers of five and six children are staying away from the sacraments while they have need of the rhythm method.*

A. I have a secret theory—don't tell anyone—that excessive rigorism does more harm than laxity when we are dealing with other people. And your story bears me out.

You do not need anyone's permission to practice rhythm— except your husband's, of course. You may need advice sometimes, because it is a difficult and complicated business. There are dangers in it; dangers of sin, dangers of friction and frustration. So you must have good reason to encounter those dangers. And if you keep at the practice for a long time you may be neglecting your basic duty to become parents.

If you are sure you are right, that you have good sound reason to practice rhythm, and that you can do it without sin, then go ahead and do it; it is your business, and a very intimate business. Say nothing to anyone about it. But if you are doubtful about your reasons, or if you start running into sin, then you probably need some advice. It is not necessarily your pastor who should give it to you. Maybe another priest would be more helpful—or, let us say it: more lenient.

Q. *Please explain again the other method besides rhythm permitted by the Church for couples whose families are growing beyond their means and where the wife's health needs consideration and protection.*

A. The only other licit method I know about is rugged and seldom recommended except in extreme cases or for exceptional people. It is total abstinence from marital relationship. It is probably best accomplished by the husband's joining the Navy.

Critics will say I am facetious. Some will think I show little consideration for the real problems of this couple. To these I can only reply that I cannot recommend sinful practices as a solution of problems. Other critics will protest that I show lack of confidence in the good will, spirit of sacrifice, and strength of character of our Catholic couples—or that I discount the effects of God's grace working in them. To these I reply humbly that I admire heroes the more because of their rarity.

Q. I am a convert and in all respects but one I am fully satisfied with the Catholic Church. My gripe and question is this: Does the Church say it is a sin to let five years elapse without adding to the family? My sisters-in-law all say this is true, but two of them have passed the time limit. My baby is now 17 months old, and they all are asking if there is something the matter with me. Is it not possible to have my children the way I want to?

A. That five-year angle is a new one on me. My advice would be: Don't pay so much attention to your sisters-in-law. The Church is not concerned with the spacing of your children. She merely cautions you not to break God's law in the process.

Q. Could you please state in your Question Box where a person could obtain some sort of leaflet telling about the rhythm method, and when it is permissible to use it.

A. The best thing I know on this subject is *Marriage and Rhythm*, by John L. Thomas, S.J. However it is not a leaflet, but a book, published by Newman and available through any Catholic book store.

In the pamphlet field, your Question Box editor is rather

prejudiced in favor of a light but fairly adequate publication of the Ave Maria Press: Conway, *Rhythm* (10¢). For a technical presentation there is Doctor Latz's *Rhythm: Sterility and Fertility in Women,* published by the Latz Foundation in Chicago. It does not explain the latest methods of determining fertile periods; and carries no guarantees of security.

Q. *After listening to Margaret Sanger on Mike Wallace's TV program, I want to know just why does the Church forbid birth control?*

A. First, let me ask you a question: Just what do you mean by birth control? It is a rather ambiguous term; there are many ways by which birth might be controlled. Old maids have a foolproof system. The young couple who put off getting married until they can afford a home control birth by staying apart. Heroic spouses might conceivably control conception by abstaining completely from marital relationship; and many couples, most of them quite conscientious, watch carefully the days which are believed to be less fertile for their intercourse. There are peasant mothers in some countries who nurse their babies for years, hoping that they will not conceive during lactation. Sterilization is a very thorough and radical means of birth control; and today there are a variety of drugs and instruments to substitute for Onan's early and fatal method. Even abortion could be a method of birth control.

Second, let me make a technical correction: the Church does not forbid birth control; she has made no explicit law on the subject. But she does teach very forcibly that contraception, or artificial birth control, is a serious sin because it is contrary to the natural law of God. There is a big difference, you know. If the Church made the law she might change it or repeal it. But since it is a law of God she cannot touch it, only teach it.

You will probably offer no argument when I say that the sexual organs of man and woman are designed by nature for

229

reproduction and that the primary purpose of sexual relationship is the conception of a child—primary because it is to that end that the act is directed by its nature, by the design and plan of God. It need not be the primary purpose in the minds of the people engaged in the act; they may not even think about it, or may hope it won't happen. Nature takes care of its own primary purpose as long as men do not interfere, and often it finds a way of retribution when they do.

In presuming that you will offer me no argument I remain aware that there are many people who would. Margaret Sanger denied definitely that conception was nature's purpose in the sexual act. You heard her. And she went on to make it clear that you would argue with her in complete futility about this point, because she leaves you no grounds on which to base your arguments. She does not believe in God, or the moral law, or any divinely conceived plan or purpose in man's living. I hate to be ungallant, but as I watched her pick at her ancient face before the pitiless cameras, I was forced to classify her as a frustrated hedonist. The philosophy of the hedonist is that pleasure is the highest goal of life, and that sensation, thrill, and sensory satisfaction are the means of all human happiness. No use to speak to such a person of sin.

It is very true that sexual activities have other purposes than the begetting of children: they are the emotional cement of marital union and the motive force for the sacrifices required to establish and maintain that union; they give physical relaxation and emotional normality; and they add immeasurably to the zest, pleasure, purpose and enthusiasm of natural living.

These things are good. The Church is aware of their goodness. But she insists that man is not mere animal; he is a rational animal. Beasts have no power of reasoning; so their instincts control their sexual life. In man the mind is the highest faculty, and it should dominate over all the other powers of man and control them. In other words man should be reasonable. His sexual life should be ordered by reason, not coldly and calculatingly but in accord with its natural purpose, as designed by the Creator.

230

To perform an act and at the same time directly frustrate its primary purpose is to act unreasonably. To perform the marital act and positively interfere with its generative effects is to change the essential nature of that act. It is no longer the good and purposeful act that is in God's plan of creation, but an act which man has devised in his own scheme of cross purposes.

Morality simply requires that husband and wife be reasonable in their relationship. A reasonable person understands the nature of things and treats them according to their nature. The nature of the sexual act is to procreate. So if they perform the act they must respect its nature, not distort that nature.

Sexual relationship does not always result in conception; so the evil of birth control does not lie essentially in the fact that conception does not occur, but in the positive action which is directly contrary to the purpose of the primary action. It would be just as wrong if it were ineffective and if conception took place in spite of it.

Pope Pius XI in his well-known encyclical on Christian Marriage sums up the Catholic teaching clearly: "Any use whatsoever of matrimony exercised in such a way that the act is deliberately frustrated in its natural power to generate life is an offense against the law of God and of nature, and those who indulge in such are branded with the guilt of grave sin."

This question of birth control is one which sharply, and often bitterly, divides Catholics from non-Catholics today. Not only hedonists favor the practice, but also good sincere Christian people, who are convinced of the desirability of the secondary purposes of sex for their own sake, and refuse to go along with our philosophical reasoning about the true nature and essential primary purpose of the marital act. They argue that sex is so powerful and essential that man cannot live without it, and on the other hand that reasons of health, economics, education, and social standing often make prolific propagation positively immoral.

These good people have been sold on the widely-advertised benefits of contraception in protecting the health of

231

women and children; in reducing mortality, abortions, and defective children; in creating happier homes and lowering the divorce rate; in elevating the standard of living, providing educational and social advantages, reducing juvenile delinquency, and avoiding a frightening famine-plagued over-population of the world. Some of them are also attracted by the lure that contraception is the modern, mature method of controlling life instead of being controlled by it, of planning your family and getting the children you want when you want them, rather than taking them as they come. It makes man master of his own destiny.

Some of these arguments have value to them; others are a deception, like the reduction of abortions and divorce. And even the sound arguments can be countered with arguments equally valid and powerful. For instance, there is no doubt that the widespread knowledge and availability of the means of contraception have increased pre-marital immorality and sexual promiscuity frighteningly, even to the point that our modern society finds a "reasonable" amount of this sort of thing acceptable, has dropped the notion of immorality, and speaks of pre-marital experiences. Along with this, in spite of prevention, there is an increase in illegitimacy, abortion, and forced marriages. Furthermore, the will for sterility which often invades marital life through contraception takes half the natural meaning and purpose from that life and makes it selfish and unsatisfying. This probably accounts for the fact that two-thirds of the people who get divorces have no children.

All these arguments about the benefits or evils of birth control have no direct bearing on the essential immorality of contraception itself. Good purposes or good effects do not justify a sinful act. It is this consideration alone which determines the Church's attitude on the subject. She does not propose mere numbers as the basis of the ideal family. She simply tells us we must not commit sin.

Q. Do you really believe that God will punish us women who are going through our menopause if we practice birth control? We have raised a family. Some women say that since they are having their menopause and do practice birth control they only confess it one or two times a year. I am a coward; I confess mine each time I go to confession.

But since God is a just God doesn't he understand? How will we ladies who are fifty look leading our grand-child around and be pregnant ourselves, and thinking will we live to raise our child? We ask our doctor when will we be safe on this subject, and he answers, "Oh, when you are sixty, maybe."

A. I would laugh at your question except that it involves mortal sin, and you are dead serious about it. I had thought that critical birth-control problems were reserved to the young and fecund. I didn't know that desiccating grand-mothers worried seriously about them.

You ask many questions. Let me answer them one at a time:

1. Do I really believe that God will punish you? Yes, frankly I do. He will punish you eternally in hell if you die with mortal sin on your soul. And birth control is a mortal sin.

2. You have raised a family. Bravo! The Lord is pleased in the measure that you have done it well, and for love of him. But you should not now undo all the good of the past and lose all your merit by habit of sin in your old age. Most sinners sow their wild oats early and then try to reform as age advances. What are you trying for? A second crop?

3. Those women who practice birth control regularly and confess it only once or twice a year are a pretty dishonest lot, it seems to me. You imply that they go to confession other times and don't mention it. Bad confessions! Probably followed by sacrilegious Communions!

4. You are a coward; you confess your sins every time. But I wonder if you are any better than those other women. Are you sincerely sorry? Are you firmly resolved to avoid the sin for the future? Or are you simply trying to sponge off the slate so you can begin to fill it again? No good to mention

233

the sins in confession if you intend to keep on doing them. It is to taunt the Lord in this manner: "See, Savior mine, dying on the Cross, these are the sins I have committed, and now having told you, I am going right out and commit them again."

5. "Since God is just, doesn't he understand?" You bet your life he does. He understands mortal sin: deliberate, cold revolt against his commandments, defiance of his will, refusal to trust his Divine Providence, rejection of his love.

If I wanted to treat God as sentimental, I would say he were much more apt to understand the passionate sins of the young who are pushed by throbbing ardor, beset by frightening problems, and endowed with vigorous fertility. He would not waste his sympathy on grandmothers neurotically frightened by old-wives tales, whose frigid chances of begetting a baby are about as good as those of the Kansas City Athletics to win the pennant.

6. Fifty now—safe at sixty! Ten years you plan to live in sin, ridiculously. You may be dead before it is over. You would look much better pregnant amid your grandchildren than roasted amid crackling devils. Time to think of eternity! "Remember man that you are dust, and to dust you will return."

Q. The encyclopedia says mechanical and chemical contraceptives were used by Hebrews, Greeks, Romans and Arabs. But haven't the only specific prohibitions against them come from Rome in recent years? I should think the Church would have dealt with such items specifically for 19 centuries or that if this is really a violation of the natural law, there would have been a special mention in the Old Testament. The only text I know of concerns Onan whose actions were unnatural, but did not involve anything chemical or mechanical. Are there others?

A. The Encyclopedia Britannica (under the term Birth Control) tells us that "the use on a large scale of contraceptives is a modern phenomenon." They trace its beginning from 1877 when wide publicity was given the subject by the prosecution of two characters, Charles Bradlaugh and Annie Besant, for selling a pamphlet on birth control. A Malthusian League was formed soon afterwards to continue the publicity, and it quickly became a subject of low-voiced conversation in England, Northern Europe, and the U.S.A. A marked decline in birthrate followed immediately.

Poor old Thomas Robert Malthus was a pious man, worried about problems of overpopulation and world starvation. He urged the use of "moral restraint" to limit the birthrate. He had been dead almost a half-century before rebellious mid-Victorians adapted his name to their program of teaching and publicizing artificial means of birth control.

The fanatical zeal of birth-control propagandists might be called apostolic, were it not more nearly diabolic. Liberals have flocked to the cause, demanding unlimited freedom for dissemination of information, and they have often obtained publicity by submitting to arrest and prosecution. Merchants and manufacturers have campaigned more quietly, and with greater personal profit. Sociologists, sentimentalists, and socially prominent do-gooders have worked ardently for the cause. Dr. Drysdale and Dr. Alice Vickery were the big names in England in the beginning, followed about the time of World War I by Dr. Marie Stopes. In America Mrs. Margaret Sanger has dominated the scene for fifty years. She is given credit for the name: birth control. She was the first president of the American Birth Control League, in 1921, and she has been a valiant missionary to such backward and overproductive countries as Japan, China and India.

Public attitude on this matter has changed radically during the past seventy-five years. The entire subject was scandalous in the 1880's—not only in Queen Victoria's England and the Puritan U.S., but on the brazen continent of Europe as well. Moral opinion opposed the movement widely. Now the Catholic Church is quite alone in upholding the traditional sancity of married life, and even some of her own children are inclined to rebel.

As late as 1925 the National Birth-Rate Commission in

England—made up of representatives of medicine, public health, education, sociology, and religion—published a report which set forth these conclusions.

1. Artificial birth control is a symptom of the artificial character of our civilization.

2. The ideal method of birth control is self-control— agreed on between husband and wife and carried out with love and sacrifice.

3. Real advancement lies not in contraceptives but in greater simplicity of life, and reform of our social and economic conditions.

4. Economic difficulties offer the weightiest argument for birth control (and the Commission concedes that contraceptives may sometimes be the lesser of two evils), but the ultimate remedy lies in the improvement of economic conditions.

5. There are many cases in which control of conception— considered in itself and apart from the question of methods —is medically necessary or economically advisable, but in every case of this kind all the circumstances should be weighed in the light of the best scientific and ethical counsel available.

From what non-Catholic commission would you expect a report like that today? And yet I believe that the instincts of our young people today are finding a way through the errors in which they were raised.

My research, no more profound than the quoted encyclopedia and a half-dozen moral books, leads me to believe that any mechanical or chemical means of preventing conception which might have been used prior to 1877 were of doubtful efficiency and limited popularity. The ancients probably imitated Onan in one way or another; and there are rumors that this practice was rather serious in certain times and places.

My moral books tell me that the Fathers of the Church in their early writings spoke out against Onanism, and that it has always been held seriously wrong by Catholic moralists and by official Church teaching (Vermeersch, Theol. Moralis, Vol. IV, pg. 61).

236

Actually birth control does not seem to have been a great moral problem until these past seventy-five years. My quick review of St. Thomas does not find explicit treatment of this subject, though the principles he lays down for conjugal chastity evidently imply that any type of Onanism would be seriously sinful. In fact he is a bit of a rigorist on this subject. (Summa Theo., Supplement to 3rd Part Q. XLIX, art. 1, 5, 6; and Q. LXIV, art. 7 and 8.)

My hurried survey of official pronouncements from the Holy See does not find explicit treatment of this subject until 1851, when the Holy Office declared that the practice was "forbidden by the natural law." Two years later a similar declaration termed it "intrinsically evil." Since that time there have been various replies and teachings in the same vein. In 1930 Pope Pius XI summed up these teachings very completely in his Encyclical *Casti Connubii*. That is practically the last word on the subject.

In the Scriptures, we read about Onan and his sin with Thamar, in Chapter 38 of the Book of Genesis. We are told that he frustrated the act of marriage and that God punished him with death for his abominable deed. It seems that his brother, Her, had been guilty of similar sin, "and God saw it and cut him off in his prime." But we should not judge this manner of sin a family trait; certainly the boys did not learn it from their father, Juda. (Gen. 38, 19 and 27.)

Apart from the forceful and fateful evidence of God's displeasure with these sons of Juda, I know of no reference to this sin in the Scriptures; which may well indicate that it was no frequent problem among the Jews or early Christians.

Q. Why, in this age of enlightenment, among the average groups of people in our social and business world, is it deemed the proper thing to look down on, and almost totally segregate those couples who choose to have more than a comfortable four or five children?

We have been married 17 years and have welcomed to

*our home nine gifts of God, products of our love. But we
find that our family is too large to be asked anywhere or
even to be included in the social events of our immediate
family. If we are invited it is always with a tactful reminder
to get a baby-sitter. The one place we are truly welcome is
at our parish functions, picnics and Scout events.*

A. I print your question as a subject of meditation and examination of conscience. We live in a social environment
conditioned by birth control, and without knowing it we
become infected by the virus which surrounds us. Anyway,
you can be proud of your parish.

*Q. I have just read an article in our local paper which is
going to prompt some discussion from both Protestants and
Catholics. What is the correct answer if we are asked
whether the Church will sanction the taking of a pill to prevent conception? In my own mind, I can't help but think of
all the abuses that would go with this sort of thing, but
maybe I am just plain old fashioned.*

A. I think that you are quite up to date. Your article tells
about the search being made by scientists to find some kind
of pill which can produce temporary sterility. It indicates
that no such pill has yet been perfected, but that research
continues and has discovered some promising leads. It mentions an "amphenone" which suppresses ovulation, and some
vegetable alkaloids which gave promise of being effective,
but were too toxic for practical use. It indicates that dozens
of compounds are being studied with confidence of ultimate
success.

Your article also points out correctly that the Church is
not necessarily opposed to the prevention of conception as
long as it is accomplished by natural means rather than artificial ones, and as long as it is not an occasion of sin and is
justified by sound economic or medical reasons. This state-

238

ment should give you the answer to your question. Sterility produced by pills could hardly be called natural.

Q. What sins does a husband commit when he is always running into taverns, and then lying to his wife about it, and getting mad and cursing and swearing when she says anything to him about it. I think it is stealing money from his wife and children to buy drinks when they need it so bad.

A. Moralists point out to us that drinking is not a sin, in itself. But then they quickly remind us that it can lead to many sins, and you have indicated a few of them:

Drunkenness, when the drinking becomes excessive.

Lying, which quickly makes the drinking man lose his sense of honor and self respect.

Anger, blasphemy, and irreverence, quarrelling and abuse.

Neglect of duties of state in life; in this case neglect to give good example to children, neglect to nurture them in love; neglect of duties of husband, which include love of the wife and maintenance of peace and happiness in the family; neglect to provide fully for material needs of the family; neglect to maintain the family good name and social position, etc., etc.

These are the more ordinary and "respectable" consequences of excessive drinking on the part of a husband and father. In its worse phases it can lead to crimes of various nature.

The man who neglects his wife and children for drink, who abuses them in his drinking, and deprives them of necessities to pay for his drinking, must never fully realize the extent of the harm he is doing, else he could never live with himself, even half sober. The unhappiness, and sorrow, and shame; the emotional disturbances which unfit children for normal living; the desecration of that sacred love of husband and father.

But where there is a drinking husband and father, there

239

may also be a nagging or slovenly wife, or ungrateful children whose annoyances and disobedience drive a man to drink. A careful examination of conscience is in order. And it is probably true that love and attention and kindness have kept more men out of taverns than quarrelling and scolding ever have.

11. *The Seventh and Tenth Commandments*

Just Debts. Discounts. Soliciting.
Income Tax. Fair Trade. Gambling.
Bankruptcy. Restitution. Legal
Judgment. Stolen Goods. Injustice.

Q. Please tell me how a person who calls himself a Catholic can go to confession and receive Communion and refuse to pay his just debt. My idea is that honesty is part of religion. I hope to become a Catholic but this is one stumbling block for me.

A. The Seventh Commandment of God requires that we pay our just debts. No one can be a GOOD Catholic who refuses to pay them. No one can make a good Confession or receive Holy Communion worthily if he is guilty of serious voluntary neglect in this matter.

The Catholic Church insists strongly on the strict observance of justice. We are required to give everyone his just due, and to respect the rights of others as we want them to respect our rights. But sometimes, in a particular case, it is a bit hard to know just what is right and just. What is a fair price, and a just wage, and a proper return on investments? Because it is hard to know, we have arguments, disputes, strikes, boycotts, and court trials.

241

Maybe the Catholic whom you think owes you a debt honestly does not believe that he owes it to you. It is difficult to be an impartial judge in our own case. We can sometimes talk ourselves out of our obligations and think we are honest about it.

Maybe this Catholic is not able to pay his debt right now. That does not let him out of his obligation permanently. He must pay you as soon as he can. We are strictly forbidden to incur debts which we foresee that we may not be able to pay.

Maybe this Catholic—like many non-Catholics—was not well trained in matters of justice. Maybe he is forgetful and careless and constantly delinquent. Maybe he even adopts some of the lower standards of our society: that justice is not what is right, but what you can get by with—a just debt not something honestly owed, but something you are able to collect. The Catholic Church tells him firmly that such ideas are wrong—but the Church can't MAKE him listen.

Q. What is the morality of buying merchandise at a discount, through a friend, when he must state explicitly to his employer that the purchase is for his own use?

A. Now, what do you think about it yourself? Isn't it a sin to tell a lie? And isn't such an explicit statement a lie? And are you not cooperating in his lie—getting him to tell it for you?

I wouldn't know about the monetary injustice; that would be an involved question, even if I knew all the circumstances. But my sense of smell tells me the deal is not quite honest.

Q. A person receives these stamps to use as we do Christmas seals. I have received several different ones, as Queenship of Mary, from the Holy Land, Sacred Heart stamps—all beautiful. But with a large family we just can't buy all these besides take care of our church collection, society dues, etc. What is the best thing to do? Use them anyway or throw

242

them away if one can't pay for them? Or must we return them?

A. This is nuisance soliciting. Treat it rough! If you realize what the package contains before you open it, you should refuse to accept it. Give it back to the postman and direct that it be returned to the sender. But if you have opened it, then I would say do with it what you want. You are under no obligation to go to trouble or expense to send this nuisance merchandise back to the person who foisted it on you in the hope of eliciting your generosity.

Use these stamps if you like, but I advise burning them—as a matter of taste rather than morality.

Q. At a recent meeting of one of our parish groups we were told by a priest that it is not sinful deliberately to falsify one's income tax return, if he thinks that the amount of his tax is too high, or that he cannot afford it. We were shocked at what seems to us a condonation of cheating and lying. Would you please give us your opinion?

A. Each year about this same time I receive questions about the obligation we have in conscience to make a truthful declaration of our income for tax purposes. Each year I answer it in similar manner.

It is a difficult problem on which moralists are not in thorough agreement. I believe the main reason for their diverse opinions is that tax laws are far from uniform in different countries; and the attitudes of the people in different nations are widely divergent. There are some countries in which only a very simple person would declare his full income; if he did he would be paying several times his just share of tax. Complete declarations are not really expected. In such a country I might agree with the priest you quote.

Our basic responsibilities as citizens, in this regard, is to pay our fair share of the legitimate costs of our government.

243

Our income tax laws represent a diligent effort on the part of our legislators and tax experts to distribute the heavy burden of public costs in an equitable manner. No doubt it has holes in it; the problem is simply too complicated to permit absolute fairness to everyone. But who should judge what is fair? If I am to be judge in my own case I will be prejudiced. Each of us is inclined to gripe about our obligations and to find excuses for ourselves.

That tax laws be fair they must meet three requirements:

1. They must be made by a legitimate taxing authority: our national or State government. The details of property assessments are often worked out by local boards, acting under authority of the State.

2. The purpose of taxation must be just; government money must be used for the welfare of all the citizens in an equitable manner.

3. The burden must be distributed evenly, according to the varying ability of individual citizens to support it.

All moralists are agreed on two basic principles:

1. We are obliged to tell the truth. Lying is sinful, and when we deliberately falsify a solemn declaration we lie.

2. We are obliged as citizens to pay our fair share of any just tax.

But there may be arguments as to when we falsify, and how our fair share should be rightly determined. If complete declarations are not really expected and are seldom made by upright citizens, then we could hardly be said to falsify when we fail to report all our income. If citizens generally pay only part of the tax required by law, then we would be doing more than our fair share if we paid all of ours.

Now I take it that your question refers to our own federal income tax, or to State taxes which follow similar methods of computation. What are the facts in our beloved country? We complain, and worry, and hire experts—and some times we chisel a little by concealing bits of income which we hope are well hidden, or by padding expenses which we claim as deductible. But generally we are rather careful and truthful about the whole business; and for two reasons: our economic

244

system is largely based on trust and honesty; and tax-return auditors are pretty sharp.

When do we falsify? We are not expected to be scrupulous or to fret about minute details; but we are expected to make our declaration the way other good, honest citizens make theirs—the way a good tax expert would advise us to make it. If we do that we are not falsifying; that is what the law expects.

When do we pay our fair share? When we make a business-like return, in accordance with the law. We can and should take advantage of all legitimate tax avoidance loopholes. But we cannot rightly argue that we are excused from paying all our tax because much of the money goes in graft, special favors, pork-barrel projects, and expenditures of which we do not approve. If we accept these arguments for ourselves, then we must endorse those ardent pacifists who refuse to pay taxes because they are used, in large part, for military purposes.

By our vote and our influence we do our part to keep our government honest, economical and efficient. But meanwhile someone must pay the cost of waste and corruption. It must be divided equally among us—as business losses would be apportioned among stockholders.

Some people claim tax laws are only penal laws; that they induce no direct obligation in conscience, until we are caught up by the tax collector. I disagree. The welfare and solvency of our country and the suitable distribution of its tax burdens require that each citizen have a sense of obligation, or honor, or decency. It is not a cat-and-mouse game. Penalties for tax evasion are severe, and probably they serve —more than anything else—to keep us honest. But I believe that our government relies on the common integrity of the majority of its citizens as the basic method of tax collection.

I am not prepared to say how serious this obligation is in any particular detail. I am convinced that there is no obligation in conscience to make restitution for past errors or falsifications—though it may be a wise thing to do it, to avoid penalties. I think the average tax payer would hardly be guilty of mortal sin in juggling his return—unless he really

245

evaded a large amount of tax. And in that case the Internal Revenue men will probably get him anyway.

I always sum up my annual advice with words which may sound scandalous at first: be average honest. Follow the example of the upright men of your community and the competent advice of those who can save you both tax and penalities. Have no part with chiselers and unsavory tax advisers. Be not ashamed of your declaration after it is made; be not fearful that you may get caught.

And then I quickly note that average honesty will not do for normal business affairs or personal obligations. We must be strictly honest. But average honesty in tax matters will result in our paying our fair, average share.

Q. Does the Fair Trade Act bind a dealer in conscience? If a dealer sells at a discount nationally advertised brands which fall under the Act does he commit sin? Would he be bound to restitution if he practiced this policy for some time?

A. Maybe we should first consider just what "Fair Trade" is, and the contracts and laws under which it operates. Basically, it is a system of price maintenance on nationally advertised goods which are sold under their brand name. A contract or agreement is entered into between manufacturer, wholesaler, and retailer by which minimum resale prices are fixed. The purpose is to eliminate price cutting on these brand products, which are often advertised at a set price by the manufacturer.

As a result of these agreements competition is restricted; so they have something of the appearance of a trust—agreements in restraint of trade. However, fair trade contracts are specifically exempted from anti-trust laws by statutes enacted in forty-five States and by Congress. Generally, these laws do not require a dealer to sell any article at a fixed price; they simply authorize and permit enforcement of a contract between the dealer and the manufacturer by which the price is fixed. So you don't violate the law by selling at a discount; you violate your contract.

California was the first State to enact a "Fair Trade" law, in 1931. Now all States have similar laws, except Missouri, Texas, and Vermont. In 1937 Congress enacted the Miller-Tydings Act permitting free trade agreements in interstate commerce. However, in 1951 the Supreme Court prohibited enforcement of free trade prices—in interstate commerce—against those who had refused to sign an agreement. So Congress passed the McGuire Act in 1952 to patch up this loophole and permit such enforcement.

In recent years "Fair Trade" has been taking a beating. Court decisions in various States have been unfavorable. Discount houses have sprung up like mushrooms, making enforcement of fair trade prices almost impossible, and putting a penalty on the "legitimate" dealer who makes agreements and abides by them. Many big companies, like Shaeffer Pen and Westinghouse have decided to give the whole thing up.

Now what of your moral obligation? I think it is basic that if you enter into a contract freely and fairly you are obliged to keep that contract. However, if the company with which you enter into this contract makes no serious effort to enforce it, so that you are being undersold on all sides, then you are justified in considering the contract void; since it is implied in your contract that the manufacturer will protect you against just this sort of thing. The way discount houses are operating today, it might be argued that many free trade contracts have lost much of their validity. Even if you did violate a valid agreement by selling a brand product at a discount, I doubt that you would be held to restitution unless there were a penalty clause in your contract, or damages were assessed you by the court. Otherwise it would be hard to determine the amount of harm you had done the manufacturer.

Do fair trade agreements actually fix a fair and just price? It is a very complicated problem. Twenty years ago most of our legislators thought so. Many of our courts are becoming doubtful. In the long run it does seem that fair competition and the old reliable law of supply and demand do the best job.

247

Q. Why did Christ drive the money changers from the temple? Who were the money changers? Does it mean that they were gamblers? Is it a sin to gamble?

A. The Temple at Jerusalem was an immense place. The main part of it was the Sanctuary, where God lived among his chosen people. Only a few priests ever entered there. But surrounding the Sanctuary was a large open square, enclosed by a strong high wall. This was a part of the Temple, but the people met there to visit as well as to pray. At the Paschal time people came from all parts of Palestine, and many of them brought lambs to be sold for the feast of the Passover; others brought oxen for the Temple sacrifices, or doves for the offerings of the poor people. These were taken into the Temple enclosure to be sold; and as a result the holy place took on the aspect of a stockyard at auction time.

Then there were Jews who came from distant cities, and many of these were wealthy. But they brought foreign money with them, and had to convert it into coins which would be acceptable to the sellers. And besides, the offerings to the Temple had to be made in Jewish coins; the established offering was a half-shekel. So the money-changers took Greek drachma and Roman denarii in exchange for Jewish coins. Of course they made a profit in the exchange, and apparently they often took advantage of their poor customers, because our Lord said they were making the Temple a den of thieves (Matt. 21, 13).

The money changers were not gamblers; they had a sure thing. In itself gambling is not sinful, but it can easily lead to a variety of sins. If a person has money which he is free to spend as he wishes, he may in all propriety wager it against similar money owned by someone else. Betting can often sharpen the interest and enjoyment of games and contests, and make such a simple thing as the roll of dice a breathtaking adventure.

However, greed can often enter into gambling, and greed may generate dishonesty. The race may be fixed, or the dice loaded, or the odds made unfair. The sucker may be taken and the innocent victimized. Rackets may develop, and induce a variety of crimes. Money is risked which is needed for other purposes, even for baby's shoes or the monthly rent. And gambling can become a compulsion—as bad as drink. It can take time, energy, interest, money and even health.

When a person gambles honestly and pleasurably, and remains master of his amusement—win or lose—there is no sin in it. But when his gambling starts to master him, when it leads him to neglect work, home, obligations, or more sensible amusement, then it becomes a vice and may lead him into a variety of sins.

Q. If a man owes you a debt on a note and doesn't pay it, and you allow him more time repeatedly, and he promises to pay, and this keeps on until he takes the bankrupt law and beats you out of your money, how can he be a Christian and go to church, and get absolution when he goes to Confession. This man is my brother. It was five years ago that he went bankrupt. Now he is financially able to pay, but says he has no obligation to do so.

A. I am not going to try to solve, in this book, complex problems of justice and conscience. Neither shall I try to decide disputes of theologians. I shall merely discuss certain aspects of public morality and personal honesty.

The honest man pays his just debts as promptly and fully as he possibly can. The law and the public conscience expect him to do so. If he tries to hedge or wriggle we rightly consider him a crook.

But sometimes misfortune strikes our honest man. The wind and the hail and the drought ruin him. He makes bad investments. Bandits blow his safe. His barn burns, his horse is spavined and his tractor burns a bearing. His wife spends too much money, and all ten children get the flu. He's broke. His creditors hound him. They get judgments and liens. They try to take his tools, and the clothes off his back and even his new car.

There has to be some way of protecting this poor fellow until he can get back on his feet. There has to be some way of protecting his creditors, so that they all get their just share. Otherwise the aggressive ones would get all he owns and the others would be left holding their empty notes.

The laws of bankruptcy in general aim to protect both debtor and creditors. Sometimes the debtor goes into bankruptcy voluntarily. The court distributes his assets, leaving him enough to support himself and his family temporarily and to start over again in his business.

Sometimes the creditors force a man into bankruptcy to protect their own rights and salvage what they can before he loses or squanders it all. In either case the results are about the same. The assets are liquidated and distributed under supervision of the court.

From a legal point of view bankruptcy practically liberates a man from all past debts and obligations. He starts over anew with what is left him and none of his former creditors can touch him by any legal process. They take what blood they could wring from the turnip, and frame their notes as souvenirs.

But what about the bankrupt's conscience? Is he freed of all obligations in justice before God? There are many fine angles to be considered and many distinctions made. Theologians particularly like to argue about the intent of the law and the agreement of creditors. They inquire into the honesty of the man in contracting his debts, in suffering his losses, and in going bankrupt. Was he trying to defraud his creditors or merely to protect them and himself and his family?

But after all distinctions are made the general conviction prevails in the public conscience that the man who goes bankrupt simply to get out of his debts, and then forgets all about his former creditors when he makes a new fortune is not quite honest or honorable. On the contrary, people respect the bankrupt man who uses his new money to pay off his old debts.

In this case the public conscience is right. It is a better interpreter of the law's intent than the lawyer or the theo-

250

logian. Bankruptcy in the public mind should be a means of protecting the poor unfortunate man who has failed. It should protect his family, give him another chance, and keep him from becoming a public charge. But it should not absolve him of all obligation, if fortune later favors him. No one can press him, or harass him. But his own honesty and honor will tell him what to do?

Q. What is meant by restitution? Are we obliged to pay in dollars and cents for losses we may have unintentionally and indirectly caused to property, even when we are not sure we are held responsible for those losses? When may we give to charity as payment for restitution?

A. Restitution is giving back to the owner the property which has been taken from him unjustly, or making good the damage which has been unjustly caused him.

You are not obliged to make restitution for damage you cause unintentionally or accidentally—only for the damage which you cause deliberately and wilfully. And you are never obliged to make restitution until your obligation is certain. In other words, as long as you honestly doubt that you were responsible you have no obligation.

The civil law may often require that we pay damages caused in accidents which result from our carelessness or violation of law. This is not strictly restitution, as required by the law of justice. It is an obligation which arises from the civil law which seeks to avert accidents and protect property from thoughtless damage.

When there is an obligation of restitution payment must be made to the person owed. You do not fulfill your obligation by giving the stolen property to a third party—unless he is acting as agent. Giving stolen property to the poor is simply a last restort as a means of getting it out of your hands when there is no possible way of restoring it to the owner—for instance, because you have no idea who the owner is. The poor have the next best claim to it after the owner;

251

and the thief has no claim at all. It will burn his conscience until he gets rid of it—and not by destroying it, either—by restoring it.

Q. If a person is released from her place of employment because a legal judgment was exacted against her salary for non-payment of a bill, is she still liable for the bill? If so, must she also pay the offending party the cost of collecting.

A. You might think that the poor woman has suffered enough, but presumably the debt is a just one and must still be paid. I don't believe she is obliged to pay the cost of collecting unless the court requires it.

Q. If a person took some goods and didn't pay for them, may he give money to charity instead? This happened years ago and the manager of the store has passed away.

A. Stolen goods must be returned to the person from whom they were stolen. If the identical goods cannot be returned then some repayment of equal value must be made to the person who owned them. It is only when there is no reasonable possibility of making restitution to the injured party, that the repayment may be made to the poor—who have first claim on things which cannot be returned to their owner.

I would suggest that you talk your problem over with your confessor. It may be that the value of the goods was so small that you have no grave obligation of restitution, and that the difficulties involved, after all these years, may excuse you from it. If obligation remains he may be able to suggest ways and means to you.

Q. Several years ago I lost a valuable watch. Then a short time later we took out an insurance policy on all our jew-

elry. Then after a reasonable wait we filed claim for the
value of the watch, and collected the money. It has been
spent long ago, but now I am beginning to worry about it.
How serious an act was it? Was it receiving money under
false pretenses?

A. You have reason to worry. It was a serious act of injustice, and it involved much more than false pretenses—probably a few false affidavits, a bit of perjury, and some bold-faced lies. I wonder just how you got by with it.

I imagine the time element relieves you of need to worry about the cops. But you are still bound to restitution.

12. *The Eighth Commandment*

Calumny. Gossip. Tale-bearers.
Mongering. Restitution. Detraction.
What Is Truth? What Makes Lying
Sinful? Curiosity. Sins against the
Eighth.

Q. A person in our parish has suffered calumny. This has spread far. In any grade-school catechism it says, "One must beg their pardon (being sure they know what you are begging their pardon for) and repair the injury done."

This person whom they have spread calumny about has certainly set a good example over many years in our parish. What about this matter?

A. Calumny is a strange old word for a vile form of malice. It is the reporting or spreading of deliberate lies about someone, to do him harm, injure his reputation, or hurt his standing in the community.

It is a despicable form of villainy, choice tool of cowards and rodents. It is like shooting in the back; the unsuspecting victim has no means of defense, little chance at retaliation. The calumniator can hit and run, and then hide in anonymous safety while the story he started rolls on like a snowball, hurting his victim while it revolves from eager mouth to avid ear.

Calumny violates the three basic virtues of social living:

254

justice, charity and veracity. Justice demands that we respect our neighbor's right to good name and reputation—that we treat him as we would want him to treat us. Charity requires that we love our neighbor and seek his welfare, his good and his happiness—that we love him even as we love ourselves. Veracity demands that we tell the truth, so that people can believe us and depend on us.

If everyone were to violate these three virtues habitually there would be only chaos and hatred, unhappiness, distrust, and conflict in society.

An unjust deed is more dastardly when its harm cannot be repaired. And calumny is often irreparable. Little good it does to beg the victim's pardon. The fires of scandal have burned over his reputation and your apology will give no life to the embers. Payment of damages—which is often required in libel—is like putting salve on a wound. It may ease the pain; it does not touch the root of the injury.

Sometimes it may be possible to chase after your story and tell everyone who has heard it that you are a liar—a bald, bare-faced and blatant liar. Some of them may believe you— even while you proclaim that you are unworthy of belief. But most will prefer your original story; it has more juice and flavor to it. And besides, run and protest as you will, you can never catch all the strands of your calumny; they spread as though borne by the wind, and multiply faster than the birds and the bees.

The man who tells malicious lies about his neighbor is the size of a scrawny midget, has the courage of a mouse, the facial expression of a rat, and the instincts of a vulture. The good Lord must be saving some exquisite torture for him in the lower strata of hell: his tongue will burn, his ears will ring, and his gloating will be turned to remorse, to gnaw at his putrid heart forever.

Requiescat in pace! The only way to help his vicious soul is to ignore his spicy tales, while he is yet on earth. Curiosity, cattishness, and credulity are the foment of calumny. A gaping audience encourages the gossip. Malice on the tongue is only a futile canker when there is no ear to absorb its venom.

Q. There is quite a lot of gossiping going on at our school this year. Some of it has proved to be damaging to various students. We would appreciate it very much if you would give us your views on the matter.

A. In brief, I take a very dim view of it.

The analysis of a chronic gossiper would be an interesting, though depressing, project:

You would probably find that the gossiper—whether male or female—has a nagging inferiority complex. He tries to pull his friends down to his own creeping level, and thus exalt himself by comparison with those he belittles.

You might find that he—or she—is really beat and wants to beat others down for thwacked company.

You would surely find the gossiper lacking in charity. "Thou shalt love thy neighbor as thyself!" Thou shalt not tear him to shreds by sharp, nasty words.

The gossiper is someone who lacks a sense of justice. This virtue would have us give everyone his due; it would have us treat others as we want them to treat us. Would we want our friends digging dirty little holes in our reputations, just for kicks, or laughs, or a little jealous spite?

You would find your talkative friend a little lenient about the truth. Routine facts are often dull, and when the gossiper tells his story he wants it to be sharp. So he grinds and whets fact a bit, adding that tiny note of untruth, which will grow from one mouth to the next, until it becomes a big lie.

Our gossiper is apt to be vain. He wants to be the center of attention. He likes the applause of rapt intentness. He feels important when he arouses curiosity. He gets a thrill of distinction from being the first bearer of hot morsels, putrid and petty though they be.

Often our garrulous friend is seeking vicarious pleasure. Secretly he would like to do the naughty things he is prattling about. He gets a thrill in telling about those awful others who actually did them—or are reported to have done them.

You will find your gossiper a bit irresponsible. He does not heed the harm he does or the trouble he stirs up. He is immature in his interests and pleasures; he has faulty judgment and a mixed-up sense of values. He does not know how to rate first things as paramount and put the tawdry in its place. He has poor taste. He ignores the beauties of God's thrilling world, and concentrates on the inane trivialities he finds in dark corners.

Sometimes you will find your gossiper malicious, moved to murder a reputation because of hate, spite, bitterness, or jealousy. More often he kills thoughtlessly, like a loafer swatting flies.

Usually you will find him small—maybe not in stature; maybe not in girth, but in interest, thinking and loving.

Often he is prurient, prying and peeping—in short, a nosey nuisance. After all he has to dig out his stories, cover his beat and search his gutters.

There is something of the coward in him. He always stabs in the back. He would never dare repeat face to face the cheap gossip he throws out so valiantly when his victim is at a safe distance.

Gossip gives scandal; it leads others to gossip. The first telling of a juicy story is like the first push to a long row of dominoes—or more like the splitting of the first atom in a self-sustaining chain reaction.

Gossip involves detraction. To detract means to take away. The gossiper pulls away part of a reputation, and he puts nothing back in its place. And the thing he takes away will do him no good. If he stole money he could spend the stuff. When he steals a reputation he merely soils his own conscience with the gore of it.

Q. In our neighborhood there is an old maid who, upon hearing any form of criticism about any of our acquaintances, makes it a point to let that person know the first opportunity she gets. It may be some little criticism, such as "Mrs. So & So ought to keep her youngsters home in her own yard part of the day instead of letting them bother the neighbors all the time," or "Mr. So & So's lawn is better

257

than the one next door," etc.; but her reporting of these remarks causes enmities among the neighbors. Now I always thought that to be a serious sin. What do you think? She apparently makes light of it.

A. Just as you make light of criticizing! I think tale-bearers are too mean and small to be capable of big serious sins. They know not what they do. They seem to act under compulsion, just like the rest of us seem under compulsion to criticize.

Charity is a beautiful virtue—but often so full of holes.

Q. What is the moral justification for professional gossip mongers like Dorothy Kilgallen and Louella Parsons who are publicly referred to as Catholics? Where does the difference lie between my telling someone an item about my neighbor, and their telling the world in print things most of us would not know without their well-paid efforts, and probably should not know in any case.

A. There is no moral justification for mongering a venomous product whether the motive be venal or vindictive. Character assassination is purged only of its gratuitous spitefulness when it turns professional; but its barbs become sharper, more purposeful and poisonous.

I know not how good these Catholic ladies may be in other areas of religion or morality. From brief glimpses at their columns I see no evidence of Catholicity in them.

In judging the direct harm of their detraction we must keep this in mind: much of it is published with full consent of the maligned, who consider any words printed about them as publicity. Their plea is: write anything about us, good or bad, but don't condemn us to oblivion by silence. This excuse does not take care of the scandal, however: the clever professional example given to dull amateur gossips.

Q. To say something about your neighbor that is false or uncertain is a sin. Correct? Isn't it also true that in such case you are bound to make restitution? To what extent, or just how is one supposed to make this restitution.

A. Correct and true are the answers to the first two questions. The third is more difficult.

He who steals my purse may find it financially difficult to replace the trashy stuff he has filched, but the manner and amount of that replacement can be readily determined. He who steals my good name by dirty lies often does not know how to begin to repair the harm he has done. He has simply destroyed, without profit to himself. He is faced with the necessity of recreating something—and creation is so hard that it is a divine prerogative.

And yet the calumniator does have an obligation. He must do what he can do, and he must often do it with shamefaced courage, even to the point of admitting frankly that he is an infernally condemned, malicious liar.

At first glace it might seem easy to undo a lie, simply by telling the truth. But a little thought makes us realize that it is not that simple. People who believed the lie may not accept the truth—or at least a suspicion may linger and a doubt spread its growing tendrils. And besides, lies travel so fast that pursuing truth can seldom catch up with them, because lies often have a jib of scandal for sail, while the truth must counter the tide of human interest.

Prudence and courage are the virtues most required in repairing the harm of calumny, and justice and charity should serve prudence as tools. Fears and scruples should not be around at all. Bumbling efforts inspired by scruples may do more harm than good, and be painful to all concerned. Be sure of the harm you have done, and be sure also that your means of repair are appropriate. Then use them with charitable courage—as you would want someone else to do for you in like circumstances. Don't just try to get yourself off a moral hook; try to really help the person you maligned.

The ravages of forest fires are best repaired before the

259

flint is struck. If justice, truthfulness, and charity inspire our conversation we need not worry about extinguishing the spreading flames of calumny. Talk about others as you would like them to talk about you.

Q. I was present in a grocery store when my neighbor, the wife of a professional man, was caught shoplifting. Would I commit a mortal sin were I to tell others of this? When another of our neighbors, a young married woman became so intoxicated and noisy that the police were called, this same lady told of it to many people.

A. I am afraid your sin would be mortal, if your neighbor's delinquency were not otherwise known. The thing you would tell about her is very serious. It would simply ruin her reputation. And she has not lost the right to her reputation by her misdeed.

I sympathize with you. It does seem an awful shame to skip such a good story. You may never have a chance again to be the welcome bearer of such succulent news, which would be so avidly received. You would be widely quoted, the popular center of attention. You had the news first hand. Certain of your facts, you would not fear charges of slander. How accurately you could describe the garish details! And if the story should grow and become distorted thereafter, it would not be your fault exactly.

But justice and charity and the good of your soul all demand that you deny yourself this great pleasure. You will hate yourself for missing such an opportunity. But you would despise yourself when you realized that you had ruined a woman's reputation and were unable to do anything to repair the harm you had done.

One bad thing about the sin of detraction is the impossibility of undoing the harm we have done by our true but unjust words. We told the truth, but we had no right to tell it. We can't go around telling people falsehoods to try to undo the harm. About the most we can do is try to think of

260

good things to say about this same person; but that is apt to be ineffective. People won't pay nearly as much attention to the good as they did to the evil we spoke. They may not even believe us.

The fact that this shoplifting neighbor committed the sin of detraction against her neighbor is no reason for you to join her on her way to hell. Maybe her sin was not a mortal sin. It is more harmful to reputation to reveal the sin of shoplifting than to make known a bit of boisterous carousing. The reputation of the carouser is probably a bit damaged anyway. You just add another smear.

Then too, the harm of detraction often depends upon the standing and reputation of the person who does the detracting. You are known as a truthful, good and charitable person. If you tell a story it is believed. Your neighbor is known as a bit of a gossip, and people only half believe what she says anyway. Probably the only advantage of being a notorious liar, is that it would be hard to commit a serious sin of detraction. Nobody would believe your slander.

The general rule is this: Don't go around saying things about other people that you wouldn't want them to say about you. Of course, I know that you would not do such things as they have done. But just suppose you had. Would you want everybody talking about it? Then don't set everybody talking about this poor kleptomaniac.

Incidentally, maybe you should move to a better neighborhood.

Q. I have been in several discussions concerning truth. Is it relative or absolute? Or is it both, changing with the subjects dealt with?

If a blind man holds the tail of an elephant and believes it to be a snake, is this belief truth to him? And would this indicate truth to be relative according to circumstances?

Catholics believe that the Catholic religion is the true religion, composed of truths. Also Catholics believe that if a Protestant really believes that he has the true religion, and is therefore pleasing God, that this Protestant will attain heaven. This indicates that truth can be both absolute (Catholic truths) and relative (Protestant beliefs).

It is an interesting subject, but very involved.

A. You certainly stated a mouth-full of truth—both absolute and relative—in your last sentence. Absolute, because the question really is both interesting and involved; and relative because it intrigues and baffles me personally.

Truth is existing reality. It has its ultimate source in the unlimited Being of God. And it has its created expression in the world as God made it. In this sense truth is absolute; things exist whether there is a human mind around to know them or not; and they exist in a certain way, whether we rightly understand them or not. But created truth is not so absolute that it cannot change—as creation itself changes. In your own letter you give an example of the change of one physical substance into another. It was liquid water; now it is steam. So created truth is sometimes relative to time and space—but it is real and existing apart from the mind which knows it.

You and I have the problem of knowing truth, and we have imperfect minds with which to know it. Our senses do not tell us everything about external reality: I cannot see an atom or hear the thud of electrons when they collide; and my intellect often fails to comprehend all the data that science and philosophy may offer it. I can even get fouled up about the things God has told me about himself. But my misunderstanding does not change the external fact. If the elephant steps on my toe my thinking that he was a snake will not cushion the bruise.

Now God knows our human limitations. He saddled us with some of them himself; He couldn't make us other gods. And he watched us commit sin and thus foul up the good work he had done for us. So in his fairness and mercy, God takes our ignorance and misunderstanding into consideration. The truths of religion are not so clear that we can all understand them right off; and the proofs of God's revelation

262

are not so readily convincing as to keep us from honest error. So God often accepts good will in place of understanding. And he accepts good faith as a substitute for the true faith.

Subjective error never changes objective truth, but sometimes it has to serve our practical needs until we get a better understanding of reality. Often we can escape harm: the elephant doesn't step on us—or the snake doesn't bite us; but it is none the less an elephant—or a snake.

Q. I have been wondering about what makes lying a sin.

A. What is a lie? According to common definition it is an "assertion contrary to your mind." You say something as true which you do not believe to be true. Maybe it actually is true; your statement may conform to external fact, but not to your own belief regarding that fact. It is still a lie.

To tell a lie it is not necessary that you intend to deceive; neither is it necessary that you actually do deceive the persons who hear you. Maybe you have such a reputation for lying that no one quite believes what you say. That doesn't make your falsehood any less a lie.

Truthfulness, also called veracity or honesty, is the virtue which helps us to speak the truth. It inclines us to make our words conform to the belief of our own minds. Like other moral virtues it can be violated either by excess or defect. We would sin by excess of veracity if we went around telling everything we know, just because it happens to be true. We would bore our friends and disgust them. We would violate secrets, ruin reputations, provoke enmities, and incite riots. We sin by defect of truthfulness when we tell a lie.

Every lie is a sin. But again, what is a lie? Not every joke or fictional narrative is a lie. Woe the poor story teller! Not every equivocation, evasion, or circumlocution is a lie. Otherwise we would never be able to keep lawful secrets from nosey neighbors. Not every conventional compliment or standardized cliché is a lie. When someone asks you, right in the presence of the girl, "Don't you think Mahitabel is beautiful tonight?" you don't reply, "I think she looks

263

ghastly," even though you are positively aghast at the sight of her. And when someone asks you how you feel this morning, you don't give them a detailed diagnosis of all those aching symptoms; you smile wanly and answer, "Oh, just wonderful, thank you!"

Speech has a social purpose. God created us human beings to live together in harmony and trust. We cannot live happily and securely with people unless we can believe what they say. Neither can we live confidently with people unless we can trust them to use discretion and to keep a secret occasionally. Sometimes we have very strict obligations to keep secrets. Truthfulness must find a way to observe both obligations.

The very fact of my speaking should carry with it an implied promise to my listeners that I will tell them the truth, as I understand and believe it. Because of this promise I rightly expect people to believe me—and they will if I have established my reliability, so that my promise of the truth has meaning. I am a traitor to my neighbor's trust when I speak falsely or insincerely to him.

On the other hand, if an unauthorized person tries unjustly to pry a secret from me, he is not asking me to be a witness to truth but a traitor to trust. He should rightly expect me to evade as best I can. And my answer which misleads him carries no promise of truth. I am simply observing my social obligations; keeping myself trustworthy by guarding my secret.

The truthfulness of a statement cannot be analyzed except in the light of its social import and acceptance. Words are creations of convention. "Yes," might just as well mean "no," if it were so understood. Truth cannot be measured mechanically. A lie can only be determined by semantics—and circumstances. The honest, upright, trustworthy, reliable man knows the difference intuitively. The scheming, evasive, scrupulous, hedging, or anxious person is either not sure— or does not care.

Q. I have lived in a rural community where we had a party-line telephone. It was customary for all the people on the line to listen in to conversations whenever they wished. We simply accepted it and took it for granted and consequently discussed nothing of a private nature. Now we are supposed to have private phones, but they are connected through a switchboard. This is a private switchboard and the operators are not supposed to listen in at all. Consequently we have felt safe in discussing matters which might be strictly personal and private. However, we have recently found that the operators are opening the switch and listening in. Is this right? Aren't they committing sin by doing this?

A. It is definitely unjust and a sin against the Eighth Commandment to pry into the secrets of other people in this way. Each person has a right to his own secret thoughts, to his own private affairs, to his reputation and to his property. It is contrary to justice to violate any of these rights. Deliberate eavesdropping, reading of other people's letters, listening in on telephone conversations and other invasions of privacy are contrary to justice. Even though the sin involved may often be minor, the whole procedure is very despicable. It indicates a smallness of character and lack of honorable principles.

If the person who listens in on this telephone conversation then proceeds to reveal the secrets she (or he) has learned, to the embarrassment or harm of someone, she (or he) is further violating justice, and probably in a more serious manner.

The person who listens in on a private switchboard for the purpose of obtaining information, prying into secrets, or satisfying curiosity, is definitely guilty of sin. She (or he) is violating the ethical code of the company which employs her (or him), and is betraying the confidence of the subscribers. Again I say it may not be a mortal sin, but it is a very disgusting practice to all right-minded people.

The meddlesome curiosity which causes people to listen in to conversations on party-lines is a petty, disgusting thing, but it probably is not a violation of justice in most cases, because the parties talking do not expect privacy. It is merely a method by which the subscribers on a party-line decrease the value and efficiency of their telephone service to themselves. It is really remarkable, with the radio gushing out all through the day personal and domestic tragedies, intrigues and romances, that women (or men), should still have enough curiosity left to pry into the petty affairs of their neighbors. Don't you often wonder if they have no business of their own to mind?

The person of broad mind, strong character and alert intellect is interested in ideas; the person of medium mind and average character is attentive to the events of the world; but the narrow-minded little scatter-brain finds most of life's thrills amid the offal of his neighbors' activities.

Q. I do not know where to draw the line in talk before it is calumny, detraction, or uncharitable talk about the known faults of others.

A. The best solution would be to let truth and charity guide your conversation. Then you would have no scruples about distinctions. However try this for simplicity:

Calumny is a lie.

Detraction is the truth, but it detracts from your neighbor's reputation.

Uncharitable talk is the harrowing of a reputation already plowed over—or under.

13. *The Laws of the Church*

*Q. This past week end while visiting out of the city—and in
another diocese, of course—I encountered the strangest as-
sortment of impressions concerning the laws of fast and
abstinence. Here are some of them:*

"I am a housewife; so I am automatically excused from the
law of fast."
A. Automatically false.

"I tried to fast for a couple of days, but I couldn't; so I am
just not fasting."
A. A weakling!

"I am a mail-man, and three years ago I was dispensed
from the law of fast; so I am still dispensed."
A. Who dispensed you? Are you sure he made it permanent?
He should not have.

267

"Being dispensed from fasting, I am then allowed to eat meat as often as I wish on an ordinary day of Lent."
A. This is the first correct statement of the bunch.

"When the priest dispensed me from fasting, he said, 'now don't ask any other priest, because he may not see fit to dispense you.' Does this dispense me indefinitely?"
A. No, only for the length of time specified by the priest when he granted the dispensation. If no specific time was mentioned, you may presume that the dispensation lasts as long as you confront those particular difficulties of health or work which provide cause for the dispensation. A dispensation without sufficient cause would be invalid. In doubt you may properly presume that your dispensation lasts through all the present Lent—but rarely more than that. A priest would hardly grant a dispensation now for next year.

"I fast, but I save my dessert from my main meal and eat it later in the evening as refreshment at a party."
A. Ah, a chiseler!

"I have school-aged children who carry their lunches, and I include meat even on Fridays all year."
A. How do you like the feel of that mill-stone about your neck? It should be a rough and cumbersome specimen since the children you scandalize are your own. What a mother!

"Priests don't ever fast, because they have to answer sick calls in the night and they couldn't do it if they were fasting."
A. Calumny!

"Sisters don't ever fast, because their work is too hard."
A. Some Sisters deserve a dispensation . . . but I don't know how many get it.

"A priest said from the pulpit, 'There isn't anybody in this parish who has to fast.' "
A. Report him to the bishop.

"When you cook pork and sauerkraut together, you are not allowed to eat that sauerkraut on Friday, yet when the grease comes to the top you can fry potatoes in it."
268

A. These culinary details confuse me. Personally I think I would eat that sauerkraut.

"Many cans of mushroom soup or mushroom sauce include in their list of ingredients "chicken fat" or "beef extract." Is it permissible to eat these soups or sauces on Friday?"
A. Not the soup; but the sauce would be all right.

Do I seem to be inconsistent here? The law of abstinence (Can. 1250) forbids meat and meat extract to be used as food —or as an integral part of food compounds. But it expressly permits "condimenta" made from meat fats. My Latin dictionary translates "condimenta" as spices or seasonings. My English dictionary adds the word "sauces" as a synonym, and defines condiment as something used to give flavor and relish to food.

Q. A non-Catholic friend has asked why Catholics can eat fish on Friday. I know why we don't eat meat, but why we can eat fish I couldn't explain.

A. Now that seems like a simple question, but when I tried to explain it I found I had better consult the books, and the more books I consulted the more I found I needed to consult; and after exhausting local library sources I find that I still do not have a very good answer.

Isn't it strange how we take habitual things for granted until someone confronts us with a direct question about them; then we suddenly find that they are not as simple as we had always assumed. Anyway it has been interesting to see the surprise on faces of my priest friends when I pinned them down with this simple question.

On the other hand maybe we try to seek an answer much too profound and positive to a question like this. If the eating of fish on Friday is simply taken for granted in all the books, it must be that Catholics have always eaten fish because they like fish, find it available, and have never been forbidden to eat it. And history books do not record negative things, like the non-existence of a law forbidding fish.

269

Anyway I learned many things during my investigation. Here is a brief summary on part of it, as pertaining to your question:

Until recent times there was no clear distinction between fasting and abstaining; for many centuries the Church had no law of abstaining from meat except as a part of the broader law of fasting. In the earliest centuries Christians had a general sense of the duty of fasting, in a spirit of penance and mortification; and they observed various fasts, but always on a voluntary basis, without any laws on the subject; and for a long time there was no uniformity in the customs of fasting in different parts of the Church. It was left to individual piety and local custom.

Early customs of fasting were usually quite severe: all day long no food was taken, and often little or no drink, until after Vespers—about the ninth hour of the day, or 3 p.m. Then the one meal of the day was eaten; and generally it was a restricted meal: no meat, cheese, milk, or eggs. But people were very hungry by that time. Vegetables, fruits and cereals were not very satisfying; so quite naturally they started looking for substitutes, and fish was the most natural thing available. It was not considered flesh meat; people did not consider it forbidden on fast days.

I have found no clear evidence that there was ever a law—even a local law—in the Latin Church forbidding fish on fast days. In the late third century there are evidences of a fast —probably during Holy Week—which excluded fish; and in the ninth century we find people in a certain locality in Italy fasting three days a week on vegetables and fruit. But these were exceptions and were probably only local customs, not laws.

As some of you probably remember, there was a law in rather recent times which limited the use of fish on fast days, in that it forbade fish and meat to be eaten at the same meal. This law remained in effect until 1918. The very existence of this law shows that great changes had taken place in fasting customs. In earlier centuries such a law would have been ridiculous: naturally you couldn't eat fish and meat at the same meal on a fast day, since you couldn't eat meat at all on such

270

a day. But gradually, in the middle ages, meat had come to be permitted at the principal meal on certain fast days; and on the other hand, by the ninth century, certain former fast days, like Friday and Saturday each week, had simply developed into days of abstinence; all the other features of fasting had disappeared and only the avoidance of meat remained.

Q. In a recent column Dr. George Crane wrote that "the use of fish on Friday was primarily started in a bishopric made up largely of fishermen. Fishing was so good that the price collapsed. A depression was in the making. So the bishop of the area wisely decided to stabilize the market by declaring Friday a day when fish alone could be eaten. That smart ruling 'pegged' the price of fish and restored the economy . . . it has since been carried along as part of the Church ritual by Roman Catholics and High Episcopalians."

A. Just a few weeks ago I wrote a whole column on the origins of our custom of eating fish on Friday. In preparing that article I did quite a bit of study in dusty old books, and I found only one hint of anything to justify this gratuitous assertion of Doctor Crane's. After the reformation in England there were civil laws enacted which forbade the eating of meat on Friday, and it does seem that these were partially inspired by the motive of assisting the fishing and ship-building industries. However you must go back about 1600 years earlier if you are to trace the origins of Church laws on this subject.

With equal disregard for historical accuracy Doctor Crane's article continues: "Moses gave the veto of hog meat, although Abraham, Isaac, Jacob and Joseph for 400 years had no objection to pork. But Moses probably saw his fellow Egyptians sick or dying after a big roast pork banquet. Not realizing the hogs had been infected with trichinosis, Moses logically decided pork was dangerous, so placed a Church veto thereon, which still continues, even though government meat inspectors weed out all infected hogs at our modern meat packing plants."

271

If you must read Doctor Crane, please don't take him seriously—at least not on historical and religious matters.

Q. My understanding is that meat may be eaten any number of times on an ordinary week day of Lent by anyone between the ages of seven and 21. Am I correct?

A. Your understanding is correct.

Q. I am a convert and I am confused by some of the things my Catholic friends tell me—particularly my boy friend who is a student at a Catholic college. They say that if I have thoughtlessly ordered meat in a restaurant and then, after I am served, remember that it is Friday, I may go ahead and eat the meat, rather than waste it or incur additional expense. They also say that if I had prepared this meat for family dinner and then remembered, after it was all done, I could serve it to the family and they would be permitted to eat it—again to avoid waste and additional effort.

A. Your friends are laxists. The law of the Church (Can. 1250 and 1252) forbids the eating of meat and extracts of meat on Fridays and various other days of abstinence. The law makes no specific provision for the exemption of anyone in any circumstances. But the Church has always been reasonable about her laws; she wants them to help us spiritually, not burden us harmfully. So without making it official, she has always benignly tolerated a sensible interpretation of her laws. She smiles with favor—as far as her own laws are concerned—on old adages like "necessity knows no law" and "laws do not oblige under great inconvenience." She knows that some laxists, like your friends, will take advantage of her leniency, and make those adages ridiculous. But better that than to impose impossible burdens on us.

The law of abstinence is a serious law of the Church. It binds under pain of mortal sin. We cannot be frivolous in

272

finding reasons to excuse ourselves from it. There must be a real, serious, grave inconvenience—something similar to the inconvenience which would excuse you from attending Mass on Sunday. It need not be an overwhelming or extreme hardship; but neither may it be something silly or trivial in comparison with the severity of the law.

If you are really hungry and down to your last buck and the purveyor of victuals will allow you no reasonable substitute, then eat heartily and starve not. Similarly, if your refrigerator is broken, your butcher's account sadly in arrears, and your poor children famished, then let them eat your luscious stew before they languish. But let's be honest with the law and not make a joke of its leniency.

Q. If on days of partial abstinence a Catholic forgets and eats meat for breakfast or at lunch, is it all right for him to eat meat at the principal meal? If not, I want to state that this can be very upsetting to the one who cooks for a family.

A. On days of partial abstinence meat may be eaten only once—period. Even this once is a dispensation from the previous law which did not permit it at all. Apparently one favor whets the taste for another.

Penances are not accomplished without inconvenience, and even occasional hardship, but the spirit of love and reparation will prevent these from becoming very upsetting. (In fairness to my readers I should note that there is a contrary opinion on this question. I cannot accept it myself, but anyone else is free to follow it if he finds it reasonable.)

Q. In regard to snacks between meals and alcoholic drinks in Lent. Is it an act of self-denial and mortification, or is it a sin?

A. Snacks between meals are forbidden by law, under pain of sin, to those between the ages of 21 and 59, who are not

273

excused or dispensed from fasting. You abstain from alcoholic drinks during Lent as a mortification or self-denial, and there is no sin involved in taking a little drink between meals—unless you take too much.

Q. The men in the armed forces are exempt from the law of abstinence except on Ash Wednesday, Good Friday, Holy Saturday, and the Vigil of Christmas. If they are 21 they must also fast on those days mentioned. Am I right? Also what about the vigil of the Immaculate Conception, since it is now observed in place of the vigil of the Assumption?

A. There is no mention of Holy Saturday in the most recent dispensation; only three days are excepted from the general dispensation, from BOTH fast and abstinence: Christmas Eve, Ash Wednesday, and Good Friday. That means that members of the armed services must fast and abstain on those three days, but are not obliged on any other day, not even on the vigil of the Immaculate Conception.

Q. As a source of protein I take an envelope of plain gelatin in fruit juice. Would this be permitted on Fridays or days of abstinence?

A. Yes. While gelatin is a meat product, it is not popularly considered as meat, and the Church accepts general popular interpretation of which things are "flesh meat," and thus forbidden on Friday.

Q. Now that Lent is fast approaching I know you must be getting the same old questions concerning the laws on fast and abstinence. I hope you won't get too discouraged with me for sending another one. I would very much like to know to what extent an expectant mother has to observe the

274

Lenten regulations. Also, the mother who is nursing her baby.

I know that a person doing hard manual labor is excused from fasting, and recently I have heard that a woman with quite a few children is not obliged to fast either. To me, this seems like a very poor excuse for not observing the lenten fast. I have six children and will have the seventh soon, but I don't feel that just being the mother of six children should give me special privileges.

A. Just keep on thinking as you do, and some day you will get your special privileges anyway—in heaven. The Lord must love you.

Generally mothers, whether pregnant or nursing or blessed with six children, are obliged to observe the law of abstinence—unless their doctor should prescribe meat as a need of their diet.

Many moralists will tell you that both pregnant and nursing mothers are excused from the law of fasting—as simply as that. I am more strict in my opinion. I think it depends on the individual and the circumstances, general health and the stage of pregnancy or lactation. Fasting laws are not very strict any more; and it may be possible for mothers to follow them without any harm or excessive difficulty. If they can, then I think they are obliged. If they cannot—or if the doctor advises against it—then they are certainly excused. Of course, they might speak to their pastor or confessor and get a dispensation. And always in case of doubt they can follow the more lenient opinion of moralists, and consider themselves excused.

Q. Is a milk shake or a malted milk classed as a food or drink? Can they be consumed between meals during Lent?

A. Most malted milks and milk shakes would be classed as drinks—except the ones you eat with a spoon and have to chew. But that does not mean that you may consume them between meals during Lent—presuming that you are past 21

275

and obliged to fast. Not at all! I can drink beef broth; but that doesn't keep it from breaking my lenten fast.

The Church has become more lenient in recent years about the lenten fast; but she hasn't thrown all self-denial into the ash-can. Fasting would be a fattening pleasure if we could have about six malted milks each day of Lent—in addition to one full meal, and a discreet little breakfast and lunch.

In most countries even plain milk is considered a food, which breaks the lenten fast if taken between meals. But that is because these people seldom consider milk a simple beverage, as we do. So concession is made to our custom; milk is permitted. But that is about the limit. You have to stop somewhere if you are to fast at all.

Probably confusion is caused by the Eucharistic fast, which permits you to take liquids up to one hour before Communion. As far as the Eucharistic fast is concerned you may consume anything you can drink—as long as it is non-alcoholic. Malted milks and beef broth are fine up to one hour before Communion—as long as it is not a fast day.

Those under 21 do not have to fast; so they can have their malted milks if they want. They should find some way of doing penance, however.

Q. Is a mother who has quite a few children and does all her own work in the home, without ever any outside help, obliged to fast? I don't mean to eat meat twice a day, but to take a bite in the afternoon if she works hard? Is it true that a mechanic and school teachers and travelers are not obliged to fast?

A. Our fasting rules are so flexible now that I hesitate to say that any entire group of people is excused. I would think the mother you describe might come first in line to be excused, ahead of mechanics, teachers and travelers—who might follow in that order.

The law of fasting is an integral thing—a unit. If you are excused from part of it you are excused from all of it. So if you are permitted to eat between meals you may have meat

276

several times a day also. Of course we can deny ourself, voluntarily. But once we are excused from fasting, on an ordinary day of Lent, there are no limitations at all—short of gluttony.

Q. *On Fridays and days of complete abstinence is it permissible to use bacon drippings for frying eggs and potatoes or for use as seasoning for beans, etc.?*

A. Yes, it is permissible.

Q. *We were discussing the evening Masses during Lent. Two of my friends agreed that they were nice, but said they just couldn't receive Holy Communion at the evening Mass because they would have to eat by 4:30 and couldn't have anything else until breakfast the following day. They say they just get too hungry. I am a convert to the Church and I realize that I don't always understand Church rulings, but surely the lenten fast is not more important than receiving Holy Communion. It seems that my friends are defeating the purpose of the lenten fast.*

A. Possibly your friends could solve their problem by deferring their evening meal until after the Mass. Otherwise, I will have to side with them. The law of fasting during Lent is ancient and definite. The privilege of evening Mass is recent and optional. The Church makes no exemption from the lenten fast for those who want to receive Holy Communion at the evening Mass. Apparently they must make additional sacrifices if they wish to avail themselves of this privilege.

Q. *We just received a can of Reese-brand fried grasshoppers from Japan. Very seriously: are these "meat" or non-meat.*

A. The custom of a country or region determines whether a certain food is meat or "non-meat," and I don't believe we Americans have any uniform established custom regarding the eating of grasshoppers. However, we do consider rattlesnakes, turtles, frogs and snails to be "non-meat," so I think we can put your hopped-up locusts in the same class. The problem does not threaten to become widely critical.

Q. You may not get to answer this until after Easter, but it might be well to get my problem settled before next Lent rolls around.

According to your column, abstention from alcoholic drinks during Lent is looked upon as mortification and self-denial, and there is no sin involved in taking a little drink between meals, but eating between meals is forbidden.

Now I don't mean to be facetious, but do you mean to say that Holy Mother Church teaches that a Catholic can have a Manhattan between meals during Lent, but woe be to him if he dares to eat the cherry?

A. Even facetiousness can illustrate a point or two. I assure you that you can eat the cherry—and even have a canape on the side—with no woe other than gastric.

How come? What of that rule of not eating between meals?

All right, I will ask you one: How can you eat between meals when you are supposed to have only one meal?

If we are to find answers to our questions we should review the law of fasting. It is found in Can. 1251 of the Code of Canon Law and forbids us to have more than one full meal on a fast day; however, it does permit us to take a bit of food in the morning and evening, as long as we observe the approved customs of our country regarding the quantity and quality of the food thus taken. For clarity we might divide it into parts:

1. One meal without restriction as to amount and kind of food. It can be a feast—a banquet.

278

2. Breakfast and lunch, which should, in principle, consist of light foods in small quantities. Actually, our American customs, approved by our bishops, permit everything but meat at these two meals, as long as the two together do not, in quantity, equal a full meal. In some countries eggs, cheese and fish are not allowed.

3. Between meals we may drink but not eat. That means that we must not take things which are primarily nutritional, whether they be in liquid or solid form. Under this heading would come things like soup and malted milk. But we can take things which are primarily considered drinks: to quench our thirst. We Americans usually classify milk and fruit juices as drinks, though they would be forbidden in stricter countries.

4. This law of fast is not intended to develop either scruples or chiseling. It wants wou to do penance, to deny yourself, to feel your denial a bit. But it is not concerned with an odd ounce at lunch or a passing thoughtless bite between meals. And sometime in the course of centuries a lenient Catholic populace developed the convenient custom of taking a little bite with their drink, with the popular excuse that they did it lest the drink harm them. If the quantity is small and not often repeated it does not break the fast.

Your Manhattan will not break the Church's law of fasting —but it may break the divine law of temperance, if taken in excess, and cause you to lose all the merit of your fasting.

Q. How can Catholics be bound under pain of mortal sin to carry through practices of the Church, when the things forbidden are not in themselves of a sinful nature?

A. I presume you refer to things like abstaining from meat on Friday and fasting during Lent.

The Church was given authority by Jesus Christ to make laws for the common good of her members:

"All power in heaven and on earth has been given to me. Go, therefore, and make disciples of all nations . . ." (Matt. 28, 18-20).

"As the Father has sent me, I also send you" (John 20, 21).

"Amen I say to you, whatever you bind on earth shall be bound also in heaven; and whatever you loose on earth shall be loosed also in heaven" (Matt. 18, 18).

"If he refuse to hear even the Church, let him be to thee as the heathen and the publican" (Matt. 18, 17).

Sin is a violation of law. Most of our sins are directly contrary to the law of God. But when we break the law of the Church we are indirectly defying God who gave authority to the Church to make laws.

Q. I have been trying to determine how the Catholic practice began of not eating meat on Friday. I haven't been able to find the complete answer in any reference books. The Catholic Encyclopedia, is too staid and wordy for me to fully understand. Recently a non-Catholic friend tried to tell me that it all began back in the middle ages when the Popes allegedly owned or monopolized the fishing industry. To encourage the sale of fish the Pope made it a church law that meat could not be eaten on Friday.

Just how did the practice begin? Was it a custom before the Pope made it obligatory? What was the Pope's motive? Is there any truth in my friend's story? Is there any biblical basis for the fast? By the way, did the good B.V.M.'s ever teach me this—and I forgot it—or was my education in Church history sadly neglected?

A. First of all, I hope to be less staid than the Catholic Encyclopedia, but I do reserve the right to be equally wordy.

Secondly, your friend is a teller of fish stories. His history is a batch of old wives' tales—and fish wives, at that.

I am sure you understand that Catholics are not required to eat fish on Friday. They are, rather, forbidden to eat flesh meat. So fish is often chosen as a substitute, though some people prefer eggs, cheese or vegetables.

The practice of not eating meat on Friday we call abstinence. To abstain means to hold back or refrain from using

280

and enjoying something. We usually apply the word to food and drink, and one might abstain by going on a diet or becoming a teetotaler. We can abstain from all food; this was the historical notion of fasting. Or we can abstain from certain kinds of food, like meat; and this is what the Church law means today when it commands abstinence.

In the general sense of refraining from food, or from certain kinds of food, we might say that the custom began with Adam, except that he rather observed it in the breach. Anyway, the Lord God gave him a law of abstinence: "From the tree of the knowledge of good and evil you must not eat."

The practice of abstinence, in itself, is called by moralists an indifferent thing: it is neither good nor bad. But motives or circumstances may make it virtuous or vicious. If you abstain out of vanity you do wrong. If you abstain out of obedience or for love or penance, your act becomes good. If your abstinence harms your health or impairs your work, it is bad. If it clears your brain and reduces your waistline, good motives will make it virtuous.

The law of abstinence was given to Adam to teach him obedience, so that he might be aware of his dependence on his Creator. But when Adam broke the law he became a sinner.

As a consequence, for him and all his children abstinence acquired additional purposes: it is a way of doing penance, in an effort to repair the harm of sin and to restore the order of God's justice upset by sin. Also, it is a means of spiritual mortification, by which we bring our disordered desires under control of good sense.

Practically, every serious religion in the world's history has recognized the need of penance and mortification. We even find that need stressed in the ethical systems of great philosophers who had no special religion. Some of them were not supernatural enough to recognize the value of penance as a reparation for sin. But all agree with St. Paul that just as an athlete must train rigorously for a big game, so we must all exercise spiritual discipline, keeping in good moral condition, if we are to endure in the race of life towards its goal of happiness.

Mortification is defined in my dictionary as a subjection of the passions by abstinence and other discipline. The means of mortification may come to us from three sources. The ones of greatest value are imposed upon us by God, in the form of trials, afflictions, disappointments, sufferings, hardships, sorrows. We practice mortification by accepting troubles with love, resignation, and spiritual adaptation. Thus they serve God's glory and our own advancement in sanctity. Simone Weil, who knew suffering intimately, found the greatness of Christianity in the fact that it did not seek a supernatural escape from pain but found a supernatural use for suffering.

The second source of mortification is law, like the Church's law of abstinence. Its advantages are threefold: the choice of means is made with wisdom and experience; the virtue of obedience gets opportunity for profitable exercise; and we avoid many of the dangers inherent in choosing our own preferred brand of hair shirt.

We can, of course, and we should, choose private mortification in addition to that imposed by God and by law. But we must be careful that the choice be prudent; that it does not detract from the fulfillment of our duties; and that it does not become a source of self-satisfaction, by which we glory in the spiritual glamour of our own accomplishments.

Whatever type of mortification we practice we must keep our thinking straight about its nature and value. We do not suffer for the good of suffering, because suffering is not good in itself. We suffer for love. We are not saints because we suffer; we suffer to become saints. We do not give up the use of God's created things because we think something evil is in them. The reasonable use of all God's creatures is good and holy, but reason requires that we use them for God and not for themselves. So also our abstaining from the use of God's created things must be done for God and not for the sake of abstaining. And we must keep always in mind that mortification is not holiness; it is a means of holiness.

The idea of penance is not uniquely Chirstian, but only Christ gives it that touch of divine value which makes it really useful in repairing the harm of sin and removing its

282

vestiges. Because he was God as well as man Jesus suffered with infinite merit, redeemed all men from sin, and made adequate reparation to God for the harm of sin. But he is also the head of a Mystical Body of which Baptism makes us members; from our close union with him we have a part in his sufferings. Fused with his redemptive agony, our little mortifications are tinted with merit; our petty crosses merge into his Calvary cross; and our penances partake of his powers of reparation.

The cross was not only for Christ; it was for all Christians. Unless we share his cross we cannot share the redemption which resulted from the cross. There is no presumption in those bold words of St. Paul: "What is lacking of the sufferings of Christ I fill up in my flesh."

The practices of fasting and abstaining, which have been common among Christians from the very beginning, find their examples in ancient Jewish history and custom. You are familiar, in general, with the dietary regulations of the Jewish law. In the books of Genesis, Leviticus, and Deuteronomy you will find details of the various types of flesh, fish and fowl which were forbidden as unclean, and there was a special prohibition about eating meat with blood in it. The Jews also had days of very strict and complete fast, like the Day of Atonement.

The Apostles had their problems with the early Christians; many of these had been Jews, accustomed to the dietary restrictions, but others had been pagans, who saw no reasons for such restrictions. In order to pacify both groups a compromise was reached at the Council of Jerusalem and as a result we have the only "abstinence" law of the New Testament in Acts 15, 29: "That you abstain from things sacrificed to idols, and from blood, and things strangled."

Our Lord's forty-day fast in the desert was an inspiring example to his early followers. The Christians at Antioch were fasting when the Holy Ghost came and chose Paul and Barnabas, and they fasted again before these two were ordained (Acts 13, 113). St. Paul advised fasting and abstaining, and practiced his own recommendations (I Cor. 9, 25, II Cor. 6, 5; II Cor. 11, 27).

In the early Church there seems to have been no clear distinction between fasting and abstaining. Today the word fasting refers primarily to the quantity of food we eat—on a fast day we may have only one full meal—while "to abstain" refers to the quality or kind of food. In the early Church the reference was more often to fasting; and it sometimes meant no food at all—or very little food—or restricted foods, e.g., without meats. The custom of fasting was common among Christians from the very beginning. St. Clement of Rome was almost contemporary with the Apostles. He says, in his Second Epistle to the Corinthians: "Fasting is better than prayer." The Didache, or Teaching of the Twelve Apostles, one of the earliest Christian documents we have after the New Testament, says: "Let not your fasts be with hypocrites, for they fast on Mondays and Thursdays, but do you fast on Wednesdays and Fridays." The writings of the Fathers of the Church are replete with such references.

From earliest times Friday was the favorite fast day among all Christians. It was observed in memory of the death of Christ on Friday, in an effort of the faithful to unite their penance and self-denial with those of the Savior. Very early, in the Western part of Christendom, this Friday fast was prolonged through Saturday. Eastern Christians—the Greek Church—agreed on Friday, but couldn't see that Saturday fast, and yet they were stricter in their fasting laws and had more fast days than the West. They insisted that Wednesday and Friday should be the weekly days of fast. The Greek Church early developed a distinction between fasting and abstaining. On their strict fast days they were permitted only bread, salt, water, fruits and vegetables. On their abstinence days they were forbidden meat, fish, eggs, milk, cheese, oil and wine. In later times, one of their points of argument with the Latin Church was that the Westerners permitted eggs and fish on abstinence days.

The process by which fasting on Friday became less strict until finally it was reduced to mere abstinence from meat was apparently a gradual one—merely a custom among the

284

people. And the process by which these customs became written laws was a gradual one too. At first the laws were local; then they became more general. The earliest evidence I have found of a law forbidding meat on Friday for the whole Church was during the time of Pope Nicholas I (858-867). I am quite sure he owned no fish markets or shrimp boats.

Today fast and abstinence laws are neatly distinct. Fasting is primarily concerned with the quantity of food eaten, and allows only one full meal a day; it puts no limitations on the quality or kinds of food at that meal. Abstinence is not concerned with how much you eat, or how often; it requires that you avoid certain kinds of food, namely flesh meat and most of its products.

However, this precise distinction is a recent legal development. In spite of the words of St. Paul to the Romans that it is good not to eat meat, in the early centuries there was no idea of simple abstinence from meat apart from fasting; but on the other hand, avoidance of meat was usually an integral part of fasting.

Customs were diverse in different places and different centuries, but in general, early methods of fasting were quite severe. No food was taken all day long, and often little or no drink, until after Vespers, about the 9th hour of the day, or 3 p.m. Then the one meal of the day was eaten. It was a restricted meal: no meat, and probably no animal products like cheese, milk or eggs. But people were hungry after their day of fasting; vegetables, fruits, and cereals made a lean diet. So naturally they sought a substitute for meat. In the popular mind there was a definite distinction between animals, birds, and fish. In some places, at one time or another, birds were eaten on fast days, but generally they were grouped with land animals and considered flesh meat. Fish were different and became the generally accepted substitute for meat.

Seldom has fish been excluded from the fasting diet in the Western Church. In the late 3rd century there are evidences of a local fast (probably during Holy Week) which did not permit fish; and in the 9th century people in a certain lo-

285

cality in Italy fasted three days a week on vegetables and fruit. But those were exceptions. It is doubtful whether there was ever an explicit law of the Church which forbade fish on fast days, except for a rather recent law, which some people remember today, which prohibited fish and meat at the same meal on fast days. That law was in effect until 1918. It gives evidence that in the course of centuries meat had come to be permitted at the principal meal on some fast days.

The rigor of early fasting gradually diminished. Hungry people became impatient; so they gave in to the urge to say Vespers early. By the 10th or 11th century the one meal of a fast day was being eaten at noon. But that had a disadvantage. By evening, people were hungry again.

The monasteries were the principal sources of fasting customs. In the evening, the monks usually had a conference, which was called a collatio. It was hard for the monks to sit patiently through those conferences, hungry as they were. The custom developed of having something to nibble on before or during the conference; and this nibbling became an evening snack, called a collation. This happened about the 13th century; it was not until five or six centuries later that coffee and a bit of bread were permitted in the morning. Now fasting has become a rather comfortable thing, adapted to the special needs of the individual.

As the method of fasting became easier the number of fast days also diminished. By the 11th century, Wednesday had ceased to be a fast day everywhere, except during Lent and Ember weeks. Saturday had replaced it, but as early as the 9th century both Friday and Saturday had ceased to be real fast days; they were only days of abstinence. You could eat as much as you wanted on those days, but no meat. Abstinence had always been a part of the fast; it ended up as the only part to remain. As a counter trend, on other fast days meat came to be permitted at the principal meal. These were fast days, but not days of complete abstinence.

You may think that the Reformation did away with fasting and abstinence; but not so. Changing customs were gradual in most places. In England under Edward VI and James I abstinence was enforced by parlimentary laws, and Elizabeth

I issued proclamations on the subject. It was made fairly clear that one purpose of those English laws against flesh meat on fast days was to aid the fishing and shipbuilding industries.

Presbyterian Scotland had fast days before communion; and the Puritans brought the practice of occasional fasting to this country. The day before they left Leyden was a solemn day of fast, and after their many misfortunes in the year 1623 they had a similar fast day in the colony. The last general fast days observed in this country were in 1849, because of the cholera; during the Civil War, when fasts were kept by both the North and the South; and June 1, 1865, in commemoration of Lincoln's death on April 14 of that year.

Q. What is the latest you can arrive at Mass, and when is the earliest it is permissible to leave? Of course all of us try to arrive at the beginning and stay until the end, but sometimes we do arrive late, and sometimes we are obliged to leave before the end. I have always been taught that it is necessary to arrive before the Gospel and remain until the "Ite missa est," but here again, is it the Gospel that the priest reads during the course of the Mass or the one he reads when he delivers the sermon?

I have even heard Catholics say that as long as you arrive before the Offertory the Mass counts.

A. This chiseling gets me. Not your question so much as the frequent attitude of our people on this subject. I have nothing against casuistry when rightly used, but I lose patience with people who wrack their brains trying to draw fine lines between mortal sins and venial sins. And we have far too many people who get into the habit of coming late to Mass, because "it is all right if you get there before the Gospel"—or who leave early, because the essential parts of the Mass are over after the Communion.

The law requires that we hear Mass on Sunday. That means an entire Mass—from the prayers at the foot of the altar to the last Gospel. To deliberately omit any portion of the Mass is contrary to the law, and therefore a sin.

The Church is not a stickler for tiny things. So she would not consider you guilty of sin if you missed one short prayer. But it would certainly be a venial sin to miss the prayers at the foot of the altar.

Your question really means this: How much of the Mass may I miss without being guilty of mortal sin? You would have us disregard venial sins—counting them as negligible, instead of the second worst thing on earth. Now do you see why I burn?

You commit a mortal sin if you miss a "substantial portion" of the Mass. You would thus be guilty of mortal sin if you came after the Offertory is finished; that is, after the Orate Fratres. Or if you came right after the Gospel (the one read at the altar, in Latin) and then left right after the Communion. Or if you missed the Consecration.

The Church is willing to accept sound excuses. An honest reason will keep you from being guilty of sin in missing a part of Mass—or all the Mass. The reason must be serious in proportion to the portion of Mass you miss. An ordinary reason would excuse you from missing the prayers at the foot of the altar, unless you made it a habit, and disturbed your devout neighbors. A really serious reason would excuse you from Mass entirely. But carelessness, tardiness, and dilly-dallying are not good excuses for getting in just before the Gospel. And lassitude is not a reason for leaving after the Communion.

Q. Will you please tell me when Mass may be heard in a hospital chapel, and when not? I am under the impression that on Sundays and holydays of obligation it is necessary for an ordinary layman to hear Mass in a Church under ordinary conditions.

A. Canon 1249 answers your question precisely. I translate it in my own words:

"A person fulfills his obligation of hearing Mass by being

present while it is celebrated in any Catholic rite, out in the open air or in any church or public or semi-public oratory, or even in private cemetery chapels; but not in other chapels, unless they have a special privilege from the Holy See."

Most hospital chapels are semi-public chapels. You can fulfill your Sunday obligation in any of them.

The proper thing to do on Sunday is to go to your own parish church; that is where you really belong. There you hear the sermon the pastor has specially prepared for you, you hear the announcements of parish activities for the week, you are kept informed of the financial and spiritual status of your own parish, and you have opportunity to make contribution to the support of the Church. Besides you will make your pastor happy.

Good reason will permit you to go to another parish—or even to a hospital chapel. But since this chapel is only semi-public it is also semi-private; and you should be sure that you are entirely welcome there by the people for whom the chapel is intended—especially the Sisters. We must not intrude. Hospital chapels are not built to accommodate the public; so we are presuming on the hospitality of the Sisters when we make use of them.

Q. Suppose that a family has lived in St. Mary's parish for a number of years, and then the bishop sets up a new parish and they find that they are not within the boundaries of St. Mary's. Are they bound by Canon Law, under pain of mortal sin, to attend Mass in the new parish, or is it optional? Some say it is only courtesy, and that we can attend Mass at any parish we desire.

A. You are definitely members of the new parish. However, Canon 1249 of the Code of Canon Law states that anyone may fulfill the obligation of hearing Mass by assisting at the Holy Sacrifice in any Catholic rite, either out in the open air or in any church or chapel, except in some private chapels.

It is definitely a courtesy and a bow to right order and authority that we should cooperate with the wishes of our bishop and pastors. So you would do something pleasing to God if you would gradually break your ties of custom and sentiment and form the habit of assisting at Mass in your new parish. The bishop has the right and duty to change boundaries and establish new parishes as the good of the Church and the welfare of souls may require (Can. 1427), and it is not possible for him to take into account the wishes and attachments of all the parishioners.

Many spiritual ministrations are strictly parochial: baptism, marriage, communion for the sick, and viaticum for the dying. Your children may not be baptized at St. Mary's unless your new pastor gives permission, and I would strongly advise you not to ask that permission. Your daughter may not be married at St. Mary's without similar permission. And you may not count on the priests of St. Mary's for spiritual care when you are sick; that is the right and duty of your new pastor. As a general rule, funerals take place in the parish of the deceased, though there is more room for choice in this matter. As the Church is established and maintained in this country your new parish is entitled to your financial support. St. Mary's has no claim on you.

Q. Can a person who does not attend Mass or receive his Easter Duty, or any person married outside the Church, have a Catholic burial if he has received the Last Sacraments before death?

A. Yes, but he had better not count on that last chance. It is very dangerous to travel daily down the speedway to hell, planning to jump off just before the precipice of death.

Q. How can the Catholic Church express a great respect for man's intellect and at the same time fence his intellect with an Index of Prohibited Books?

I have heard a Catholic student with some pretensions to learning rather breezily explain his ignorance of two masterpieces—Gibbon's Decline and Fall of the Roman Empire, and Flaubert's Madame Bovary—on the ground that "they're on the Index, you know." Another Catholic acquaintance to whom I mentioned this incident told me that he had himself been "given permission" to read those works.

Why should a mature, intelligent man (or any man, for that matter) have to ask permission to get acquainted with some of the world's greatest books? Isn't the Index really an outmoded disciplinary tool that ought to be dropped?

A. When we try to explain the Index to our non-Catholic friends, one of our first problems is that of semantics. The terms we must use are loaded: liberty of conscience, freedom of thought and expression, censorship, authority, permission, subjection, and obedience. They are catchwords, in the sense that they release a catch on assorted prejudices and emotions, letting them fly loose to entangle our thinking.

Liberty and freedom are slogans of patriotism; our fathers and our brothers have died for them. Any authority which would curtail them is traitorous. Censorship brings visions of an eagle-beaked Puritan of ancient vintage, poking his prurient nose into our private pleasures, and threatening to burn us at the stake if we don't desist—or at least to burn our books. Authority implies the authoritarianism of the dictator. Permission brings memories of childish subjection; and obedience hints at servility.

No exercise of authority, no laws or censorship can make sense until we have a comprehensive grasp of true liberty and freedom, and see these precious rights in their proper positions in the scale of values. Freedom is not the ultimate goal of human life; we aim at happiness, in this life and in eternity, and freedom is a valued means of achieving that aim. But it can only be a useful means if it remains in harmony with right and truth.

There are current in our modern world various concepts of liberty. The most extreme is that of the existentialists,

291

who live in a world devoid of meaning and rattle around in it without purpose or moral restraint. They make their decisions without the aid of principle, with no firm sense of values; and they acknowledge the right of no earthly power to influence them. They have the freedom of the space man, unrestrained even by gravity; and it must leave them lonely and insecure.

A more populous second group like to call themselves liberals, but we might dispute their right to that title, which is claimed by all who are free and tolerant and love liberty. They might rather be called liberalists. They believe that a man's freedom should be limited only by the strict and proven rights of other men. They accept law as a restraint on liberty, but they hold that no law of state or Church should attempt to determine man's obligation to himself or to his God. Truth imposes no necessary limits to the liberalist's freedom; man must be free to believe error, if he wishes. And goodness inflicts no restraints; the liberalist defends his right to choose evil, foolish and immature though the choice may be.

We Catholics prize liberty as much as anyone. Through the centuries the Church has often stood alone in insisting that man has within himself the principle of true liberty; a free will. And she has always upheld man's basic right to use his free will, unhampered by arbitary restraints. But she does insist that we have definite personal obligations to ourselves and our God. True liberty is that which best serves our purpose in life; it is not freedom from law, but freedom under just law. It does not chafe under reasonable restraint; it rather rejoices to have competent help and guidance.

Catholics take as much delight as other Americans in those glorious words of our Declaration of Independence: "We hold these truths to be self-evident, that all men are created equal, that they are endowed by their Creator with certain unalienable Rights, that among these are Life, Liberty, and the pursuit of Happiness." But pursuit of happiness is the main objective, and it requires that liberty be in harmony with right, and that license be balanced with discipline.

Church censorship does not make sense until we understand the Church's divine foundation and purpose, and the teaching authority which was given her by Jesus Christ. We Catholics hold that the Church is the Mystical Body of Christ: a spiritual extension of himself, of his love, authority, and sanctifying power. When the Church speaks we recall the words of Jesus to his Apostles: "He who hears you hears me." So when the Church tells us not to read a certain book it is as though our divine Master gave us that command.

The Church is first of all a teacher. Jesus gave her a solemn commission that she should make disciples of all nations, preach the Gospel to them and teach people to observe all that he had commanded. Any good teacher is concerned about the truth; she wants to keep it intact and to see that it is taught faithfully. She is concerned about the textbooks she uses, and she will surely eliminate from her courses those writings which distort the facts.

Most of us are deeply grateful to teachers of our youth, who inspired and guided our studies, and taught us to discern between the true and the false, the good and the bad.

To the Catholic the Church is such a teacher, but she is much more. She is maternal; she is a loving parent who looks out for the spiritual welfare of her children with the competence which comes from centuries of experience, and with the sureness which comes from the authority Christ gave her.

When a non-Catholic becomes critical of the Index he should keep this in mind: the Church is not trying to impose her laws upon him or his friends who are outside her membership. For all practical purposes, her laws are for us, her members; and we accept them freely, not with blind servility, but with reverence for the divine origin of the authority behind them. If I did not hear the kindly voice of Jesus speaking through the decrees of the Holy Office when it forbids certain books, I might scream in protest. But as it is I accept these decrees with love and alacrity, even though I may not see the reason for some of them—and may not like some of them.

The Church's obligations as a teacher are peculiar; her truths were revealed to her, and they often cannot be verified

293

by experiment, research, or logic. She must be careful to keep them intact, and solicitous in teaching them correctly—especially in view of their critical necessity for eternal happiness. Realizing the importance of books as a teaching medium, the Church has long been concerned about them: anxious that the good ones be widely used, careful that the dangerous ones be wisely restricted.

The Church's earliest concern was with the books of the Bible; she guarded the inspired books carefully to keep them intact, and she was critical in holding them separate from an abundance of apocryphal writings which sought to usurp their sacred place.

The pagan classics gave concern to early Christians, who often esteemed their literary value, but were anxious about their harmful influence on faith and morals.

However, it seems that the first book officially condemned by the Church was the Thalia of Arius, whose heresy was proscribed by the Council of Nicea in 325. Later Pope Anastasius condemned the works of Origen, who was a great philosopher and teacher of the early Church, but whose errors were judged dangerous to those not sufficiently educated to discern and deal with them. Pope Leo the Great condemned writings of the Manicheans, in the middle of the 5th Century.

It was not until the invention of the printing press that the Church became greatly involved in the censorship of books. And she was not the only authority concerned about the abundant and wide-spreading products of this new invention. Henry VIII censored books in England, Charles V did the same in the Netherlands. At Paris, the Sorbonne was more competent, but also more comprehensive, in exercising its authority.

The first catalogue of forbidden books was prepared by Pope Paul IV in 1559. Then the Council of Trent revised the Church's legislation on books, and laid the foundation for our present laws. And on the basis of this new legislation, Pope Pius IV revised that early Index and brought it up to date, in 1564. There have been various editions since that time; and the entire legislation of the Church was modernized by Pope Leo XIII in 1897 and by the Code of Canon Law in 1918. In the edition of the Index which appeared in 1948 there were listed 4,126 condemned works, the great majority of them are ancient books of theology and philosophy, obscure and little known in our modern world.

The most practical book I know on this subject was written by Father Redmond A. Burke, C.S.V.: *What Is the Index?* Much of my information has been gleaned from it. According to my count, Father Burke lists 112 authors who have had all their works condemned. Of these 88 wrote on theology, eight on philosophy, one on politics, one on law, three on religion, and four on history. Three are listed in the field of literature and four in belles-lettres. The ones in this last category are the best known of the lot: Maurice Maeterlinck, Anatole France, Emile Zola, and Pietro Giordani. In literature I recognize only one name: Jean Paul Sartre, one of the most recent added to the Index. (The works of Andre Gide have been condemned since this edition of the Index was published.)

Among the theologians whose total works are condemned I fail to recognize even a half-dozen names: only David Blondel, Giordano Bruno, John Lightfoot, Albericus Gentilis, and Hugo Grotius—and these last two I know from law rather than theology.

There are bigger names among the philosophers: Francois Voltaire, Rene Descartes, Thomas Hobbes, David Hume, and Benedetto Croce. John Gentile is also on the list, but his subject field is not indicated.

Sigmund Freud never got on the Index, and neither did Karl Marx. But in 1949 the Holy Office issued a decree which pointed out that the writings in the Marxist press are designed to undermine Christianity, and so are forbidden by the general law of the Church.

As for Gibbon, I really do not know why he is on the Index, but it is probably because of his contempt for Christianity, and for things Catholic in particular. He was inclined to be lofty and cynical, and consequently to give offense. His facts are apparently accurate, but his interpretations often reflected his ironic opposition to Christianity.

Gibbon was very popular and highly fashionable in his day. And his volumes were often cited as arguments against the Church; they were recommended as antidotes for those who had any idea of becoming Catholic.

Gustave Flaubert is considered the father of the modern novel, and he is celebrated for the purity and force of his style, for the validity of his scenes and the verity of his characters. Madame Bovary presents a sordid story with some very real but stupid and vulgar characters. Possibly it was placed on the Index because of the notoriety it received from a public trial in which the author and publisher were accused of presenting an immoral work. The defendants were acquitted; and the passages which were then alleged as pornographic would seem quite tame to readers of modern novels.

That you may better evaluate the force of the Index, I will translate for you part of Canon 1398 of the Code of Canon Law: "The forbidding of a book means that, without proper permission, it may not be edited, read, kept, sold, translated, or in any way communicated to others."

You object to obtaining permission, but we do not, because we recognize the authority of the Church as our teacher and maternal guide. But anyway, you will note that the prohibition of books is conditional—subject to authorization from proper Church authorities. And provisions are made that the bishop can grant this permission quite readily to most persons who are qualified and have good reason to read some book on the Index. It is not the Church's intention to condemn these books to complete oblivion; it is rather to warn the unwary and to keep the books out of the hands of those who are not able to handle them competently.

And it should also be noted that the Index lists only a small number of the thousands of books of the world which richly deserve condemnation. You will find on the Index none of the junk which litters our gaudy book stands, none of the modern novels which would make Flaubert blush, few of the philosophies which make Kant seem so solid, and little of the theology which makes Luther seem orthodox. Incidentally, you will not find Luther's name in the Index. But

296

this does not mean that the reading of his works is permitted. By general laws all books of heresy and heretics are forbidden, along with books against religion and sound morality. I would need a separate article to explain these general laws and the Church's requirement of her authorization, or Imprimatur, for the publication of certain types of books.

The Index is published in various languages, but it really makes little difference except for the preface. The titles of the various condemned books are given in their original language, and most of them seem to be in Latin, with French apparently holding second place. There are quite a few in Italian, some in German, and an occasional one in Spanish and English. I find a few titles in Greek and Hebrew, and there is one which seems to be in Arabic.

An indication of the practical importance of the Index emerges from a conversation I had with nine of my fellow priests while I was writing this article. None of them had a copy of the Index in his library; they had all seen it at one time or another, but had little precise knowledge about it. My own edition of the Index dates from 1929, and has been little used in the intervening years, except to answer questions presented to me. I had to visit our university library to find a recent edition.

Our university students do have need, occasionally, to read books on the Index. They explain their cases to me and I refer the request to the bishop, who grants the permission readily, merely advising them to be cautious in their use of the books and not to pass them on to others who do not have permission.

And it is probably salutary for the mature and intelligent man to recall occasionally that his powers of critical discernment are not without limit; and that he can gain much spiritual merit by the exercise of humility, in submitting to the teaching authority of the Church. After all, the person who boasts that he can read anything is not really mature; he bears resemblance to the braggart who can eat anything—or drink anything.

14. *The Sacraments*

*Q. My friend—a seminarian—told me that in case of an
accident a person can be baptized on the arm if the head
cannot be reached. Then I started looking through my first-
aid kit to see what I could use to give the sacrament of
baptism. I found tincture of merthiolate, aromatic spirits
of ammonia, and olive oil. Could I use one of these in an
emergency? Anyway, I now carry a small bottle of holy
water in my kit.*

A. Your seminarian friend would not get an A in my class unless he explained to you that baptism on the arm is of doubtful validity. In an emergency baptize on the arm, by all means, if you cannot reach the head—or a central part of the body. But if you do baptize on the arm, and are later able to get at the head, then the baptism should be repeated conditionally on the head. When I say conditionally, I mean that you repeat the ceremony of baptism with the idea that if the first one was not valid this one will be.

No use to even try to baptize with any of those medicines you mention. It would be invalid. Stick to water—and it need not be holy water.

Q. *My niece is getting married and her future husband plans to become a Catholic. She plans to have her uncle and aunt as godparents for her boy friend. However, her uncle and aunt do not always go to Mass on Sundays and holydays; they just go when they feel like it. May she have them as sponsors for her boy friend?*

A. I take it that you are not the aunt in question. They are probably from the other side of your niece's family.

There is no law against their being sponsors. Maybe the new responsibilities will encourage them to more faithful practice of their religion. And their adult godson need not imitate their negligence; he may rather provide them with inspiring example.

Q. *I am shocked at your answer about the Catholic girl who plans to have her aunt and uncle as sponsors for her boy friend when he becomes a convert. They do not go to Mass regularly, but you said that it was all right for them to be sponsors. It was taught to me and I have read it many times that only those who are good Catholics themselves may be sponsors for baptism.*

299

A. It is desirable that good practical Catholics be chosen as sponsors in baptism, especially for children, because they assume responsibility for the spiritual welfare and Catholic education of their godchild. But the law does not exclude poorer Catholics from being sponsors, and we have no right to make our own laws in the matter. The law of the Church, in Canons 765 and 766, makes the following requirements for sponsors in baptism:

They must be baptized themselves, and have the use of reason and the intention of being sponsors. You cannot make a person a sponsor without his knowledge and consent.

They must be Catholics, not members of any heretical sect, not excommunicated or under other Church penalties.

They must not be father, mother, husband or wife of the person baptized.

They must be chosen and appointed either by the person being baptized or by his parents or guardians; or if none of these is able to designate the sponsor then the baptizing minister will do it.

They must hold the child at the time of baptism, or be otherwise in physical contact with the person baptized. Usually a hand is placed on the shoulder of an adult at the moment of baptism.

They are supposed to be fourteen years old, but the priest who does the baptizing can permit younger people to be sponsors if he judges advisable.

They must have an elementary knowledge of their faith.

They may not be novices or professed religious, unless they have permission of their superior; and a priest may not be sponsor without permission of his bishop.

These laws are made by the supreme authority of the Church; it is presumptuous for us to add our own. If the law does not require that the sponsor for a baby be a good practicing Catholic then certainly we should not demand that the sponsors for an adult convert be in all ways exemplary. I strongly advise that you choose the best sponsors available, but I do not recommend that you be more Catholic than the

300

Church. Advice is not law; and sometimes there may be good reason to settle for less than the optimum.

Q. When our infant son was to be baptized I asked some good friends—I thought they were—to be godparents. They refused. I am a convert and I never heard of anybody refusing to be a godparent, which to me is an honor. When I choose my children's godparents I think it over carefully. Am I committing a sin to let their refusal bother me so?

A. No, you are not committing a sin because you are trying honestly to get over the hurt caused you by this rebuff. Of course I do not know the reason for their refusal; I can only guess. And the most charitable motive I can attribute to them is that they are over-impressed by the duties of a godparent and afraid to assume the obligations of this office.

We must not make light of these obligations, but we should be realistic and sensible about them. The person baptized becomes a spiritual son or daughter of the godparent, who are warned by Canon 769 to be careful that their godchild live the type of life they promised for it in the ceremony of baptism. Canon 1335 places upon them—together with parents and guardians—the obligation of seeing that their godchild receives religious instruction.

In themselves these obligations are serious, but they actually become effective only when (1) the parents or guardians evidently and gravely neglect their duty, and (2) circumstances are such that the godparents CAN do something about it. In our American society it is seldom possible for godparents to step into a family circle and supply the deficiencies of parents in the religious education of their children. Where prudent judgment indicates that some good can be accomplished the godparent is obliged to do what he can. But no one is obliged to do the impossible, or even to attempt it when it is evidently impossible. Much less need we fret about our duties under impossible circumstances.

Love and zeal will prompt the godparent to do good for his

godchild, but neither love nor zeal will have a chance when good friends refuse to accept the obligation.

What are the duties, obligations and privileges of godparents? In case of the parents' death must the godparents assume the duties of the parents in providing for the child or children? On the other hand, in case of the parents' death, CAN a godparent adopt the child or children if no legal guardian was specified in the parents' will? Does a godparent have a right to adopt the child if there are other relatives (grandmother, aunt, etc.)?

A. The godparents' duties are restricted to the spiritual welfare of the child. They do not assume obligations for its material care or adoption. The Church law states that in baptism the godchild is commended to their spiritual care and that they assume an obligation for its Christian education, especially when the parents fail to provide that education or are taken away in death. These obligations are not absolute; their practical application depends on circumstances. Sometimes it is impossible to step in and aid the negligent parent; and in our modern shifting population the child may often be taken far from the godparents' influence. No godparent is obliged to follow the child across the country or to adopt it in order to give it a religious education.

There would be no religious objection to the adoption of the child by the godparents. I doubt that the civil courts would give them preference over relatives, unless they showed superior qualifications otherwise. But if there is no contest, and they qualify as adoptive parents, the Church would give its blessing.

Q. In my catechism I find the admonition that an adult, who is in danger of death and has not been confirmed, should have that sacrament administered to him, if at all possible. What of a child, particularly one who has not re-

302

ceived his first Communion? I know that the Orthodox Church gives confirmation at the time of baptism. Should one ask one's pastor to confirm a five year old child who has leukemia.

A. Yes, I would advise that the request be made, and I am sure that the pastor will be pleased to administer the sacrament.

Not only the Orthodox, but our own Eastern Uniate Churches give confirmation immediately after baptism. During the first three centuries after the time of our Lord the bishop was nearly always the one who baptized; so after the baptism he went right on and gave the sacrament of confirmation. Then parishes grew up and were put in charge of priests who were not bishops. In the East these priests followed the custom of the bishops and gave confirmation right after baptism. In the West the priests baptized but waited for confirmation until the bishop would come to confer it.

Consequently, in the Latin Church generally, confirmation is reserved to the bishop and can be conferred by another priest only with special authorization. Such special authorization is often given to priests in mission fields and to those who hold certain positions or dignities, e.g. a Cardinal can confirm even if he is not a bishop, and certain abbots and other prelates can confirm in the territory under their jurisdiction.

A few years ago Pope Pius XII gave special authorization to pastors to confirm in their own parishes those who were in grave danger of death. In virtue of this privilege a pastor may confirm either an adult or a child; but it must be a case, like your leukemia, in which there is practically no hope of recovery.

I might mention that it is not at all unusual for babies to be confirmed even in the Latin Church. The custom was fairly common up until the middle ages, and is still found generally in Spain and various parts of Latin America. The law on the subject reads as follows (Can. 788):

"While the administration of the sacrament of confirmation is properly deferred in the Latin church until about the seventh year of age, however it may be conferred before that age, if the infant is in danger of death, or if the minister judges it advisable for serious reasons."

Q. I have recently heard that under Canon Law parents have the obligation, under pain of mortal sin, to see that their children receive Holy Communion at the beginning of the age of reason (which may be as early as 4 years old). This would apply to their Easter duty at this time.

I would appreciate help in understanding why this is not promulgated by the hierarchy of the Church, so it could be practiced.

A. It is true that the law of the Church states that everyone who has reached the use of reason must receive Holy Communion at least once a year, during the Easter time. However, there is a general presumption of law that children do not have the use of reason prior to seven years of age; this presumption may give way to fact, in a particular case, where the reception of Holy Communion is concerned. But it is a good norm to follow, until the opposite is clearly proven.

The use of reason is a relative thing. Babies can think a little bit. At what stage of their thinking should they receive Holy Communion? Canon 854 of the Code of Canon Law gives us the norms:

(1) Children who are not old enough to understand and appreciate this sacrament may not be given Holy Communion. (As a general rule, we do not consider them old enough to understand and appreciate it before the age of seven. The exception needs to be proven before the priest can permit them to receive.)

(2) In danger of death, children can and should receive Holy Communion if they are able to distinguish the Body of Christ from ordinary food, and can pray with reverent adoration.

304

(3) Outside the danger of death, they must have a more complete knowledge of Catholic doctrine and a more thorough preparation, so that they may at least grasp those mysteries which are necessary for salvation, and be able to receive devoutly.

(4) A priest must help the parents decide whether or not a child is sufficiently prepared to receive Holy Communion. (So there can be no serious obligation on the parents as long as the priest says the child is not ready).

(5) Finally, it is up to the pastor to see that no children receive Holy Communion before they have the use of reason and are sufficiently instructed. Of course he also has the duty of seeing to it that they do receive as soon as they have the use of reason and are rightly prepared.

So I would say that parents should not worry much about this obligation until their children are seven. Let the pastor do the worrying; the obligation is primarily his. Besides parents are always inclined to think their own children precocious. Only a fond and doting parent would think a four-year-old ready for Holy Communion—unless he were an absolute genius, in danger of death.

Q. Why would it be more beneficial for us to receive Holy Communion during Mass rather than before Mass? There have been a few discussions in school on this subject.

A. By its nature Holy Communion is a part of Mass. The Mass is the continuation of the Sacrifice of Jesus on the Cross —it brings his sacrifice to us so that we have direct and personal part in it. We have a personal part in it in three ways.

(1) We unite ourselves to Jesus in offering the Sacrifice to the Heavenly Father in adoration, love, thanksgiving, reparation and petition. We are all one with the priest, who represents Christ, in offering that Sacrifice.

(2) Then we offer ourselves together with Jesus, as victim of the sacrifice—and we thus become an offering acceptable to God, because of our association with the Sacrificial Victim of Calvary.

305

(3) And finally we receive into our souls the fruits and benefits of the Sacrifice; and the greatest of all those benefits is Jesus Christ, who gives himself to us in Holy Communion.

So Communion completes our participation in the Mass by bringing into our souls the spiritual benefits of the Sacrifice of Jesus on Calvary.

It is only when we are prevented from receiving at Mass, or have some sensible excuse for receiving at other times, that the Church would have us go to Communion outside of Mass. However, the benefits of receiving at any time are so great that the Church is very free and generous on the subject.

Q. Would I be allowed to request that at my own requiem Mass my wife, children and friends be allowed to receive Communion during that Mass.

A. You would certainly be so allowed, and if anyone objects refer him to Canon 846 of the Code of Canon Law, which states, in general, that any priest may distribute Holy Communion during any Mass. The only exception is that of Canon 869 which permits the bishop to forbid this distribution of Communion in individual cases for good sound reason.

Q. We may drink coffee, cocoa, etc. up to an hour before we receive Holy Communion. Is this approximate, or is it an hour before Mass starts? May we take the 20 minutes, or so additional that Father takes to get to Communion after Mass begins?

A. It is not approximate; it must be exact. You may not receive Holy Communion 59½ minutes after you had a drink of coffee. However you do count the time to your own Communion—not to the beginning of Mass. The priest must be fasting from coffee, cocoa, etc. a full hour before his Mass

306

begins—but you can take that extra 20 minutes, or whatever it is, before you actually receive. But be careful. If you miscalculate, even by a fraction of a minute you may not receive Communion. Leave yourself an extra five minutes to be sure!

Q. When a convert goes to Confession for the first time, does he tell the priest that this is his first confession? How is it worded?

A. Yes, He simply says: "Father, I am a convert; this is my first confession. I was baptized two weeks ago, and since that time I have committed the following sins." He can choose his own words.

Very often converts from some Protestant denomination are baptized conditionally when they were received into the Church. They usually go to confession right after their conditional baptism; and they might say something like this to the priest: "Father, I have just been received into the Church and baptized conditionally. My first baptism was in the Methodist church ten years ago, and I want to confess the sins which I remember since that time."

Q. Do priests feel like hearing a non-Catholic's confession, and would the non-Catholic say he isn't a Catholic and then go ahead and confess?

A. A non-Catholic may not receive the sacrament of Penance; but speaking for myself, at least, I am entirely willing to have a non-Catholic consult me in the confessional, to open to me as much of his conscience as he wishes, and to seek my counsel, advice and enouragement. If a non-Catholic does go into the confessional he should make it perfectly clear to the priest that he is not a Catholic.

Q. If a person forgets a sin in confession, can he go to Com-

*munion a week, or two weeks, or must he go to confession
again just as soon as confessions are heard in his church?*

A. He can go to Communion as often and as long as he
wishes. If the sin he forgot to confess was a mortal sin, then
the next time he does go to confession—whenever it is—he
must mention this past sin. But if it was only a venial sin he
had better forget it completely right now.

*Q. When a priest doesn't give you absolution, but gives you
a penance, does this mean the sins are not forgiven?*

A. If he didn't give me absolution I wouldn't accept the
penance.

How do you know he didn't give you absolution? Did he
tell you? Refusal of absolution is a rare thing; and there
would surely be much discussion of it beforehand. You
would have to understand fully why the absolution was refused—and there wouldn't be any question of a penance.
Absolution is refused only because the person going to confession is not rightly disposed to receive it.

*Q. Can a person receive Holy Communion without going
to confession as long as they don't have mortal sin, or are
they supposed to go to confession every several weeks or so?
Lots of people do a lot of gossipping; still they go to Communion: it's no mortal sin.*

A. You are not obliged to go to confession at any set intervals
within the year; and you may go to Communion as long as
you are not guilty of mortal sin. Most of us, however, need
confession almost as much as we need Communion—especially if we do much gossipping; confession could help us to
quit it.
308

Q. I have heard the term "general confession" used, and I would like to know just what a general confession is, and which people use it most.

A. A general confession is a resume of the sins of your past life, or of a certain period of your past life. Sometimes I think people who like to use it most are those scrupulous persons who are always worried about past confessions, and always wanting to go back over the past for reassurance. For a short time after such "general confession" they feel a little more confident because of new evidence that the old sins are forgiven. But then they start worrying again, probably worse than ever, because they have stirred up the heap of their anxieties.

Scrupulous people should rarely make general confessions —and then only on the advice of a wise and prudent confessor.

General confessions are often used by pious people who want to advance more surely in sanctity, who review their past that they may do penance for it, and that they may profit in the future through the memory of forgiven errors. Such calm and sane general confessions may be helpful at retreat time, or before great status-changing events like marriage and ordination.

No one should ever make a general confession in a spirit of half-mistrust of the efficacy of former absolutions. When you make a good honest confession, and the priest speaks the words of absolution, as the minister of the sacrament of penance, he floods your soul with the grace of God's forgiveness. You need never be forgiven again for those same sins.

In spiritual things, as in the business world, it is well to keep current. Put the old files in storage and disturb them as little as possible, remembering only the lessons you have learned from past mistakes. All heaven and earth cannot erase a jot of them; but God's mercy has forgiven your guilt in them. Don't question his love by asking repeatedly if he really meant it.

309

Q. If I am given seven "Our Father's" and seven "Hail Mary's" as a penance in confession must I say them in any particular order? May I say one "Our Father" and one "Hail Mary" and then repeat that double prayer seven times? Or should I say all seven "Our Father's" and then all seven "Hail Mary's"?

A. Choose your own order; and it might help to vary it occasionally. The confessor could prescribe a special order, but he rarely does.

Q. It is a problem for a deaf person to go to confession; they say I talk so loud (I can't help it). Isn't there any way to write our sins and have the penance written out? Why is it so easy for a man to go to confession anywhere, but a woman must go in church (except for last rites, I know). I think confession should be made easier for a deaf woman, don't you?

A. Yes, I do think so, but I don't know exactly how to do it in every case. It is permissible, when the deafness is serious enough, to write out the confession and to have the penance written out.

Also the hearing of confessions of women outside the confessional is not restricted to the last rites. It may be done in cases of "infirmity, or real necessity." I believe that many good priests consider deafness to be an infirmity which justifies hearing the confession of women in the sacristy, or some other proper place.

Q. Is it possible to go to confession, be really sorry for a sin and really want to stop committing the sin, but still know that you will do it again? Is this a good confession?

A. Theologians tell us that we must have a firm positive intention of not committing a sin again in order to be honestly sorry for it and make a good confession. It is evident that such firm positive intention cannot exist alongside a definite plan of committing sin. Neither can it exist alongside a nebulous plan of probable sin which you keep hazy lest you admit your real intentions to yourself. In other words, you must be honest and not try to kid yourself—or God.

However, when we are dealing with sins of weakness, especially those which have become a habit or an emotional escape, we may have a determination as firm and honest as we can possibly make it, and yet know pretty darn well that sooner or later we will do it again. We have full confidence in the efficacy of God's grace, but from sad experience we also know our own weakness—and we don't expect miracles. Right now we are strongly determined, but we know that in the past our determination has never stayed at the sticking point. And still we make a good confession.

Q. A deaf person, after 40 years, developed a fear that past confessions were not made good; so she made a general confession, using a "Guide for Confession" book, and wrote the sins down the best way she knew how and asked the priest to read her confession, and received absolution. Now a year later, after reading the Catholic papers and books about sin and confession, she again fears that maybe she didn't confess everything just right. Should she make a general confession again? She loves her religion, but confession is such a nerve-wracking ordeal. My particular problem is that I am afraid the priest will ask questions and I will not understand. Many times I answered yes or no, and was not too sure what he asked.

A. It is very sad that good people become so afraid and worry about confession. It is the sacrament of the Lord's goodness, love and mercy. It is the last place in the world to expect his wrath and vengeance. Read Luke 7, 36-50. Do you find Jesus harsh, severe, or demanding with the penitent woman? She was evidently a sinner a hundred times more guilty than you

311

have ever been. But he did not make her get out a "Guide for Confession" book and write all her sins down. He did not grill her to make sure she got every detail just right. He simply said: "her sins, many as they are, shall be forgiven her, because she has loved much" . . . "Thy faith has saved thee; go in peace." He was a little rough with the Pharisee, who was not going to confession, but with the penitent he was gentle, kind, considerate and forgiving.

Then read John 8, 1-11. Do you find the Master strict and stern with the poor adultress? He apparently took delight in confusing her persecutors. But she was sorry for her sin; so he simply told her: "I will not condemn thee. Go thy way, and from now on sin no more."

His attitude towards you is similar when you go to confession. He will say something like this: "Dear lady, you are not really a very bad sinner, are you? But even if you were, I would forgive you quickly, because you do love me very much and are honestly sorry for your sins. I love you very much too; it was for you that I gave my life on the Cross. Now you are receiving the benefits of my death through this sacrament of my love and mercy. So don't be afraid; go now in peace and confidence; and I will help you to sin no more."

Why should an attitude like that frighten you? Can such kind and gentle words scare you? Are you afraid to be loved?

Please don't ever worry about your past confessions, and don't be repeating them or making general confessions. They were all perfectly good. How do I know? Because you wanted to make them good, and honestly tried; and when you have that attitude you simply can't make a bad confession. Can't you take my word for it?

Q. Could you tell us the moral obligation to reveal chronic or crippling physical and mental disease to the future marriage partner? I am thinking of such things as hemophilia, epilepsy, diabetes, T.B. These ills usually do not change a person's appearance, but they can bring huge medical bills in the future, financial stress, and can sometimes be passed on to the children, and cause all kinds of strains on the future spouse and family. May the innocent party in a case of this kind obtain an annulment?

A. I would not try to give specific advice to an individual in answer to a general question of this kind. I would want to talk to that individual and hear the whole story, and probe the individual's conscience and sense of responsibility.

In general, honesty is the best policy, and justice requires that we do to others as we would have them to do us. Marriage is a union of two minds and hearts, as well as two bodies. How can two minds be united when one deceives the other about something which vitally concerns the other?

Secrets may sometimes be rightly kept, when they concern things which will remain secret and which will not greatly affect the happiness of the marriage. But the things you mention will later come to light, and when they do they may destroy trust and confidence, and ultimately ruin love and happiness.

In health problems of this kind it would be well to consult your doctor and be guided by his advice.

In any case, the deceived party cannot get an annulment.

Q. Are two people in their sixties too old to be thinking of marriage? Each one is alone and would like to have a suitable companion. Neither one has ever been married. Or would it be better for them to remain single?

A. Since life begins at 40, they are really only in their twenties—a delightful age for marriage. And since two can live together as cheaply as one it is an awful waste for them to remain apart.

Q. My friend is going to be married. She made a serious mistake when she was very young. She says that she can wear white at her wedding and I think she shouldn't. Not

313

many people know about her mistake, and she argues that many women now are wearing white gowns when they are two and three months pregnant. So why can't she? If she can wear a white gown and veil, when did the Church law on this change?

A. The Church law doesn't tell a bride what she may or may not wear at her wedding. It is naturally expected that she will be modest and decent, and conform to the accepted customs of her country. Certainly the Church would not expect a repentant and reformed sinner to give public testimony to her fault. Let your friend wear what she wishes; I am sure she will look beautiful in white.

Q. My husband insists that when his grandparents married —a mixed marriage—only the children of one sex (I am not sure which) were to be raised as Catholics. Since we are a mixed marriage this is not the first time I have heard a reference to such an arrangement. Was this ever a practice anywhere?

A. In earlier days there were some local abuses—half-tolerated by the Church in some areas of Germany, for instance—by which boys were raised in the religion of the father and girls in the religion of the mother. Such arrangements never had the official approval of the Church.

Q. If a baptized Catholic has been married to a baptized Presbyterian in a Presbyterian church wedding and is later divorced, can either party marry again to a different partner in the Catholic Church? Is it a mortal sin to keep company with either of these persons?

A. I'll bet you are keeping company with a baptized Presbyterian. Right?

314

It is never possible to give a firm answer to a question of marriage nullity without having all the evidence on the table. However, you and I both know that Catholics can only be validly married before a priest; so it would certainly look like this marriage in which you are interested was invalid—which would leave both parties free to marry again.

Now don't rush off, on the basis of that statement, and start keeping steady company with this young lady (or gentleman). Take the matter up with your pastor, first, and have him refer the problem to the bishop. And even if you do obtain a declaration from the bishop that this person is free to marry, there still remain a couple of problems which deserve calm consideration:

1. Why was the first marriage a failure? Was it entirely the other person's fault? (Of course it always is!) What assurance do you have that this person's second marriage—to you—will be more successful than the first?

2. What about that mixed marriage problem? That needs some prayer and consultation, as well as objective thinking.

Q. When Our Lord said: "The man who puts away his wife, save on account of immorality, etc.," does that mean that a man or woman cannot get a separation from each other except for reason of immorality? I understand, of course, that divorce and remarriage are not permissible, but what about other causes for separation, such as unending quarreling and nagging?

A. The Church law regarding separation of husband and wife is found in Canons 1128—1132 of the Code of Canon Law:

Husband and wife must live together and maintain conjugal life, unless a sufficient reason permits them to do otherwise.

For reason of adultery, the innocent party may separate from the guilty one, and make that separation permanent. However, he must be really an innocent party—not guilty of

315

adultery himself. And he must not have given his consent to the sin, or later condoned or forgiven it. He is considered to have condoned and forgiven it if he takes his wife back, with full knowledge of her guilt, and continues to live with her as a loving husband—or if he just lets the matter rest for six months, without throwing her out, leaving her, or making formal accusation against her.

All that is said above is true for the innocent wife also. Just change the pronouns. There is no double standard in this matter.

The innocent party may later take the guilty one back, even after their separation has been formally authorized by the Church.

Adultery is the only thing which automatically permits permanent separation, but there are a variety of things which permit temporary separation—for as long as the reasons continue. In these cases the separation may actually be permanent, if the reasons never cease. The difference is that the guilty party does not give up all right to reunion, and the innocent one must take the guilty one back when reform is established. These reasons are:

1. One spouse joins a non-Catholic Church;
2. One spouse educates the children as non-Catholics;
3. Either husband or wife becomes a criminal and a reprobate;
4. There is serious danger to either soul or body from the cohabitation;
5. Cruelties are such that they make conjugal life too difficult;
6. Other reasons similar to these.

Usually before one party may separate from the other for any of these reasons the matter must be presented to the bishop, who is to judge the sufficiency of the reasons and authorize the separation. The only exception is when the existence of one of these reasons is certain, and there is danger in delay.

In case of separation, children are to be given into the care of the innocent party. If one party is non-Catholic they are to be given into the care of the Catholic party. In either

316

case, however, the bishop can make other arrangements for the good of the children, as long as their Catholic education is secured.

In none of this is there any provision for civil divorce. The Church law simply ignores such procedure. The bishop will sometimes tolerate it if (1) it is necessary to protect property or other civil right, and (2) the parties, or at least the party obtaining it fully understands that it gives no right to remarriage and sincerely promises to live and act as a married person should while living separate from the other spouse.

Q. After ten years of marriage, and having adopted two children, I am now expecting a baby. Will you please tell me what are my responsibilities as to the baby's burial in the event of a miscarriage?

A. First of all, congratulations to you, and to your husband. I hope you may have no trouble at all, but may have a strong and healthy baby. And if you should have a miscarriage, the problem of burial would be the last thing about which you need to be seriously concerned. First give thought to baptism if the foetus is discernible and if there is reasonable chance that it is alive. Immerse it in water, and as you open the membranes which enclose it, say, "I baptize you in the name of the Father, and of the Son, and of the Holy Ghost."

Canon 1203 of the Code of Canon Law requires that the bodies of the faithful deceased must be buried; and their cremation is disapproved. But your little aborted foetus is not one of the faithful, if it died before being baptized; and it is hardly a body, in the ordinary sense of the word until it has taken on very definite development and growth. I am sure that the law of Canon 1203 does not apply to the tiny aborted foetus with anything like the same rigor it has for the grown body. And I base my opinion largely on an instruction given by the Holy Office, on Aug. 3, 1897, regarding the disposal of amputated members. The preference is,

317

of course, that they be buried, if it can be done reasonably and without great trouble or expense. But the Holy Office is really very tolerant about other methods of disposal.

It is quite possible that your miscarriage will be completed in a hospital—if you should be unfortunate enough to have one. In that case you can leave the problem of disposing of the foetus to the hospital. It will probably go to the laboratory and be examined by the pathologist. Then, even though it is a Catholic hospital, the odds are that it will be decorously and properly cremated.

Of course, if it is a definite baby in size and features, then you will naturally want to bury it as your own child. In most states you will require a burial permit, a cemetery lot, and the services of an undertaker.

15. *Sanctions*

Meaning of Excommunication.
Public Sinner. Sacrilegious Communions. Denial of Sacraments. Religion of the Excommunicated. Marriage before¹ a J.P. Secret Sins.
Limbo. Requirements for Heaven.
Desire for Hell.

Q. Please explain about excommunication. It worries me.
If a person through fear or ignorance failed to receive the
sacraments for years, would he be excommunicated.

A. Quit worrying. Excommunications do not sneak up on
you; they always challenge you openly. You could never be
excommunicated for anything you might do through fear or
ignorance, but only for a crime which you commit deliberately, with full knowledge that excommunication is the
punishment provided for it by law.

The Church will never punish you for doubts or worries
or even intentional errors in making your confession. About
the only excommunication a Catholic layman would be apt
to incur would be for procuring an abortion, marrying before a minister, marrying after a divorce, or having children
baptized or educated in a non-Catholic religion. Of course,
you might fight a duel, but it isn't popular anymore.

Excommunication prevents a person from receiving the
sacraments and from sharing in many spiritual privileges of

319

Church membership. It is always taken away as soon as the sinner has given definite evidence of repentance.

Q. In a local daily newspaper we saw a picture of a notorious Hollywood star and her children in a Catholic Church apparently praying and attending Mass.

Why wasn't this scandalous person ejected from the church during Mass? We believe she is a public sinner, and after reading your articles on excommunication we believe this should have happened.

A. Probably this beautiful transgressor is no worse sinner than that poor woman of Jerusalem about whom Jesus said: "Let him who is without sin among you be the first to cast a stone at her."

Our Lord was not commending her actions when he concluded, "Neither will I condemn thee. Go thy way, and from now on sin no more." He was merely showing mercy, and reminding us that we should examine our own consciences before we start throwing stones at sinners. Thank God, none of our sins get the publicity given to this movie star. But the good Lord in his heaven sees all, and maybe he finds some of her flamboyant sins no worse than our secret ones.

We may readily agree that she is not a model Catholic—far from it. But I have no reason to believe that she is excommunicated. If the Church started excommunicating all sinners—even public ones—her ranks would be sadly depleted.

Excommunicated persons are deprived of the right to receive the sacraments and to gain indulgencies; but they may still use and receive the sacramentals, unless there has been a formal public decree of excommunication issued against them, and that is very rare. In theory excommunicated persons are deprived of the right of assisting at Mass, but the Church law is explicit that they are not to be thrown out when they assist privately—like the ordinary layman. The only exception is for a special type of excommunicated person, called in Latin "vitandus"—to be avoided.

320

No excommunicated person is "vitandus" unless the Holy See publicly proclaims that he is excommunicated and must be shunned—in religious matters—by all Catholics. Such procedure is extremely rare.

Most people have a fearful idea of excommunication, as though it were some cruel form of medieval torture. Actually it is a stern reminder by a loving and motherly Church that some sins are very serious, that for our own good and the welfare of society we must avoid them, and that we need to repent quickly and thoroughly if we have committed them. The Church law calls excommunication a medicinal punishment; its purpose is to help the sinner recover his spiritual health quickly and thoroughly—and to prevent a relapse.

Q. I read in your column about absolving excommunicated persons, especially for the sin of abortion. I know a person who got absolution from that crime the first time she went to confession. What must she do if the confessor who gave her the absolution didn't write to the bishop for faculties or permission to absolve her? If this person felt she was in the right and lived in the faith ever since, for many years, has she made sacrilegious Communions?

A. If this person was honestly sorry for her sin and was absolved, then her sin was forgiven, and that is all there is to it.

Oftentimes the person who is guilty of a crime does not incur the excommunication which the law provides for that crime. There may be various reasons, but the most common is that this person did not fully understand, at the time, that this penalty was provided. In matters of this kind ignorance of the law excuses from the punishment.

If the person did not actually incur the penalty of excommunication, then any confessor can absolve her the first time she goes to confession with honest sorrow.

Often the particular confessor may have faculties to absolve from various excommunications. Maybe the bishop has

321

given them to him for a particular occasion, like a mission, or a retreat, or during the Easter season. Maybe he has received these faculties because of a particular position he holds.

Anyway that is not for the penitent to figure out. It is for the priest to worry about. If he gives you absolution, you are absolved. The Church supplies any lack of authority or jurisdiction he might have.

Since your friend was absolved at the time she went to confession there can be no question of sacrilegious Communions. But, for the sake of argument, even if she had not been rightly absolved, her Communions would not be sacrilegious—because she received them in good faith. You cannot commit a sacrilege without fully knowing and intending it. Those things do not creep up on you unaware.

Q. I saw by the paper the other day where a young lady that was a queen candidate for something or other was told by her bishop that if she appeared in public before the judges in a bathing suit he wouldn't permit her or her mother to receive the sacraments for a certain period of time. Does he have the power to do this?

A. First of all, I don't think it is proper for us to be passing judgment on the official acts of a bishop—especially one in a remote part of the country, where the problem is really none of our business—and especially on the basis of newspaper reports, which are notoriously inaccurate in matters of this kind.

I seriously doubt that the bishop has threatened to deny the sacraments to these women for a certain period of time. Denial of Holy Communion may not be used as a punishment. It may be done only because the person is evidently unworthy to receive the Sacrament; and as soon as this person repents and becomes worthy and repairs the scandal given, then Holy Communion may no longer be denied. It would hardly be possible to fix a definite time for repentance, reform, or even the undoing of scandal. So I am guessing that this part of your report is wrong.

While the bishop may not directly deny the sacraments as a method of punishment, he can impose a penalty of excommunication on a person who violates a law—and this excommunication prevents the person from receiving the sacraments. Usually a bishop imposes excommunication only after he has warned the person ahead of time—and then the law is violated with full awareness that the punishment will be incurred. That might well be the case here.

However, even an excommunication must be removed when the person has honestly repented and repaired the harm and scandal as far as possible. So it could not be imposed for a definite period of time.

Canon 855 of the Code of Canon Law states that those who are publicly unworthy are to be prevented from receiving the Holy Eucharist and a person may be publicly unworthy because he is excommunicated, under personal interdict or openly infamous. There is no difficulty in knowing which persons are excommunicated or under interdict, but there is some latitude of interpretation as to who is openly infamous. The term is generally taken to include those who live in invalid marriages or in concubinage, those who lead a notoriously dissolute life, or practice a profession forbidden by civil law—and finally those who would give scandal to people generally if they were permitted to receive.

This last group leaves some leeway for personal judgment. For instance, if some woman were to present herself at the Communion railing in dress which was frankly and shockingly immodest and startlingly contrary to the accepted customs of the locality, she should be refused Holy Communion for this reason. And I would judge that it is for similar reason that this bishop is refusing the Sacrament to our little bathing beauty. In his judgment her participation in a vulgar display of feminine charm and vanity would be a source of scandal, because it would seem to give Catholic approval to immodesty. He may have had other reasons which he judged sufficient to cause him, in the interest of public morality, to forbid her to make this publicized display of herself.

323

I can understand his forbidding the sacraments to her on this basis, until she gives satisfactory signs of repentance. And as for the mother, it must be that the bishop judges her guilty of scandalous encouragement and cooperation in the plans of her daughter. He could hardly make it a requirement that the mother prevent her daughter from participating; most mothers don't wield that kind of influence with their daughters—especially with those who are pretty, vivacious and forward enough to be in beauty contests.

Q. When a Catholic becomes excommunicated what religion would he be? If you are once a Catholic doesn't that imprint remain on your soul, so that you are always a Catholic, good or bad?

A. The excommunicated person remains a Catholic, unless he has given up his faith or been guilty of heresy. He is simply a bad Catholic who, because of his crimes, has been deprived of many of the privileges and benefits of membership in the Church. As soon as he repents and straightens himself out he will be absolved from his excommunication and restored to good standing.

Q. What is the punishment for a Catholic who marries before a minister or a justice of the peace? Some think all he has to do is go to confession and all is forgiven. Then he may go out and marry any Catholic before a priest and everything will be perfect in the sight of the Catholic Church.

A. The Church law states definitely that a Catholic can only marry validly before a priest and two witnesses. His attempted marriage before a minister or a justice of the peace is only a fake and a pretense—no real marriage at all. Besides, if he goes before a minister for his ceremony, he is excommunicated.

Now your question supposes that he has tired of his bargain and rid himself, by legal means, of the woman with whom he had been living—in concubinage, as we might bluntly call it. Should the Church refuse him the right to repent and be forgiven? She couldn't refuse a murderer or a thief. His crime is much less. Of course, if he is excommunicated the matter will have to go to the bishop, and a special penance will be imposed. But otherwise, if he honestly repents, God will forgive him. Shouldn't we?

A shady past does not disqualify a man from marriage; it should only be a stern warning to the girl who thinks of marrying him. And remember, this man never did have a real wife—just a partner whom the state considered his wife.

Q. Most of us shudder to think of our secret sins being revealed at the Last Judgment. But what of those sins which are acceptable to society, like birth control and malicious gossip? Will they be shown in their true ugliness?

A person can be consistently guilty of both these sins and still be a social leader in almost any Catholic parish. What of the people who sacrifice themselves and their families to avoid these sins? The women who bear children despite poor health and poverty? The people who don't criticize in return for criticism? And those who do not seek revenge? Are they idiots?

A. Probably the only ones who will not greatly mind having their hidden sins revealed are those who are truly humble. They are honest during life, never trying to create false impressions or maintain a fake front. They are discreet and do not go around bleating and moaning about their secret sins. That type of humility is only a guilt complex seeking an excuse, or the salve of sympathy.

The Last Judgment will be the supreme moment of truth. We can be sure that all sins will appear in their veritable colors. The weak and wasted will trade their shame for true sorrow. The snobs and Pharisees will crumple before the

325

accusing eye of Truth and the scorn of those they tried to deceive.

You will find an inspiring answer to your final question in our Lord's own words (Matt. 5, 3-10): "Blessed are the poor in spirit . . . the meek . . . they who mourn . . . they who hunger and thirst for justice . . . they who suffer persecution for justice's sake, for theirs is the kingdom of heaven."

To Almighty God the wisdom and cleverness of the world is often eternal foolishness; and the idiots of the world may later know God in his infinite perfection.

Certainly Jesus was not advising us to be idiots when he told us: "But I say to you not to resist the evildoer; on the contrary, if someone strike thee on the right cheek, turn to him the other also, and if anyone would go to law with thee and take thy tunic, let him take thy cloak as well; and whoever forces thee to go for one mile, go with him two" (Matt. 5, 39-41).

"Love your enemies, do good to those who hate you, and pray for those who persecute and calumniate you"—not that you may be idiots, but "that you may be children of your Father in heaven" (Matt. 5, 44-45).

Q. It is my understanding that Limbo is for children only. Adults who have lived according to their convictions, though not baptized with water, have baptism of desire, and thus are eligible for heaven. The fact that they have tried to live good lives automatically creates a baptism of desire. This, with sorrow for any wrongdoing, offers one a good chance for Heaven. Am I right or wrong?

A. In general outline you are right, but you have simplified it too much, and made it seem too easy. Stop and think how hard it is for us who have the faith and the sacraments to keep ourselves in the state of grace and on that steep and narrow road of virtue! Am I to believe that some un-baptized person with vague good intentions and a general sorrow for wrongdoing will whizz past me on the wings of his convictions while I plod along with my penances, prayers, and the daily strength of Christ in the Eucharist?

Let us say rather that salvation is possible for the person who has a baptism of desire, but it is precarious and difficult. The baptism of desire does not result from a casual set of easy convictions. It supposes deep sincerity and an honest love of God. It means, in accordance with ability, at least as much sorrow for sin as we would need for an act of perfect contrition.

Q. I have been told that if a woman dies in childbirth she will go right to heaven. Will you let me know if this is true?

A. The basic requirement for getting to heaven is that we have sanctifying grace in our souls. Childbirth cannot supply that, if it is lacking. It is possible to imagine that a mother might be in the state of mortal sin when she gives birth to her child. The pains of labor would not necessarily make her repent. Even the threat of death might not make her love God.

Another requirement for getting into heaven is freedom from venial sin, and forgiveness of all the temporal punishment due for past sins. Childbirth cannot forgive venial sins, except as it increases the mother's love for God and leads her to repentance. The pains and dangers of childbirth may well be a means of taking away temporal punishment for sins—provided that they are accepted in the right spirit: with love and penance and resignation. Even then we may wonder if they replace all the pains of purgatory.

God surely loves the mother who is working with him to bring a new person into the world. But she does not necessarily love God. And their love must be mutual to be sanctifying.

Q. I know a person who has asked the Lord to take him to hell, many times. Are these sins pardonable? This person now is very sorry he has said this. Can he be forgiven?

A. A person can be forgiven any sin if he is honestly sorry for it because he loves God and does not want to lose heaven. I am very doubtful whether your desperate friend committed a great sin. He probably was not serious in his foolish request; he meant no blasphemy; did not really despair. He was only discouraged, disgusted, disconsolate, and indiscreet. He was also frustrated by failure to find adequate expression for his desperation. No one in his right mind would seriously choose hell; though many of us who think we are rational make deliberate choices which have hell as a consequence.

16. *Modern Problems*

Q. Can you help me straighten out my thinking on racial integration? Until the recent Supreme Court decision I never gave it a thought. Since the Church has become involved in it, I find myself wondering what view it takes on various aspects of the situation. For instance, what is the view of the Catholic Church on interracial marriage—which might be one of the results of complete integration. Also, in social gatherings for young people, such as dances, etc., does the Catholic Church believe that integration should be complete and unbiased? Should white and colored boys and girls mix in dances, as escorts, etc.?

A. Your questions are the ones which drive our Southern friends frantic. Their favorite rationalization against permitting Negroes into white schools is that it will be a step on the way to interracial marriage. And when that dirty word is mentioned they start shooting in defense of Southern womanhood.

Basically you are right in believing that this is a social problem rather than a religious one. But no aspect of social relations can be completely divorced from moral principles. Furthermore, the Church lives in society, and is made up of the same human individuals who constitute society. She brings people together in churches, conducts schools and hospitals for the members of society. So she is constantly called upon to put her own principles into practice.

The same rules of justice and charity which regulate your individual relations with your neighbor apply to the complicated relations of millions of you's with millions of neighbors. We each have rights and duties. But they are human rights and human duties; not white rights and white duties, or Negro rights and Negro duties. Our rights are inherent in our human personality, not in our color.

The Church is usually in no great haste to change established social custom. She has a long history of tolerating abuses rather than stirring up conflict. But when the issues come out in the open and her sound principles are challenged or denied she must speak up loudly and firmly.

Right now there is in our country sharp, and often bitter, controversy as to what rights a colored man has. What would you have the Church do? Pussyfoot? Hedge? Both doctrine and morality are involved in this controversy, and on the basis of both doctrine and morality the answers are very clear and certain. The only possible controversy among Catholics would involve means and methods, speed or delay. In these circumstances, even though it heighten the conflict, the Church must speak out firmly. She must fulfill her divine mission of teaching the truth of Christ, even though some of her stubborn, hard-headed members get sore and leave her.

So the Church insists on the equality of all men before God, and their equal rights before the law. In our modern society this implies that there can be no distinction, on the basis of race or color, in the fair and equal use of public facilities, such as schools, streets, parks, and the voting booth. It means that equal protection must be provided human life and liberty regardless of color: fair police action, just and equitable procedure in the courts, and freedom from mob threats and violence. It means equal economic opportunity, freedom of speech and assembly, freedom of worship, opportunity for decent housing, opportunity for education and self-development, and all those other rights and privileges which we prize so highly as American citizens.

The Church is not committed to undue haste in solving problems which are rooted deep in social custom and prejudice. She does feel that she should lead the way cautiously. But she knows that you can't force men against their perverse will in matters of this kind. She can teach and admonish, however, and pray that grace will mellow perversity.

In your individual personal relations, justice and charity seldom dictate your choice of friends and companions. Social equality demands that we show people the courtesy, respect and consideration which they deserve by reason of their personality and behavior, without regard to color. It does not demand that we ask any particular person or group or class of persons into our home, or make them our drinking companions. You don't consider yourself guilty of sin if you refuse to date Protestants, Jews, or pagans. On the contrary, your pastor urges you to keep company only with your own, lest you run the danger of a mixed marriage.

Interracial marriages are not forbidden by law of the Church. Some moralists believe that in our actual American society they are forbidden by general moral law because of (1) the dangers to matrimonial harmony which result from diversity of background, tradition, and social attitudes, (2) the tensions that are produced between families and friends, (3) the social ostracism which will be a burden on marital life, and (4) the problems which will be created for the children.

So while interracial marriage remains basically a matter of personal choice, it is in our society highly inadvisable, and any priest will feel in duty bound to point this out to you, if you consult him. And if marriage is inadvisable then the

331

type of association which would lead to marriage is likewise inadvisable—and the objections are just as strong for the Negro as they are for the white person. To see it from the other side: Protestants should not keep company with Catholics; Negroes should not keep company with whites—for their own good. And there are always exceptions to every general rule.

Q. The question of interracial marriage came up recently in a discussion in our history class. I would appreciate it very much if you would please set us straight on what the Church's viewpoint is on this subject.

A. I am taking your question to apply to a marriage between a Negro person and a white person. Many of the things I write here are not applicable to other interracial marriages in most parts of the United States.

One basic point should be made thoroughly clear: There is no law of God against interracial marriage, and no law of the Church which forbids or discourages it. There is no biological argument against it—unless you consider it an argument that the child will inherit various characteristics of each parent, including color.

Many of our State laws forbid marriages between people of different races. Marriages between Negroes and whites are forbidden in 29 of our 49 States—even in such northern and liberal States as the Dakotas, Nebraska, Oregon and Nevada. Orientals and whites are forbidden to intermarry in 15 States. And whites may not marry American Indians in four States. At least one State has the double standard: in South Carolina a white man may marry a Chinese woman; but a white woman may not marry a Chinese man. In North Carolina a Negro may marry any Indian except a Robeson County Cherokee.

A California law forbidding interracial marriages has been declared unconstitutional; and it is quite possible that the future of all of them is in jeopardy. But meanwhile they present various legal problems of nullity, and in many States other serious penalties as well. I think we can say with certainty that these State laws have no moral validity for baptized people—but the hard fact of them is inescapable.

In practice, there is one valid objection to these marriages: the rigid reality of prejudice. Social opposition is strong; interracial marriages fly in the face of our established custom. And society is bitterly determined to see that those who defy its customs shall pay dearly the price of their nonconformity. It will persecute the defiant couple all the days of their life, and will put a curse on their children to the third and fourth generation. Mutual friends will be few, in-laws will do battle, housing will be unavailable, brickbats will be thrown, and jeers will rival sneers in integrated schools.

Prejudice is a hard and heartless fact. We may hate it, but we can never equal its hate. It is an ignorant man's substitute for thought. It excludes charity and is blind to justice. It is tenacious and often ruthless. Yet we must live with it. We may fight against it with harmless arguments, but when we frankly defy it we find it harshly inflexible. We might as well batter our heads against an opposing wall.

By profession and instinct I am an idealist, especially where justice and charity are concerned. I would like to be able to counsel a man to marry whomever he wants: to ignore narrow prejudice, to rise above carping reactionaries, and to scorn superstitious taboos. But when people actually come to me for advice I find it better to put my ideals under the restraint of unpleasant facts: social facts, man-made facts, immoral and unjust facts, but inexorable realities, none the less.

Marriage is a life-long project. Even the best union will encounter difficulties and problems. But when we multiply and magnify the obstacles to its success we all but doom it. Defiance of evil custom is a fine and laudable action in the man who has courage and strength to carry it off. We all admire the hero and revere the martyr. But matrimony should not be a martyrdom. And after the glamour of romance wears thin will the defiant hero have courage to persevere? Or will resentments gnaw him into acerbity and remorse ruin his resolve?

Q. After reading your discussion of interracial marriage I felt that you should hear from one of "those" marriages. My husband and I have been married 12 years. We find that we are definitely not social cast-offs, have many friends of both races, and friends in our neighborhood. Our children, who are three in number, are not jeered or called names. Perhaps we just live in a civilized community, but we have not been persecuted in any way. Our housing problems were no more difficult than anyone else's. And after all these years there has been no suffering.

Oh, yes, by the way, after 12 years the "glamour" has worn off, and the result has been a deeper, more understanding love and companionship than ever. It has not resulted in regret or resentment at all. Neither of us feels we are martyrs, because we love each other.

I must also mention that our in-laws are friendly and visit each other when they find it possible.

Now I can find no "great price" that I have paid for my marriage. I find that my children have not been cursed because they are products of an interracial marriage. We enjoy life as any other couple. With our faith in God we have learned to ignore the few ignorant, prejudiced people with whom we have come in contact. It doesn't take a stiff spine to rise above that type of thing, merely an open mind. There will always be prejudices and hatreds in this world; and why should we deprive ourselves of happiness because of this? They are the ones who will later suffer in hell for their injustice.

When we married we were prepared to "give up the world" for each other, and I might add that we still are; but so far we haven't had to give up anything. Maybe we are just one in a million, but I don't think so. There are many couples like us.

A. Never have I been so pleased to be refuted. But I did hedge my generalizations by stating that no type of marriage is doomed to failure. Your letter helps prove my prudence in leaving an avenue of escape. And you prove much more: that the success of the marriage depends on the partners, on their personalities and temperaments, their love and unselfishness, their willingness to make sacrifices and overlook the petty things of life, their faith and trust in God, their confidence in friends and neighbors. Some of these things are explicit in your letter; others are implied.

I think all of us—and married couples in particular—can learn a great lesson from your letter. Success and happiness in life depend ultimately on ourselves—with the help of God. Too often, we blame failure on external factors: on prejudices, enmities, and discrimination—on bad luck, bad weather, and poor tools. We seek alibis rather than reasons— find excuses instead of shouldering the blame. Each man's happiness must come from within himself. And marriage adjustments must start with the first person singular; it is difficult to force the partner into adjustment and impossible to greatly alter the attitudes of our friends and neighbors.

And I thank you for reminding me that an open mind may often serve better than a stiff spine as a cushion against life's jolts.

Q. In the list of sins which you gave recently you made no mention of discrimination like that in Louisiana. Against which commandment does this come? It must be a sin or people could not be excommunicated for it.

A. It certainly is a sin, and it fits under various commandments. It breaks at least five of the ten:

THE FIRST Commandment requires that we exercise the virtue of charity, by loving God above all things, for His own sake, and our neighbor as ourselves, for the love of God. Those who bar a Negro priest from the altar certainly have a strange way of showing their love for Christ's personal representative. Those who try to bar little black children from Catechism class and beat up their teachers should listen

335

again to the gentle words of Jesus: "Suffer the little children to come unto me, and forbid them not, for of such is the kingdom of heaven."

THE FOURTH Commandment obliges us to respect and obey the authority of Holy Mother Church. It was contemptuous violation of authority which was the immediate cause of Archbishop Rummel's interdict on the parish at Jesuit Bend. A similar spirit of contempt and revolt caused Bishop Jeanmard to impose his excommunications. Both these penalties are medicinal or remedial in purpose. As soon as they had accomplished their purpose of correction they were removed.

THE FIFTH Commandment deals generally with the virtue of justice in matters of personal rights, such as life, health, liberty and equality. When you deny a man that measure of equality demanded by human dignity you kill him in part—in his spirit at least.

This Commandment also forbids scandal, and those Catholic people in Louisiana gave nationwide scandal, which the prompt action of their bishops largely repaired, with a good lesson taught.

THE SEVENTH Commandment demands, among other types of justice, that which we call distributive. It demands that all the members of society participate fairly in the common goods, benefits, and facilities of society. Discrimination violates distributive justice and the seventh commandment most flagrantly.

THE EIGHTH Commandment demands respect for a man's honor and standing in the community. Discrimination debases him—insults him—dishonors him.

Q. I am a colored convert to the Catholic religion, and accepted it as it was taught to me by Father B. He explained about some of the parishioners, but I had no idea that the priest and Sisters would tell us that they can't accept us at a school because we are colored.

In our parish the only sodality is the Altar and Rosary,

and the colored women are not welcome to join. My daughter is graduating from eighth grade in June, but the principal of the Catholic high school tells me they have no colored there. I am puzzled, and whenever I ask why all they tell me is: "It is unfortunate"; and some won't even answer.

What explanation do you give a child who wants to know: "Is there white Catholicism and colored Catholicism"?

I have four children, three in school and one to go next year. I would appreciate it if you could better explain this to me.

A. Maybe just the publication of your letter will do more good than any words of mine as a subject of meditation for clergy, religious, and laity. I might say, thankfully, that this letter does not come from our diocese; but it does come from a place far north of the Mason-Dixon line.

For my questioner, who is naturally puzzled, my only explanation is that many Catholics do not live up to the things their Church teaches—and some priests and Sisters are too ready to compromise on principle to conform to social customs and demands.

There are problems, of course, in some areas. We cannot change ingrained customs and prejudices over night. But we don't need to share them or encourage them.

I can understand why "some won't even answer"; they have no answer. They know it is all wrong, but they don't know what to do about it.

My only practical advice to you is to be patient and to pray, and to offer up the insults and injustices you suffer, in union with Christ's similar sufferings on Calvary.

Q. I assume there is no challenge to the statement that the Church has for a good long time tolerated the separation of the races in matters religious in the South.

That being so the parishioners of the segregated congre-

gations certainly have had reason to think such conditions were not in conflict with the position of the Church, have they not?

If the above are true why does the Church suddenly threaten or invoke excommunication for adherence to what it has itself so long permitted? Could it not more charitably use a gradual approach?

A. How gradual should the approach be? It is probable that the snail's pace of the past century has served to create the false impression you point out.

Can even a gradual approach be without incident amid the turbulent hatreds and fears now being fanned by demagogues in certain areas of the South?

I had opportunity to visit a little corner of the South recently and to talk to serious people who discussed objectively the problems ahead. No thinking person should try to minimize those problems which are rooted deeply in tradition, social custom, and passionate conviction, mingled with fear. But I carried away the impression that if spouting politicians and professional hatemongers could be capped like gushers, there would be hope for eventual and fairly peaceful solution.

The Church has been proceeding with gradual force for some time in various parts of the South. The progress has flamed incidents, but in time the embers hardly glow. How many years ago is it that the Archbishop of St. Louis had his faithful followers swarming violently about his head seeking his scalp? They have long since been peaceful. The Bishop of Raleigh, a forceful Southerner, had to personally confront a rebellious congregation a few years ago to bring about integration at Mass. Archbishop Rummel's recent interdict is far from the first flame he has kindled, but his progress has been notable. And the Bishop of Lafayette apparently achieved his purpose with a little temporary and salutary excommunication.

Your point is well taken, but I fail to see that the Church is going too fast. Her progress is usually characterized by an oft-quoted motto: *festina lente*—make haste slowly. She has often been too slow in the past, but her pace, already increasing in recent years, has been abruptly accelerated by the Supreme Court. Would you now have her lag behind and let civil authority teach her the message of Christ? Before she might silently tolerate without scandal. Now that the question is sharply raised she must speak clearly or seem to side with error.

You might wish that problem of school integration had never been raised; it is often more comfortable to ignore social evils when we do not suffer from them personally. But now that the issue is openly joined, Catholics are obliged by clear indications of justice and charity to align themselves definitely against all forms of enforced segregation—at least in principle. In some cases you may rightly argue the need for time and prudence in subverting established customs, and the futility of the law in trying to force the stubborn and inflamed will of the majority. But the difficulties of achieving justice do not alter the principles involved. It may often be impossible for a man to obtain his rights; but that does not permit us to deny that he has the rights, before God and in accord with the vaunted equality of our Constitution.

In much of the argument on this sensitive subject we find it hard to distinguish between sound reason and convenient rationalization. In a matter so complicated it is easy to make prejudice plausible, and to confuse convention with morality. The basic principle is clear and simple: it is unjust to discriminate against any group or individual by reason of race. We are guilty of sin if we demand that one racial group accept an inferior position and deny them equal public advantages. To segregate them against their will is definitely to deny them equality.

It is for this reason that I have been saddened to see Catholics, in my own liberal community taking a leading and scandalous role in eliminating Negroes from barber shops and appealing to the courts to enforce racial restrictions on housing.

339

Q. On the second Sunday of each month the men of our parish are urged to attend the Holy Name Mass. At the conclusion of the Mass a pledge is made that they will observe all civil law. The law of the State of Iowa, according to popular interpretation, prohibits bingo, regardless of "nom de plume" or subterfuge; yet many Holy Name men are urged to manage such games. Please explain how one can take such a pledge and then in good conscience participate in such activities.

A. First of all, let us eliminate the pledge. It doesn't add anything to the moral obligation we all have of observing the civil law. It simply emphasizes that obligation. Of course it does contain a promise; so if the pledge were made in bad faith it would be a false promise. A person would be guilty of a lie. But if it were made in sincere good faith and then broken, there would be no sin from breaking the pledge—though there might be sin from breaking the law.

Our moral theologians are not in agreement as to the obligation created in conscience by some of our civil laws. All agree that the legislature of our State and the Congress of the United States can make laws which bind us directly in conscience. But the question is, in many cases: Do they intend to so obligate us—under pain of sin and before God?

It might be argued that our legislators are not much concerned with obligation in conscience. They know that such obligation would produce very unequal results in the enforcement of laws. Some people would obey conscientiously from religious motives, others would obey because of patriotism or respect for order and the good of society, and others would scorn the whole business, laugh at the laws and do as they blightingly well please. So the legislators provide penalties stiff enough and police numerous enough to see that their laws get obeyed.

Other moralists hold that regardless of the explicit intention of the legislators the common good requires that laws be obeyed by the general populace out of respect, or obedience, or some such superior motive inspired by love of God

340

or country. The penalties are there primarily to take care of the irresponsible or malicious characters who have no dependable sense of duty. Consequently these moralists would say that most civil laws do bind us in conscience, under pain of sin.

Most of these stricter moralists would admit that there are some laws which require no direct obligation in conscience for their proper enforcement. The most obvious example is a parking ordinance. No one believes that he commits sin by over-time parking, but he knows well that if he finds a red sticker on his windshield he will have to pay his fine.

Some people believe that our Iowa laws against gambling are in the same class as parking ordinances—mere penal laws which create no direct obligation in conscience, but simply require that you accept your punishment if you get caught.

Other people think that this is the gangster's way of looking at laws—that it tends to create a general disrespect for all laws, and hence undermines the common welfare.

Some people even maintain that our Iowa gambling laws are unjust and create no valid obligation, because they deprive us of our natural right to the free disposition of our own property. Others say, no, that these laws are made to protect the common welfare of our people from the organized rackets which pursue gambling and seek to control it.

What is the answer? I don't think it is clear-cut. On the one hand, it is not for you or me to decide that a law is unjust. That is a question for our courts to decide, by due process.

On the other hand, you and I both know that our little personal game of gin rummy in no way threatens the common welfare and is a legitimate exercise of our rights as free citizens—regardless of the intemperate threats of an ambitious attorney general.

But when it comes to public bingo games conducted by a Church organization I think we must give due consideration to the effect our action will have upon general respect for law and hence upon the common welfare. We cannot lightly dismiss the whole matter as a mere penal law. There is a question of scandal—in the strict sense of the word—of lead-

341

ing people into general disobedience. If the games are conducted in such way as to stay within the letter of the law and that fact is apparent, then all right! Few of us have much sympathy with this law in many of its applications. But if the holding of the game is a flouting of the law, made possible by local laxity in enforcement, then I think we should give thought to higher obligations—or campaign to have the law repealed.

Q. What right do priests have to interfere in labor-management relations? Aren't they a little out of their field? I think that these matters should be left to men who are working in that field, i.e., Chamber of Commerce, N.A.M., etc.

A. Your question looks like a "plant" to me. Else why didn't you include the Communist Party and the W.C.T.U. in your list of competent agencies? Who ever accused the Chamber of Commerce of competence in the field of labor relations? Who ever suspected the N.A.M. of lack of prejudice? Ever hear of the N.L.R.B.?

The QUESTION BOX does not dodge questions because they are "plants," or issues because they are hot. We are quite willing to help grind axes, and we prefer double-bitted ones. Then, watch out for the chips!

The Church is vitally concerned with the moral aspects of labor-management relations, in which justice and charity are directly involved. The Church is the divinely appointed teacher and arbiter of justice. Christian charity is her primary field of activity.

The Church has similar vital interests in various secular fields where ethics and morality are involved, e.g., in medicine and surgery, where the fifth commandment often rules; in family relations, where the fourth and sixth commandments are concerned; in law and business, which are particularly regulated by the seventh commandment.

There are secularists galore who would try to drive the Church from all such fields, and take from her other precious

342

rights which have been her own for centuries, e.g. education. There are those who demand: What right do priests have to interfere in problems involving abortion, or birth control, or euthanasia, or fraud, or delinquency. It is the same as asking: What right do priests have to preach the moral law of God?

The Church is concerned with men, as individuals created by God and endowed by Him with spiritual and immortal souls. The Church was established by God to save those souls. It is her task to lead men to God. Labor is not a commodity; labor is men. Jesus Christ died for those men. By sanctifying grace he raises them to the dignity of sons of God. He makes them his brothers, members of his Church, part of his Mystical Body.

The Church is concerned with the divinely-given rights of men: Their right to life and liberty, and to the means of salvation. She is interested in their right to property and to security in the necessary means of earthly existence. The assertion and protection of these basic rights is the duty of the Church. They involve moral principles and spiritual truths.

Bishops and priests as shepherds of the flock of Christ, are necessarily concerned with all those things which directly affect the welfare of the flock. It is well known that economic injustice carries a long train of evils, not only physical and social, but also moral and spiritual: poor nourishment, bad housing, ragged clothing, troubled family relations, juvenile delinquency, sin and crime.

The Church is properly interested in labor-management relations. So, too, the priest is interested. No one can rightly question that. But you evidently propose objection, by your question, to the priest's direct intervention in labor disputes, strikes, picket-lines and disturbances. You want to use the axe, which we help you grind on opponents in local controversy.

So we proceed to sharpen both bits of the axe. We are out of the field of principle now. We are discussing means and methods. Here there is room for argument and disagreement. Much depends on the priest's qualifications, his ability to really help settle the dispute. Much depends on his accepta-

343

bility to both management and labor. Can he do any good? Or will he only aggravate the antagonism? Is he fair in his judgment, and well informed of the matters in dispute? Does his presence help calm violent tempers and lead to reasonable discussion? Or is his very collar inflammatory? Does he really contribute to justice and charity? Or does he stir up prejudices? Does either side really want him around?

There is no doubt of the priest's right to act in such matters. That right is clear and we must defend and uphold it. Sometimes it may be a duty. But you and I have the right to disagree about the advisability or propriety of some particular priest's action in some particular dispute. We are free, and should feel free to express our opinion on actions which are public and controversial. But let us not question motives or sincerity. We simply disagree. Either one of us could be wrong. Maybe we are both partially wrong.

The priest must always be conscious of his responsibilities to his parish, to the community, and to the Church in general. How will his actions be interpreted? That very consciousness can make a coward of him. It can make him afraid to sponsor right and justice in the face of ingrained prejudice. Forceful action on controverted issues will always stir antagonism. Should the dormant canine be left to slumber? Or should he be roused and vanquished?

Most of us like things peaceful and friendly. We have to defend our Church so often against prejudiced attack, that we resent having any issue raised which further burdens our apologetics—however much we may be right. Priests on picket-lines are controversial. But so are labor disputes. Sometimes good sharp controversy clears the air, and lets justice and charity emerge from the smoke.

Most of us are as prejudiced in labor-management issues. One of us sees all capitalists as greedy, grasping, grinding grafters, who never give a worker a break, if they can first break the worker or his union. To this partisan only the laboring man can be right, however red his union bosses, however selfish and short-sighted his demands. Another of us sees all unions as guilds of gangsters, all labor leaders as racketeers, every strike as Communist sabotage, and every

344

picket as a bright red hoodlum or a sadistic goon. This one naturally asks: "What part have priests with gangsters, Commies, hoodlums and goons?

It would help a lot if we could keep our judgments calm and factual. Management is made up of a group of your neighbors; you would like most of them. Some are probably good Catholics; most are honest and think they are fair. Many are generous. But all are strongly interested in their business and their profits. And some may be prejudiced against the demands and tactics of organized labor.

The ordinary member of a labor union is the fellow next door. He pays his dues to his union because it looks out for his welfare and his wages. He probably does not often go to meetings, and he may sometimes criticize his officers and their methods. But when you attack his union you are striking at him—and his buddies. He seldom picks weaklings to head his union, or to represent him in negotiations. And it may be that rugged characters can sometimes muscle into organizing activities, disputes and strikes.

In the course of our history, both labor and management have used some lusty and robust methods in their disputes. Through the years their conflicts have generally worked out to the ultimate improvement of wages, working conditions, welfare, profits, efficiency, understanding and progress. They call some mean names and bash a few heads, and then they lock arms and go to work.

Management is not an ogre, and labor is not a racket; they are simply two strong forces trying to arrive at justice and understanding amid the clash of their conflicting interests. And I think it would particularly help the composure of those who are inclined to see red, if they would calmly reassure themselves that the Communist efforts to dominate some of our labor unions are now quite thoroughly squelched.

Q. My sixteen-year-old daughter has great talent in art. We are proud of her and have encouraged her. She has been in a class of high school art students, and I was deeply shocked recently to learn that all this year they have had a model posing in the nude for their drawing and painting. Is this necessary, and is it morally right? Where can I send her to school that she may develop her talent and yet not be led astray?

A. I can understand your being shocked. The age of this child makes us stop and think, and then there is the suspicion that it is a mixed class—both boys and girls of around that same age. We don't want to be prudes or allow our bourgeois conventionality to stifle talent or interfere with the legitimate demands of art, but after all . . . !

My moral books give me the principles involved in this sort of thing. Most moralists are a bit reluctant to sanction this nude posing without many restrictions. They do know that many art teachers insist that it is necessary, and they admit that the essential requirements of art can justify the dangers inherent in it—provided that the individuals concerned can handle the dangers without sin. They also admit that serious purpose of study can lessen the dangers. But they still insist on caution, prudence, and various limitations.

I have always believed that if we are to apply moral principles prudently in a given area we should be reliably informed in that area. Since I know nothing about art, I had recourse to Father Edward M. Catich, of St. Ambrose College, whose reputation in this field is firmly and widely established. He kindly took time from a busy schedule of varied work, and I am giving you the benefit of what I learned from him.

Father Catich insists that the problem posed by this question is a difficult one, because the subject is controversial. Those who insist that the nude be included in the curriculum of instruction base their argument on the fact that the human body is the subject most frequently used by the artist in his creations. They insist that the young artist cannot get enough training in drawing this subject in the nude. Those who oppose this view maintain that, by way of practical instruction, more good is achieved through the study of basic anatomy, human mechanics, and the origin, function, and insertion of muscles, than from the study of the nude.

Father Catich then began to speak on the basis of his own experience, first as a student at the Art Institute, before he began to study for the priesthood, and then later as a teacher of art. He says that this experience has proven to him that the use of the nude for the entire four years of art study—as in a place like the Art Institute—is unwarranted. Indeed it is mostly a waste of time. But let me quote his own words:

"Frankly I did not learn figure drawing until after I got out of school and had to teach the subject. While teaching I learned that a serious study of bones, muscles and mechanics is really what is needed, and not the superficial study of the nude. In proof of this position we here at St. Ambrose turn out art majors who have a sound enough knowledge of figure drawing without having studied the nude. It is not that we are Puritans or bigoted. It is simply that we have to conserve our study time and we do not feel the need for exhaustive study from the nude.

"If your inquirer had asked me about his daughter I would have tried to convince his daughter, through him, that a basic college education from a good liberal arts college is the best preparation for an art career. The technique of drawing and painting is quickly acquired, but the study-habits, discipline, learning, broadening and cultural-historical feel that one gets out of a liberal education can be had only in college. My regret is that I didn't have my college education before my art training. I did things backwards and wasted a terrible amount of time and energy. Honestly, I did not really learn the meaning of art until after I had gone through college. Of course it is difficult to tell these important things to a spirited youngster, especially a talented one, as you mention."

Father Catich goes on to insist that this young girl should have at least two years of good college work before taking up the study of art. "At the end of two years she will be more mature and her parents will have less to worry about should she be required to draw from the nude."

"Moreover there are some fine Catholic colleges that give

347

good art courses along with the college work, schools like St. Catherine's in St. Paul, Cardinal Stritch in Milwaukee, St. Mary's at Notre Dame, etc. I do not know much about eastern schools. For strictly art schools the two best in the east are the Art Students League in New York and Pratt Institute in Brooklyn—this latter one probably better for a raw beginner."

On the basis of Father Catich's information, my own moral conclusion would be that the use of the nude for the study of art at the high school level is not justified—and certainly not for mixed classes.

Thank you Father Catich.

Q. We have been showing motion pictures as part of a movie-education program. A number of times, we have shown films which features actors or directors who have been rather notorious in their moral lives. A few times, Catholics have written to me complaining about our show-ing such motion pictures. The general complaint is that it is unbecoming for a Catholic organization to sponsor such motion pictures. How do you answer such an objection?

A. There is no necessary connection between the private life of an actor or director and the quality of films he pro-duces. And we should not feel obliged as movie patrons to try to dictate morality to actors through the pressure of boy-cott. It seems to me that the Legion of Decency makes its moral ratings of films without regard to the persons involved in the production. For instance, I recall a couple of Ingrid Bergman pictures which received quite high ratings after loads of scandal had burdened that splendid actress.

Do we enjoy less the brilliant performance of a baseball player because he happens to be living with his third wife? Well, maybe a little bit. After all there is a certain wholeness about a person; we cannot entirely dissect him in our think-ing and feeling about him. Even while we cheer his home-run there remains a lingering resentment about his

348

turpitude. I might feel much the same if he were ugly in looks or mean in temperament. We do like best those heroes who are morally good, physically handsome and personally pleasing. But a good hit, a sharp throw or a stolen base remains a pleasure in itself, no matter how immoral or uncouth the rodent who makes it.

As a fan I have a right to expect a ball player to be physically fit, alert, sober and self-controlled on the field. I may gripe if he breaks training rules. But his politics, religion or personal morality do not affect his game; so they are none of my business.

In some professions we have a right to expect and demand moral integrity. A priest has the task of leading others to sanctity. No one can lead unless he first goes along the way. A teacher is rightly expected to give example as well as knowledge. And we certainly have a right to expect virtue—at least in external and social matters—from those who run our government.

On the other hand, I am only a fool if I deny myself the inspiration and pleasure of good poetry because the author happened to deviate from righteousness, in the manner of a Wilde or a Byron. And I should take a picture at its face value, even though its painter may have misbehaved in the manner of Goya, been socially defiant as Picasso, or doctrinally unsound as Rivera. Music is not made beautiful by the morals of the composer—or of the conductor.

Traditionally we show more than average tolerance for moral aberrations in the acting profession. Maybe it is their artistic temperament or the emotional strain of their work which often leads them into moral complications. Maybe their bad reputation results from their living in glass houses, with everyone watching their misbehavior—and columnists and publicity agents spreading the dirt where it will produce most fertile effects.

Of course we cannot remain indifferent to immorality wherever we see it. And we must not forget the evil effects of scandal: the tendency of fans to imitate their heroes. But on the other hand we cannot be frowning Puritans all the time: clucking reprovingly at every sin in the world, wagging our heads at every scandal, seeking to ostracize every sinner and impose virtue by fair means and foul. I am not my brother's censor, judge, or dedicated reformer.

Q. What do you think of the ethics of this TV advertising which is called subliminal projection?

A. My first reaction, as a casual viewer, is to rejoice that a way has been found to save us from the conscious suffering of the visible commercial. But then I realize that pain is the body's warning signal—to dull it is to blind ourselves to the insidious dangers of disease. When malignancy grows without hurting it escapes timely eradication.

This method of shooting insinuations into our mind under the sill of awareness is so new that we are not yet able to obtain complete and definite information on it. Some advertisers seem enthusiastic; others are apprehensive. A few seem troubled in conscience. Psychologists do not seem greatly excited; they refer you to books written 60 years ago. Surveys are inconclusive.

Whether it works or not, it does seem like a sneaky trick to try to take advantage of us in this subconscious manner. One might call it an insidious intrusion into the intimacy of the id. We admit that advertisers often do trick us with the cleverness of their visible advertising. But at least we have our eyes open; if we are smart we can learn to build up our defenses and sharpen our incredulity. If we do succumb we feel that we are at least partly to blame, ourselves. But this subliminal thing seems like brainwashing.

We are told that this unconscious suggestion cannot create desires in us; that it can only arouse and bring to consciousness those which lie dormant within us. But even so, from the moral point of view, it does not seem right that one person's will be unconsciously subjected, in this indirect, casual manner, to the will of another, especially when this other person is selfishly seeking his own interests. If completely uncontrolled this method might be used to induce to crime.

350

Suggestion is not sinful in itself. It is often done for a person's good while he is awake, and is occasionally justified in hypnotic trance. But any unconscious method is dangerous, and should be handled with scrupulous sense of responsibility—a quality rarely credited to hucksters.

What should be done? Wait and see. Maybe it is a fad which will fade. Apparently no one has yet been had.

Q. Is there any magazine or any means of finding out what TV programs are approved or disapproved? The TV programs are becoming quite a problem. You think you have something pretty good on, and all of a sudden some immoral discussion or aspersions are passed or some scantily clad woman appears and "entertains" you for a few minutes.

A. Shhh! Speak low when you talk like that or some of our neighbors will hear you and think you are advocating censorship! And that is authoritarian and un-American. Better suffer your home to be suffused with suggestion and sensuality than to risk violating the freedoms guaranteed by the First Amendment!

Actually all you are doing is pleading for decency, but that plea has somehow become associated in the popular mind with the efforts of the hierarchy to take over control of the government.

Somewhere I have seen a little publication which evaluates TV programs, along with movies, radio, and the theater. It is called "The Catholic Preview of Entertainment" (Main St., Carmel, N. Y.,) and may be of use to you.

Q. I would like to ask your opinion on a subject that generally brings amused smiles (and not-so-amusing remarks!) from the male sex: namely soap-operas, the afternoon dramas on the radio. Formerly, I believed soap-operas were silly, and that only silly women listened to them (which is

351

*probably still true!). However, now I must confess that I
am a confirmed "S.O." addict. Before the children came
along we used to get out a lot, but now there is so much
time to be alone, and so little money to do anything with
that the extent of our social activities has narrowed. These
dramas are a diversion; they do not interfere with my work.
But some of the attitudes and phrases from the programs
are definitely non-Christian, and I realize that I may be
absorbing a great deal of paganistic propaganda that I am
not aware of. All the programs accept divorce and remarriage.*

*Okay, by now you would think I would know enough to
shut the radio off; but unfortunately, I am a woman; we
females like stories of people, and soap operas are interesting.*

A. Alcoholics rationalize too. And they always thought
drunks disgusting until they started to imbibe themselves.

These soap operas seem to be an occupational hazard of
the housewife, alone with her dusting or ironing. The worst
thing about them is that they stultify; they inhibit positive
intellectual activity, demean taste and discernment and create
a world of unreality in which you float along on the surge
of vicarious emotionalism. And then, as you indicate, you
tend to absorb, by constant exposure and unconscious osmo-
sis, the amoral attitudes of the people you live with in rev-
eries several hours a day.

Why not swear off for Lent? Or if you can't be a teetotaler, at least cut down on your consumption—and choose
only the better grades of stultifiers.

Q. *My daughter seems quite impressed by a "Faith Healer"
she has seen perform on television. I looked over the copies
of the Catholic Messenger and found the article "Can Miracles Occur in Our Day?" It states that we must be "cautious
in accepting as miraculous events that have not been so de-*

clared by the Church, but we need not for this reason refuse to consider the possibility that God's power to work miracles can still be employed for the needs of His church."

My daughter was much impressed by the fact that this "healer" caused a person, who to all appearances was hopelessly crippled as a result of polio, to stand up on television and walk, cured.

I have never seen this program, nor have I read anything about the spectacular results from his prayers. I would like to know how to regard this program.

A. I have never seen the program either, and I don't want to see it. I would prefer science fiction. Certainly miracles are possible in the modern world, but I am sure that God does not work them to sell soap—or to encourage the hysterical racket of some religious faker.

Q. A nephew of mine says that he was taught at St. Ambrose, in a religion class, that it was necessary to get a dispensation from the bishop to send your children to a public school when Catholic school facilities are at hand. He says it is binding under pain of mortal sin. Our argument is based on the fact that we feel that eight years in Catholic parochial school is sufficient, and it should not be necessary to make financial sacrifice to send them on farther. Who decides when a family is financially capable of sending their children to a Catholic school? Some parents are more willing to sacrifice than others. I wish someone would clarify the Church's position in this matter.

A. The law of the Church in this matter is very clear and definite. It hardly requires clarification. It is found in Canon 1374. Here is my own translation:

"Catholic young people shall not attend non-Catholic schools, or those schools which are called neutral or secular (our public schools). THE BISHOP IS THE ONLY ONE

353

who can decide in what circumstances the attendance at such schools may be tolerated, and he must follow the instructions of the Holy See in making his judgment, and see that proper care is taken to avoid harm to faith or morals."

So it seems that St. Ambrose teaches the true doctrine, as you might naturally expect; and your nephew understood it correctly. The Diocese of Davenport has its own regulation on the subject. I quote Art. 59 of our Third Synod:

"Where the parochial school exists, parents or guardians must not violate the general Canon Law of the Church (Can. 1374) by sending their children to public or non-Catholic schools. If they persist in doing so, they sin gravely and cannot be absolved unless they make proper adjustment with their pastor or with the Ordinary." (The Ordinary is the Bishop.)

Since your question concerns the Catholic high school, in particular, I shall quote also Art. 60 of the same Synod:

"If a Catholic high school is within reasonable distance parents or guardians are OBLIGED to send their children to this school provided suitable courses are taught."

In general the bishop permits the sending of Catholic students to public schools: (1) when no Catholic school is available, and (2) when necessary courses are not available in the Catholic school. This latter circumstance will hardly be found below the college or university level. Manual training or domestic arts, in high school, may be very desirable; but the absence of them in the Catholic school is not sufficient reason for sending children to the public high school. Football is a great sport, and your boy may be adept at it, but that is not sufficient reason to ignore the law of the Church.

If your boy or girl is expelled from the Catholic school for disciplinary or scholastic reasons, then you may take for granted the bishop's permission to send him or her to the public school, until the Catholic school will accept the darling again. If you think you have any other good reason for sending your child to public school, then you had better discuss it with your pastor. If you can not agree with him, then you may take it up with the bishop. THE BISHOP IS

354

THE ONLY ONE AUTHORIZED BY LAW to decide. The pastor is simply authorized by diocesan statute to interpret the mind of the bishop, in cases in which he knows what the bishop's decision would be.

The Church can not approve secular schools for Catholic students for many reasons. I will not try to recall them all here. Hardly any of these schools are strictly neutral in religion. In our own area they are quite definitely Protestant, or irreligious. Strict neutrality is impossible. In such subjects as history, literature, philosophy, etc. no teacher can absolutely conceal his own convictions, persuasions, and prejudices. Besides, the very separation of religion from secular learning gives the impression that religion is not an integral part of life, but a sideline, something reserved for Sundays, and not to be mentioned or bothered about in affairs of the world. Neutral education, even when neutral, is fragmentary, uncertain, and lacking in answers to the important questions of life. It is education without Christ, preparation for life without Christ. It is not for a Christian, whose very life is Christ.

In particular would I disagree with you strongly about the relative importance of the Catholic high school. I think it is more important than the Catholic grade school. High school years are the most critical of the child's life. It is intolerable that parents submit him to unnecessary dangers to faith or morals during those years when characters take definite formation, convictions ripen, and temptations assail.

Who decides the financial question? The bishop. The law so states . . . clearly. At first glance that may seem a bit unfair. Can the bishop understand our financial problems? He can. They can be explained to him. And furthermore, he can probably help to make arrangements. Rarely need a child be excluded from Catholic school for financial reasons. However, I doubt that the bishop will consider a TV set or a new car more important than a Catholic education. Parents are not good judges of the situation themselves. They are apt to be prejudiced. They FEEL (as you state in your question) rather than think. They feel the sacrifices they have made; they feel the sacrifices they are still required to make; they

355

feel that the public school is just as good anyway; they feel that they are being imposed upon. Such feelings obscure their thoughts of things spiritual, moral, and eternal.

Q. I would like to know why the Catholic Church tolerates the liquor business. I, for one, think the liquor business is damning more people's lives and sending more people to hell than any other.

What makes me ask the question is this. When I was 12 years old my grandfather died. At the funeral his brother was asked "Henry, how did you come to be a Catholic?" His answer was, "I could not join any other Church on account of my position." His position was general manager and superintendent of the Utica Brewing Co. of Utica, N. Y. His name was Henry Tebbert, and his answer has bothered me for 62 years.

A. My friend, you are a patient man. After 62 years of waiting it is high time that you had an honest answer to your question. I hope I do not fail you.

First, I suppose we have brewers, vintners, and distillers in the Church for much the same reason we have lawyers, doctors and farmers. They believe in the teachings of Jesus Christ and want to save their souls.

A second reason is that we do not consider their business entirely bad. Their enticing product undoubtedly contributes to the temporal and eternal damnation of millions, as you say; but it also promotes the happiness, heartiness and friendly relaxation of many more millions. It is one of the good things of life which can be readily used for evil.

A third reason is that the Church is realistic. Some evils in life must be tolerated because it is humanly impossible to eliminate them. While we are throwing the brewers out the front door, the bootleggers will be coming in the back door. The substitution would eliminate no evils, but it could result in inferior brew. Since the dawn of history men have

356

produced alcoholic drinks, and no earthly power is going to stop them.

Your question implies that the makers of alcoholic drinks are intolerable sinners who should be put beyond the pale as unfit to associate with decent Christians. Do you recall the words of Jesus while he was at table in the house of Levi, the tax collector, whom he had chosen to be Matthew the Apostle? The Scribes and Pharisees asked the disciples, "Why does your Master eat and drink with publicans and sinners?" And Jesus heard this, and said to them, "It is not the healthy who need a physician, but they who are sick. For I have come to call sinners, not the just."

The Church continues the work of Jesus, her Founder. And we who seek salvation through her can be grateful that she does not weed all sinners from her membership. We would find it cold outside, even though we would have plenty of company in our exclusion. Rather the Church follows the command of the Master: let the cockle grow with the wheat until the harvest, when it will be gathered up to be burned.

I can imagine what you are thinking. Jesus called sinners to repentance; but the makers of alcoholic beverages do not repent; they keep on expanding their vats and increasing their sales. The Church's tolerance encourages them, and thus seems to encourage the evils of drink. Many other Churches condemn the brewers roundly for the harm they bring on society.

So we must get down to the basic question: is brewing immoral? Are alcoholic drinks vicious? Is the whole liquor trade a crime?

We should begin our discussion of these questions by frankly admitting that the various industries which produce alcohol in one potable form or another contribute to a long list of personal and social evils which afflict the world. If alcohol did not exist there would surely be less crime, sorrow, poverty, ill health, and evil temper in the world. We would be rid of the sad plague of alcoholism, which makes helpless addicts of its millions of victims. We would no longer be disgusted by drunkenness, which dulls man's intellectual discernment, eliminates his inhibitions, and lowers his sense of morality.

However, we must be careful about blaming the manufacturer of a good product for all the evil uses to which perverse men may put it. Should we exclude arms makers from Church membership because guns are sometimes used for murder? Should we excommunicate chemists because they make poisons, or atomic physicists because their H-Bombs threaten us with destruction? Maybe we should reject automobile manufacturers. Their powerful products cause thousands of highway deaths every year.

If we will consider the matter calmly and without prejudice, we will realize that much good comes from alcoholic drinks. For centuries they have been used as a staple and satisfying part of daily diet by the people of many nations. Millions of discerning men hold the taste of fine wine to be one of the exquisite pleasures which mother earth affords her children. If it is morally right to savor a good dinner, then it is also right to add to it those drinks which make its taste complete.

Then there is the matter of conviviality. If alcoholic drinks were entirely removed from the world's scene, conversation would be inhibited, many hearty friendships would fail to develop, social gatherings would remain tense and formal, and self-conscious men would seldom relax. International diplomacy would be less challenging, and if possible, less successful; salesmen would have to learn their art anew.

So you see there are two sides to the alcohol business, the good and the bad, the right use and the misuse. For every alcoholic tippler, and drunken gutter bum, there are probably 20 temperate drinkers who make pleasant and moral use of the various extracts of the hop, the vine, and the malt.

And how do we know that mankind would be better off without these often pernicious products? We have no proof, because no nation in history has ever seriously tried to do without alcohol. We once made a pretense of doing so here in the U.S., but even our legislators knew how to evade their own laws. And in some of our dry states it is aptly said that the dry voters will cast their ballots against liquor as long as they can stagger to the polls. Even if we could eliminate every intoxicant, can we be sure that restless men would not find other escapes more noxious? What about narcotics?

Our great experiment with prohibition, for all its dismal failure, brought home several important truths. A free man prizes his liberty more keenly once it has been curtailed. Laws cannot enforce morality, and they lose their effectiveness when they are contrary to the will of the people.

Moreover, bad laws, which cannot be enforced, engender disdain for all law. When legitimate public demand is made extralegal, various forms of gangsterism will arise to supply it. Man drinks no less under prohibition, but he drinks with a feeling of guilt or a smirk of defiance—and he drinks some horrible stuff.

Very few Catholics have ever favored prohibition. We revere man's rights and freedom too highly. And we don't like to see any of the good things of God's world declared evil in themselves. Even the derived products of man's industry are not morally bad. Sin comes from our abuse of them.

It is unfortunate that our stand on this subject should seem to put the Church on the side of drunkenness and alcoholism. The Church is sensitive to sin, and she knows from centuries of sad experience that alcohol can be the cause of many sins. The Church is alert to the welfare of her children; and she knows that millions of them suffer in mind and body because of alcohol. The Christian home is the primary social concern of the Church; its hearth should radiate sanctity, but alcohol can fire it with discord.

The Church has always opposed excessive use of alcohol. She may be a bit more tolerant of human weakness than you or I would be; she gets that tolerance from her divine Founder, and her maternal heart has been mellowed by ages of love and experience. I think we might outline her attitude in the following points.

1. She teaches temperance and sobriety as basic moral virtues, essential to a good Christian life. Morality requires that reason be clear and judgment fine; sobriety is the virtue which keeps them that way.

2. She teaches that excessive use of alcohol is sin. Voluntary drunkenness is a mortal sin; it means the loss of God's friendship and the punishment of hell.

3. She constantly exhorts parents to give good example and right teaching on this and similar subjects.

4. She stresses both the danger and the seriousness of many other sins committed under varying degrees of alcoholic influence.

5. She encourages total abstinence from alcoholic drink as a matter of prudence, self-denial, or penance. She particularly urges it during Lent.

6. She has frequently made use of the voluntary pledge, which is a special, dedicated form of total abstinence. It can be taken for a period of time or for life, and it has a history of helpfulness in strengthening the resolution of many good people.

7. Her priests and bishops have often sponsored total-abstinence societies; Popes have blessed them and granted indulgences for taking part in their activities.

8. The Church has practically adopted Alcoholics Anonymous in recent years. She approves and blesses their practical program, based on humility, helpfulness, and sad experience.

9. She gives her maternal sympathy to those who suffer from the compulsive sickness of alcoholism. But she is not maudlin with them; her moralists point out firmly that for them a single drink may be a mortal sin.

10. Day in and day out she urges prayer and the sacraments and the Sacrifice of the Mass. These spiritual helps are particularly useful for the addictive drinker or the weak man who tends to excess. They seldom work miracles; they do not replace natural aids, but they are the source of strength beyond ourselves; and they are the means of sanctifying all our natural efforts.

It may not be a formal part of her program but I think the Church would readily agree that there are two more things badly needed in the whole liquor business: legislation and education. We need wise, prudent, unprejudiced regulation of the alcohol industry, and its sales, taxes, and advertising. Our laws should not be inspired by crusading bottle smashers but by wise and tolerant students of social problems who are not scandalized that a man takes a drink but who are sensible of the evils of excess. They should be expert in the use of practical remedies and alert to man's rightful liberties.

Brewers have an obligation in the field of education, because their advertising helps to form the attitude of our people toward drinking. Up to now, many of our drinking habits and attitudes in this country have been really bad. Education can improve them if it is intelligent, factual and free of prejudice and hysteria. In the past most of our education has come from crusaders; it was impassioned and unreasoning, and resulted in either fear or revolt.

Amid the rigors of our frontier life men seldom developed grace. Drinking was something done in the alley or behind the barn. One took his whisky raw from the bottle, with a cough and a grimace. He was likely to be secretive about it because it brought him into conflict with dedicated nondrinkers and often with the law. Even civilized drinking, in those early days, was done chiefly in saloons.

Just when we were getting a start at being graceful about our drinking, prohibition came along to disrupt our progress. Drinking then became something illegal, surreptitious, smart and cynical. And the quality of the beverage was so raw that it could be taken only in burning gulps. A whole generation learned to drink for the effect alone: the tingle, the relaxation, the escape, the oblivion. They never thought of savoring the drink for its taste.

You and I both know that most alcoholics have personality problems. They should be helped to face life and come to terms with it; so that they can live with themselves. Then they will not need that form of escape which leads to the gutter. We must continue our studies of alcoholism, and our understanding efforts to help its victims. But it will not help to solve the problem if we begin by eliminating all brewers.

We might make a start towards solving the drinking problem if we all recognize that it is basically a personal matter. When a drunk causes me trouble, his drinking becomes my business; up to that point it is his alone. Each person should map his own sensible program, though some may need help with it. If a man does not wish to drink, that is his business, and bad cess to the host or companion who foists a drink upon him.

Still another person may like to drink, and be able to do it with grace and control. Then down with the Pharisee who points the finger of scorn at him!

Perhaps you are one of those who do not drink. In that case, more power to you!

The Church, with you, deplores the evils of alcoholic excess, and stands ready to cooperate in any sensible program to eliminate them. But she still respects the right of a temperate man to quench his thirst. She encourages abstinence, but does not consider abstinence an obligation on all men. That is why in your words, the Church tolerates the liquor business.

Q. On this matter of birth control information in New York hospitals (city-owned), don't non-Catholics have the civil right to this information, as Catholics do to play bingo? The Catholic comment I have read has never considered the right of Protestants.

A. No one has a right to do something wrong; and birth control is wrong, not by Catholic law, but by the natural law of God.

However, the solution to the problem in New York is not as simple as that. There, as everywhere in this country, we live in a pluralistic society. That word pluralistic is quite popular recently; it is borrowed from the sociologists. It means that Catholics, Jews, Orthodox, and a variety of Protestants all live in the same city and State. It means that whites and blacks and a smattering of other races share the same community; and the militarists and pacifists, Democrats and Republicans, the NAM and the Teamsters must somehow find a formula for peace.

I do not believe that the problem in New York is con-

cerned with birth control information, but with the prescribing and fitting of contraceptive devices. It seems that for
many years there has been a regulation in all the public
hospitals of New York City which forbids doctors to utilize
birth control devices in these hospitals. I doubt that Catholics
are responsible for this regulation. Like the anti-birth-control
laws of Massachusetts and Connecticut it was probably put
into effect by Protestants, who were opposed to the practice
in those days. But thinking has changed, and the direct
descendants of those strict Protestants now hold birth control
to be a wise and holy and humanitarian practice. Not only is
it essential to the mature modern planning of families and
the solving of the world's population problems, they say, it is
particularly needed in some medical cases in which conception would mean "tragedy." And its proponents hold that
man vicious—hardly less than a murderer—who would with-
hold it in such cases.

Only Catholics hold firmly to the old ideas. They strongly
insist that you may never do evil so that good may result
from it. And they maintain that birth control is contrary to
God's plans for the reasonable use of sexual instincts. Their
argument does not faze their strong opponents.

It seems that for several years now there has been agitation
in New York medical circles to get rid of this regulation.
The hospital Commissioner for the city is Dr. Morris A.
Jacobs, and some time ago he made a statement about permitting all "proper and accepted therapeutic practices" in
the hospitals. Some doctors interpreted this to mean that he
was ready to disregard the old rule. So one of them prescribed a contraceptive device for a woman who was a patient
in one of the hospitals, and for whom the medical indications were definite. She should not have another child. But
Doctor Jacobs would not permit the procedure. He invoked
the old regulation, and the fat sputtered all over the fire—
and the nation.

Catholics have supported Doctor Jacobs. Protestant and
Jewish organizations generally lined up in opposition, sec-
onded by the big city newspapers and the American Civil
Liberties Union.

The basic Catholic contention is that the hospitals which are supported in large measure by their taxes should not be centers for immoral practice. The basic contrary argument is that Catholics should not try to ram their own ideas of morality down the unwilling throats of those who disagree. And they call loudly for their civil rights—even though they are not right—without much regard for the rights of others.

Something will have to give. It is generally by tolerance that we are able to live peaceably with those who disagree with us. Sometimes we have to put up with things which are wrong and offensive. We can never condone them or take part in them, but we close our eyes to them. Usually the reason for such tolerance is that greater evil would result from active opposition or attempts at suppression.

Is tolerance called for in this case? It may not be very prudent or humble of me to take a stand at variance with certain learned theologians who are right on the ground and know all the facts. But I must be honest, and I believe that little permanent good will be accomplished and much harm done by continued intransigent efforts to maintain this admirable regulation. It is the rear-guard action of a battle which has been lost all over the country.

The evils of trying to maintain and enforce the regulation will be many: bitterness will be fostered, prejudice increased, and bigots will revitalize their favorite stale chestnut. They will have horrible proof to convince their fearful listeners that the Roman menace must be crushed before its tyranny and intolerance suppress all American liberties.

The good will be limited. We will not convince anyone of the immorality of birth control by forbidding it to them contrary to their convictions. We will rather make them staunch fighters against the prohibition, and convert the condemned practice into a holy cause. Our regulations may limit the practice slightly, but effective bootlegging methods will circumvent our efforts.

However, we should not give in easily. For that reason I would praise those who have staunchly defended the Catholic position up to the present time. In our tolerance we must not give the impression that we are unconcerned, that we

364

hold moral principle of little moment, and that peace is more precious than God's law.

Certainly vociferous Catholic opposition has served to strengthen our own people, and has impressed our opponents that the matter is important to us. If we give in, it must be clear that we do so for motives of tolerance only: because we respect the sincere consciences of those who oppose us— wrong though they be; and because we realize that we cannot legislate morality effectively against the honest convictions of a large segment of the population.

And in the process of giving in we should somehow convey the message that we expect a measure of tolerance in return. I am not concerned with bingo; it is a corny bore. But there is definite lack of tolerance in the program of the Protestant Council of the City of New York, which claims to be giving its all for civil rights. They explicitly state that a Catholic nurse would be expected to assist a physician in fitting a contraceptive device, no matter how much it violates her conscience.

Such lack of fairness and logic makes tolerance difficult, but there is the more virtue in it. It is easy to love those who love us . . .

Index

368

369

370